THE DIRECTOR MURDERED

Emmanuel Igwaro Odongo-Aginya

The Director Murdered by Emmanuel Igwaro Odongo-Aginya

ISBN 978-1-952027-18-5 (Paperback)
ISBN 978-1-952027-19-2 (Hardback)

This book is written to provide information and motivation to readers. Its purpose is not to render any type of psychological, legal, or professional advice of any kind. The content is the sole opinion and expression of the author, and not necessarily that of the publisher.

Copyright © 2020 by Emmanuel Igwaro Odongo-Aginya

All rights reserved. No part of this book may be reproduced, transmitted, or distributed in any form by any means, including, but not limited to, recording, photocopying, or taking screenshots of parts of the book, without prior written permission from the author or the publisher. Brief quotations for noncommercial purposes, such as book reviews, permitted by Fair Use of the U.S. Copyright Law, are allowed without written permissions, as long as such quotations do not cause damage to the book's commercial value. For permissions, write to the publisher, whose address is stated below.

Printed in the United States of America.

New Leaf Media, LLC
175 S. 3rd Street, Suite 200
Columbus, OH 43215
www.thenewleafmedia.com

Foreword

The Director of government Medical Research Institution in Kitgum Town Uganda is murdered. A Deputy Police Inspector from the Criminal Investigation Department (CID), Regional Office in Gulu Odongkara is sent with a team of experts to go and solve the murder. In a mixed mood of going to solve the murder case in Kitgum and the infidelity of his wife with his boss the Police Inspector CID , Odongkara left for Kitgum perturbed after he observed dried blood mark on the rear wheel of his boss Mukasa official car. To establish the source of the blood, Odongkara scraped the dried blood from the wheel of the vehicle in his handkerchief and took it to their laboratory for identification. The twists and turns in the storyline expose criminals' characters which is the facde behind which they carry out and hide their motives and evil deeds. This detective novel, is a great creative work which explores human intrigues, which propels them to commit crimes and at the same time they try to cover their tracks so that, they are not caught or are criminally not liable. Odongkara uses his training skill and charm- ing personality to uncover the murderer of the Director of Medical Research Institute in Kitgum. The author cleverly blends suspense with romance the story which compels the readers to read to the end of the novel.

    I strongly recommend you read the novel *The Director Murdered* by Professor Emmanuel Igwaro Odongo- Aginya to understand the mind of the criminal and how the investigator uses his tactics and charming personality to expose the criminals.

Associate Professor of Literary and Cultural Studies Charles Okumu

Gulu University, P.O. Box 166, GULU.Uganda.Dept: Languages and Literature

Email.add:c.n.okumu@gu.ac.ug/ charles.okumu52@gmail.com
Phone contact: +256-772-961-256

Chapter 1

She got out of bed and stood naked in the full light. The red bulb they were using in their bedroom gave an exquisite contrast between her copper-coloured complexion and the triangular tuff of dark hair in her pubic region. She gave him what you wouldn't dismiss as an apologetic smile, slid on her see-through nightdress, turned the handle of the door leading to the children's room and disappeared behind the door into the children's room.

She's a charming and beautiful woman. If she were only honest and trusted, I would have loved her more. My father warned me against marrying her, but I insisted simply because of her beauty. And now I am seeing the truth of what Daddy told me about her. I may seek a divorce and have her divorced with disgrace. I can't share my wife with another man. It is either him or me. She must make up her mind. She can't sit on a fence in love, Odongokara thought as his wife put their five-year-old son back to sleep.

Otto, their son, had fallen asleep on an empty stomach before supper. Now hungry, he continued to yell for eats. She took him out of bed and walked him to the dining room to give him his share of food. While he nibbled at his meal, she sat at his side, her chin in her palms and elbows pinned on the table. She starred meditatively at one of their wedding photographs on the opposite wall.

Why did he behave like this? Is he only suspicious of my movements, or was he actually told about me? I remember I was found swimming naked with his boss the day he went out on official duty to Mable. And in our home here, Mrs. Ojuk, paying a visit on me, caught us kissing each other. I am sure he knows all about all I have done now. Should I go and confess to him, and give him my sincere apology and promise not to give myself to any other man again? On the other hand, if his sudden onset of melancholy was due to something else, I would be accusing myself, and he might just bury a bullet in my brain. I think I will wait and see. I will pretend nothing has happened. Instead, I will try hard to outfox him and lure him into thinking I have no guilt whatsoever, Jane thought, forgetting she was sitting near her son. Had it not been for the rattling of the plate on the floor, which Otto knocked down with his forehead as he fell asleep over his food, she would have sat there the whole night, trying to solve her sex mystery.

"Hey Otto, you've fallen asleep again before you've finished your food." She complained as she flicked away some fragment of bread from his head and arm. Otto only stirred in her arms and flung his limbs limply, like those of a dead child. She took him to bed and returned to clear the table. She put the plates away and went back to their bedroom.

Odongkara was snoring lightly. She knew he was asleep and did not want to disturb him. *It's better to let him sleep. Maybe he will be all right tomorrow when he wakes up,* she thought and tiptoed across the room to her side of the bed. She snapped on the bedside lamp and turned the lampshade toward her husband, so that he was in darkness while her portion of the bed was brightly illuminated. She wiped the sand from her feet, slid in the bed beside Odongkara, and pulled the blanket over her with the stealth of a guilty woman and thought, *let the sleeping tiger lie.* She glanced at the table clock, ticking meekly at their bedside. It was midnight. It was five to ten when she went to feed Otto.

I have been up for such a long time. No wonder Otto slept over his food, and here, Odongkara is snoring heavily. He's a lovely, handsome, kind man. I don't know why I am misbehaving like this. I hate Mukasa even if he's my tribe's maid. I am going to tell him next time we meet that I have reached the end of the road with him, and we can't go on cheating like this. I am a married woman, and what I am doing is adultery. I cannot go on doing it perpetually. I am guilty like Lucifer. And I don't derive any sexual satisfaction from Mukasa. I must stop this nonsense immediately, Jane thought with remorse and shed a few drops of tears.

The Director Murdered

Odongkara drove the police Land Rover from the police station to his house. The gate to his home was half-open. He glanced at his wristwatch, it was eleven o'clock. The policeman on guard wasn't at the gate. He got out of the Land Rover, left the door open, walked to the gate, and opened it wide. As he swung open the gate, he thought he saw a black car parked behind a flower shrub near his house through the poorly dimmed headlamps of his Land Rover. His heart banged. The blood raced through his body.

Who could this be? A visitor or someone lying in ambush for me? This second thought made him fidget. He slipped off and crawled under the fence. He turned off the headlamps of the Land Rover and cut off the idling engine. *Whoever has parked the car must be some- where in the compound. Why no light anywhere in the house, no police on guard, and the time is eleven thirty now? Isn't this odd? I will find out what is going on. Maybe the police officer on duty is guarding other areas, or he is lying dead somewhere with bullets riddled body.* He thought.

Odongkara stealthily crouched under the fence and checked every dark, suspicious area in the compound. But nothing stirred, only lizards and rats ran from him. *Well, it looks no one has been killed, and no one is around. However, I shouldn't risk exposing myself in the open. Let me see the number plate of the car.* He took of his white shirt and the vest and hid them under the fence, so he became like charcoal on a blackboard. He crawled furtively on his chest, his .38mm police automatic revolver clenched in his hand, until he was only a few feet away from the car. He remained quiet as a stone near the car for a good minute to detect any movement inside the car. But nothing moved except the sound of his heart thumping in his chest. The snapping metal on the body of the car indicated it was parked not many hours ago. He crawled forward and came right next to the car. The number plate, UP 128, was unmistakable. It was the official police car of Mukasa, the officer in charge of the Gulu police station.

What the devil could he be doing at my home at this hour of the night? Why on earth has he parked here? Maybe the policeman on duty is sick but yet he can't take up his duty himself unless he's getting out of his mind. There are other police constables who could come out here to guard, not him. Certainly not. I have got to find out why the car is parked here. Should I go and get a witness, or can I go it alone? No need, the car is my witness. Whoever drove the car here is going to be answerable for the eventualities of tonight's episode. But what if he gets me in a tight corner? There might not be any clue to trace him. People who leave evidence like this are no fools. They always trick you by putting a clue right under your nose. And when you handle it unwittingly, you regret it too late. Whatever the case, my hand is on the plough now. I have to use my senses and solve this mystery alone. I don't need anyone's help.

Odongkara swore under clenched teeth and dragged himself on the ground, pulling on some long grass growing on the lawn. He slithered and lay parallel to the car, and waited. But nothing stirred in the car. He raised himself up and knelt on one knee, his finger on the trigger of the gun in the firing position. He hid his face with the frame of the car door and peered inside. There was no one.

What is this about? What is the motive? I don't understand. He tested the door of the car. It was unlocked. This puzzled him further. He opened the door a millimeter per second until it was wide enough for him to climb in. He slid behind the steering wheel. His knees knocked the bunch of keys stuck in the ignition, and they jingled in the air like the tinkling of wind chimes. He could not understand. *Is this a very carefully planned trick, or is this man just an idiot? Why all this carelessness if he is not being very witty for me?* Odongkara found himself getting angry with all his findings. *I am going to remove the keys and dig around a little before I go and wake my wife to find out what has happened and why this car is here. If the person who parked this car to lure me to it like a butterfly on a rose were around, he would have moved by now. Or maybe I haven't reached the very spot where he intends to crucify me. Anyway, let me march on. I will watch every inch of the ground on which I set my toes.* He pulled the keys, put them in the pocket of his trousers, and got out of the car.

He went round the compound again nothing indicated the presence of anyone outside.

Well, I have done enough in the compound. Next let me try the house. But before, I need to confirm there is nothing unusual happening there. He walked towards the children's windows. All he could hear was the alternating snoring of the children enjoying their sleep. He tiptoed towards their bedroom windows. He thought he heard strange movements, which sent a tickling wave up his spine. The bed squeaking at the rhythm of some movements. He thought he didn't hear well. He pressed his ears on the wall. The wall was kind enough. It did not only amplify the squeaks of the bed but also the familiar sensational romantic noise from his wife, which was unmistakable. It was like the voice of his mother calling him. He felt the earth vibrating under his feet. He started sweating. He touched his pocket for some more slush. They were there.

Whoever is there is a dead duck tonight, Odongkara thought and moving like a cat stalking a mouse, he walked to the door thinking. *By any luck I will find the door open and the idiotic, son-of-the bitch will be riddled with leads very soon.* He knew how to open the door without making a noise. Luck was with him. The door stood ajar. He lifted it, carrying it above the floor and slowly walked in the living room like a ghost. He came and stood at the door to their bedroom, and gently turned the handle of the door, swearing hell, his heart thumping in the chest nearly suffocated him. He knew where the switch was, while moving to put on the light he kicked something, which tinkled down like an empty glass. The couple in bed automatically knew there was an intruder. He put on the light, and saw what he was expecting to see, which he refused to accept was true. A man he knew well was buried between the legs of his wife shoring in the air like horns of cows. For one moment he thought it was funny and he wanted to ask them to keep on as he watch on, but, gripped by sudden hysteria, he found himself pulling on the trigger of the pistol. Bang, he fired again bang, and the couple rolled off each other not voluntarily but involuntarily.

H-e-e-e-y He shouted as he stirred in bed glad to find that it was only a dream? But he was worried. *I - I hate to murder anyone. Why such a dream? I think it's because of what I was told about her. Some people always dream of what they worried over before they sleep. Could this be the case?* He thought, turned towards Jane and fondled her. The urge of narrating to her the dream was overwhelmed by the skepticism of how she would interpret the story. She might think it's a made up story and not a dream. He decided against it, laid on his back awake until six o'clock. Later he fell into a deep sleep which lasted up to seven o'clock in the morning one hour beyond his usual waking hours.

Jane woke up at six o'clock their routine. She flung the blanket from her shoulders and rested the hem just below her longish breasts. But still had all the feminine warmth in them. Their looks were still enchanting enough to make any man's mouth water.

She yawned, rubbing her eyes with her fingers and looked at her husband coiled under the blanket, his knees only a few millimeters from his chin as if he was ready for a lumber puncture. *Why is he still sleeping up to now? He has never slept beyond six o'clock. Is thereanything wrong? Well he was from a journey yesterday but he didn't look all that tired.* She shrugged at the thought and threw the blanket from her breasts down to her feet and kicked it away. She laid on top of the bed on her back staring at their other wedding photograph hanged on the wall in the bedroom and looked at her husband still snoring near her. *We looked wonderful there.* She thought and wanted to wake him up and apologize to him for what she had done. *I am sorry for what I did with this bastard Mukasa. I can't disappoint my husband because he doesn't belong to my tribe. I love him and he loves me.* She drew her legs up and laid in lithotomic position the see through nightdress was folded up, resting on her abdomen. She picked the netted hem and feelingly began to move her finger along. *This is a gift from him for my birth day after our wedding.* She thought, kissed it, got up and went to prepare breakfast.

It was while she was in the kitchen that their telephone in the living room buzzed. Br-br, br-br. *Who is this ringing so early?* She thought and walked out to attend to it. She lifted the receiver with her wet hands holding it with two fingers only.

"Hello, good morning. This is Inspector Odongkara's house. Can I help you?"

"How nice to be greeted by you darling, the first thing in the morning of a Monday of the first of January 1971."The voice wasn't strange to her. She recognised it well enough. If she were still the same, she would have probably said, "how nice to be telephoned by you darling the first thing in the Morning of Monday of January 1971. But, because she was beginning to abominate that person at the end of the line with all his pumps, she felt rage. She kept quiet and didn't reply a word and hung up. She walked back to the kitchen annoyed when the telephone buzzed again. She walked back and stood near it and stared at the buzzing telephone the way you would angrily look at a fly over your delicious dish at lunch hour. *What the hell is this bastard up to? Doesn't he know I am married and he is married too? And here he's behaving like a secondary school boy in love. I thought he was intelligent, but he's just a clown*, a cow. *No common sense at all.* She didn't know whether to lift the receiver or not. But when she thought of her husband in bed she decided to take it up. Had she been alone she would let it buzz.

"Hello" She retorted rudely. "What is in the air baby?"

"Look here you ... ," she stopped short as she heard the bed in their room squeaked.

"Can I help you?" She asked trying to steady her voice as the husband continued to rock in bed. The man at the end of the line came to his senses and suspected that the husband might be near.

"Yes please."

"What do you want?" She asked in a harsh voice. Mukasa could not belief his ears. He thought he was dialing the wrong number and not Inspector Odongkara's house. He thought he wasn't talking to Jane the lady he was romancing with. He even had the audacity to ask if the number he was dialing was extension 13.

"What number did you want?" "Extension 13."

"I hope you're awake enough to see the number you are dialing?"

"Yes I'm, but ... "

"But what? Please can I help you? I am very busy in the kitchen and I must get the breakfast ready. I don't want that nonsense anymore. I am not joking. I am different from now on. Forget all we have been through, and please don't try again. Okay?"

She nearly hung up, when the man at the end of the line sighed and said, "I don't take a "no" for an answer from any woman neither do I take them seriously when they threatened as you have done. In fact to me that is very encouraging indeed. Anyway, is your sugar up?" He asked contemptuously.

"He is."

"Can I talk to him?"

"Hold on the line for him."

"I am holding. She left the receiver on the table at the side of the telephone set and walked to their bedroom. She turned the handle of the door slowly and carefully as if she was expecting to find her husband with another woman in bed. She walked in and closed the door behind her. She stared at him and walked to him slowly.

The first telephone, which buzzed, had wakened him up and he was lying on his back resting. He wondered what was up.

Who is this ringing very early intermittently? Is the telephone out of order or the caller is not sure of the number. Well she'll let me know. He thought and shrugged and continued to lie on his back in the bed naked.

"Good morning honey." She greeted him.

"Good morning honey, how are you?"

"Why are you sleeping late today? Is there anything wrong?" She asked ignoring his question and walked towards him and stood akimbo just an inch only from the bed. Her pink see through night dress revealing her sex just at the angle he wanted it to be shown and her aroma defused right into his nose. He found himself getting hot and the cock rising at the order of his brain. It made acute, obtuse and perpendicular angles with his thigh and began to beckon at her. She looked at it and smiled at him romantically. Lasciviously she moved nearer the bed bent and touched the cock. It jerked in her hand like stout spring. He accentuated her to it.

"The children are waking up soon." She warned.

"A quick one will do." She looked at him with the eyes of a dreamer and gave him an erotic smile. He raised himself slightly from the bed and pulled her towards the bed with the hem of her nightdress. She meekly followed the slight jerk she needed to set her in motion. She whispered something again which he didn't care to hear. She rolled up her see through nightdress up to her waist and threw one of her legs over him. She lowered herself on him and adjusted herself. They lay near each other for a brief moment squeezing each other as if to test the texture of their skins.

"What was wrong last night?" She asked not bothered about the telephone she left open.

"Forget it, I was only tire."

"Well, if that was it then it's all right. I thought I had annoyed you with some of my rude words. I was very worried in fact." She said believingly.

"It's all over darling. You didn't do, nor said anything wrong." Odongkara told her. She kissed him on the cheeks and got up content she was washed of her mortal sin.

"Dressed up. There is a telephone call waiting for you out there." "Who is calling?"

"Mukasa I think." she said with a thick voice full of hatred for the name.

"You're not sure who called. You didn't ask who was calling?" "Well it's Mukasa. I don't know why he has telephoned so early." "Something must be on our hands again."

"You mean you're going out again?" She snarled.

"If it will be necessary. We're fed up with murder cases in the district these days. Nearly every day somewhere someone must be murdered and this bastard is stuck on my back like a leech on a cow to solve the murder mysteries for him." Odongkara snarled.

"I quite agree with you darling. I am wondering if you are the only CID Officer in this station. You're hardly home for a full day. The total number of hours you spend home in a week is less than a day. The children and I see very little of you. Certainly we're missing your love. Otto continuously asks me where daddy is and why you don't come home to stay with us. I mean, this is going to affect them. Can't you do something about this darling?"

"I too, miss you, but you know, I have to go and do the work. If I don't go, very little or nothing is dug out from most of the crimes being committed around. Besides, my position as number two in command of the CID, I have to take orders from the boss to accompany the junior officers who are at the moment second to none. They need a lot of coaching and training on the job."

"Weren't they trained?"

"Oh yes they are trained, but you know, passing an examination is a different issue, and putting what you've learnt during the training into practice, especially, in criminology are two different things altogether. A criminal is not a fool. He tries to fool you so that you look an idiot with all his alibis and words. So really, before you pin him or her, you will have kept your five senses alert. You take whatever they say for granted and analyse them word for word later when you are alone. And these boys are still very young in the field. They are good and hard working enthusiastic lads, but left alone at the moment they are useless."

"What are you going to do about your family now darling?"
"At the moment there is very little I can do, but to coach the boys."
"What about transfer from here?" "To where?"
"Where there are more competent officers who do not need your help. When we were in Kampala you were not overworking like here in Gulu."

"So you are suggesting I ask for transfer back to Kampala?" He asked and laughed as he slipped on his bathing gown over his pajama he had just put on while she had changed into her gomace. He patted her on the back and slightly pushed her in front ignoring her suggestion.

"Will you need cold or warm bath?"

"It's warm, I will use cold water. I smell the cakes, you'd better check. They might burn." He warned, and she walked fast to the kitchens holding on gomace to avoid trading on the hem. He walked and sat at the edge of the table, one foot dangling in the air, the other resting on the stool below. He collected the bathing gown between his legs and talked in the mouthpiece.

"Hello Joe, good morning and how are you?" Joseph Mukasa the Officer-in-charge of the CID was a great friend to Peter Odongkara partly, because Odongkara was married to a girl from Mukasa's tribe so that occasionally they called themselves *Semegi* (brother-in-law).

"I'm sorry I kept you waiting long Joe."

"I was wondering what was happening. You came on the line when even our police patience was wearing out. Did you have a drop too much of the beer last night?"

"No. I didn't even see a Bell labeled bottle. I was as sober as a Bishop on a Pentecost day. I was only tired. In fact, I was too tired. I almost failed to eat my supper. No coffee could refresh me. The first time in my life have I slept like a dead volcano."

"You must have been Peter. I am sorry for that."

When Jane roughened him and left him hanging on the line, Mukasa kept wondering what has blown up. *What has caused her to change so suddenly? Has anyone reported her to the husband and this call I have put through has just worsen the situation? Moreover she made a mistake she hung up on me first and I rang again. It looks as if a kid playing with phone isn't it?* He thought as he toddle with the bottom of his pen on a Radio call message he received from Kitgum reporting a murder case to the Police Provincial Headquarter in Gulu. He expected Odongkara to come on the line fuming, but the friendly greeting and voice he got as he talked in the mouthpiece surprised him and thawed his frozen heart. Mukasa had started thinking how he was going to defend himself against Odongkara, in court if news of his infidelity with his wife had reached him. He was a man who has never lost any case in court. Because of that, he was feared not only by Mukasa, but also by the rest of the Policemen in the District. They wonder why he wasn't the Provincial Police Officer in-charge. They thought probably it was because of his appearance in the Police Service. People like Mukasa got their position through, laborious slow gradual promotion of the past where you have to start from the root of the ladder and work your way up depending on your ability and reliability. But with the young generation where education put you up the ladder, Odongkara would have eluded most of the old men from their chairs, but to avoid embarrassment, they put him high enough on the ladder pending retirement of the old men by death or otherwise.

"What time did you come in?"

"Oh I really didn't check on my watch. It must have been something near to eight o'clock in the night. It was still early. I would have come to the club if I weren't tired. Where you there?"Odongkara asked.

"I was there, but I was called to the station just when I was turning hot. I didn't like the idea, but I had to. You know the motto, duty first the rest later. And also, it saved me a few quid. May be that will add onto what I will drink tonight."

"Will you sponsor me Joe?"

"If you stay around I will certainly do that Peter."

"That will be great. I think I should be in if nothing else springs up during the day."

"That's why I said if you stay around."

"Oh, well, safe you from spending more quid. May be that's why you were willing to sponsor." He joked and they both laughed. "I'm very sorry about this radio call from Kitgum, which you'll see when you come to office. It seems the boys have done it again. This time the cousin of the big man. They even claimed it on BBC yesterday. You must have heard it."

"I had no time for anything last night Joe." He replied and added; "That's not good news to hear Joe on a New Year Day like this when everyone is preparing to celebrate the Passover day. The first of January and on a Monday in a new year shouldn't be spent cracking nuts in offices. We should be lying with our families in shades of our houses and trees, in the lawns or go driving in the park."

"I absolutely agree with you Peter, that is why I sympathize with the Police and Medics. You're always on your feet when others are enjoying themselves in exotic places", Mukasa said.

Odongkara chuckled cynically in the mouthpiece and said, "I wish I could be reborn Joe, to capture these young beautiful girls I see around. I might just resort to taking some of the loose married women out for romance in those exotic places and returning them to their husbands."

Mukasa felt a sword through his head right down his coccyx. He fidgeted in his chair and looked blankly at the portrait of the president in front of him. He wanted very much to abandon that topic, but he was not all that dull. He knew that Odongkara was pulling his legs. Therefore, any silly talk was going to expose him in the hands of the ingenious Inspector Police CID Odongkara who seems to have eyes which see through human minds. Even where he sat he felt nervous as if Odongkara was at his office telling him that, "tomorrow we are in court, because I have caught you with my wife." He felt warm water dripping from his armpits flowing down his ribs into his trousers. His nose began to run. His eyes watered as if he wanted to cry. He tried to talk, but no words came. He forced laughter, which was dry and naked like the sound of breaking wood.

On his part Odongkara bit his lower lip and raise his eyebrows and smiled, knowing that he had thrown a scare in the big pig. The laughter he gave told him a million of things. He knew the sound of his mirthful laughter and the cracking one he had just blown in the air was far from it. If they were near he would have read a lot from his reaction. Even then he knew quite well that he was as guilty as Adam. Just a matter of asking him, why you want to break our marriage? And the pig will run out of his skin yapping for mercy and forgiveness. He waited for the reply. At last he came on the line again.

"I think you're too decent to do that Peter. I don't believe you have a gut to run any married woman. You is not the type who can do that."

"Oh, well people change my friend, and acquire new skills. All I have to do is to be a great friend of someone who has the knowhow and he will show me the tricks. Mukasa nearly told him to shut up. But he stayed on precariously.

"You're a Police Officer who is fighting such crimes and you cannot go on encouraging it."

You go with my wife you idiot and you forget you are a Police Officer? I could ruin you and you'll never forget me for the rest of your remaining life. Anyway, so long as I haven't the proof, you may meddle around, but watch your step Odongkara thought. Talking ostentatiously Odongkara pinned Mukasa again. "Don't you know that the law makers are the law breakers? You make it and you know exactly where to snap from to save your neck from the gallows. That is why some Dictators claim they are above the laws of their states. How do you like that Joe? Isn't it interesting to be above the laws?"

"I wish you and I could do that but we can't." Mukasa remarked.

Complacent with his talk with Mukasa, Odongkara thought it wise to abandon the topic and pick on another easier one for him, which won't be heavy going.

"How was it here in the station when I was out?" Odongkara inquired.

"We were quiet except for minor cases of road accidents, burglary and assault, otherwise there was nothing major really which required you type of brain." He said with relieve and giggled trying to gain control of himself again.

"Back to our Kitgum news. Will you come to the office after your breakfast so that we discuss what we can do. I have contacted all our colleague and they confirm, they're coming. I am sorry Peter. You will have to spend your New Year Day out in Kitgum."

"I have already seen that Joe. And I regret that my wife is so eager I spend it home with her. She has made all sorts of arrangements. Well duty first the rest later. You take care of my home." He said casually.

"I will take care of my sister of course. He said and giggled foolishly. So long for now Peter. See you when you come down here."

"Are you in office?" "Yes."

"You won't go back for break?" "Not before we meet."

When they were talking, Jane was busy in the Kitchen like a weaver bird carrying food for its nestlings. She had made cakes laid the table and done all sorts of beautiful things a guilty lady would do to win the love of her husband. Odongkara put the receiver on its cradle. He got up staring at a handkerchief resting on the arm of the chair. He walked and picked it and examined it the way you would look at a fossil you have unearthed as you dig. He put it back and turned to go to the bathroom.

Jane saw him picked the handkerchief and looked at it curiously and put it back. Her heart missed several beats.

So the idiot forgot his handkerchief behind?" She thought. Small beads of sweat appeared on her nose. She wiped them dry and forced herself to talk.

"It belongs to Mukasa. I think he forgot it here yesterday when he came to check on you." She said nearly out of breath.

The Director Murdered

"Why are frightened like that honey? Is it because I have found a strange handkerchief in our house. People forget things don't they? I was talking to Mukasa just now, he sounds someone with a heavy cold and I don't doubt he needed a handkerchief to carry around.

I will let him have it when I meet him in Office at 8 o'clock. And by the way darling, I might not spend my New Year Day at home with you today. We have a case to follow up in Kitgum. Mukasa got a radio message from Kitgum that the cousin of the President seems to have been gunned down by the Uganda Black Devil Movement, UBDM and I am sure beyond doubt we will be there this afternoon. Didn't he tell you this yesterday?"

"No he didn't." Well no one trusts any woman with such news or he hadn't got the message when he called in to check on me."

"But darling are you going away again?" She said ignoring his remark and moved near to him. She, under normal condition would have clung round his neck. But because of the handkerchief of Mukasa and twice she was found romancing with him, she felt like asking the Almighty to bury her in the stomach of the earth there and then. She felt guilty touching her husband she is disgracing with her adultery.

"I think I will," he answered, moved near and held her waist without any passion. On her part she moved on him like a metal to a magnet, clung on him excruciatingly and began to weep.

"Why are you never at home with us?"

"Duty." When I retire I will sleep with you day and night until our bones decay.

"I want it now." "No time."

"I am fed up of staying alone."

"You could pay a visit to Mrs. Mukasa Mary. She's a nice woman. I am sure she will give you a good company." She opened her eyes, the lips quivered in an attempt to say something but she couldn't. She had no courage to say it out but after a while she said, "I will stay alone."

"Will it be a bad idea to ask Mukasa to take you out with the children when I am out?"

"Don't do that."

"Why? I mean, if you're lonely you need someone to occupy your mind for a while don't you? Mukasa and the family are our family friends, aren't they?"

"We will miss you, but I will be all right alone with the children."

"Darling don't be worried. I am not suspicious about the handkerchief I have found now. And I will be out of mind to suspect you with that old man Mukasa. What do you get from a man like him although women are known for their stupidity in sex? I am trying to make you happy when I am away." He said and hugged her and kissed her. It was a cold kiss. The type one gives to an unknown companion in pubs. She was still groping for his lips when he was already a foot away from her.

"I don't mean you're suspecting me for anything, but I just don't like Mukasa's family." She said getting convinced about what her husband had said.

"Why don't you like them? I find them a nice family and very helpful too."

"I think it make me look tribal if I associate myself too much with them. I'd rather stay with people of other tribes other than them."

"Nonsense darling, staying with people of your tribe doesn't mean you are a tribal. It's when you hate other tribes and treat them as sub-human then you become one. Here we are in Acholi land I am thronged by them on all sides. Other tribes are dotted here and there. Most of the time I am with my fellow Acholis does that necessarily mean I am a tribal? No; not at all. May be you have another reason for disliking Mukasa's family. If that is the only reason then keep yourself with them when I am out. You'll need their help and advice in difficulties."

"Okay darling as you advised, I will stay with them. But I will not go out with him."

Odongkara at the door to the bathroom, turned and looked at her and sneered and said, "Do what you think makes you happy when I am away. It's all right with me. Let me take a quick bath. You get everything ready. I am getting late for Mukasa and the group. Wake up the children and prepare them for breakfast. I might go away without talking to them again."

"I will do that." She said and went to the children's bedroom and woke them up, took them to the sink and washed their faces and brushed their teeth and they were soon dressed waiting anxiously to meet their daddy.

As he bathed, Odongkara tried to banish the thought of sharing his wife with an old man an equivalent of his father's in age, but in vain.

She seemed to think from all I have been saying that I know nothing about her infidelity. Or, she knows I know but just does not bother about it. Those tears are meaningless to me. I am not going to point it out to her at the moment. Why does she not like Joe's wife and family she of course has no reason. That excuse of tribe just came. To her, she thinks she's very smart when she talked like that. And I am sure she believes I am convinced. That statement would convince an idiot not me. Now the question is what next? Stay with her? Seek divorce. If I divorce her what will become of the two children. They will of course stay with me. But how happy will they be without their mother? I have already got enough proof to fire her. But the children. I will only stay with her in spite of all these, when she changes and apologizes for all these and promises that she won't go with this old man again." Odongkara thought as he bathed. The thought of killing Mukasa in order to make his family a happy home sneaked in his head, but he could not yield to it. *I think if the worse comes to the worst, I will divorce but, not kill anyone because of a woman. I won't do that.*

He walked out of the bath and toweled himself dry and sat on the dressing stool looking at himself in the mirror in the bathroom. He looked puzzled. He put on his dressing gown over his pajamas and walked out of the bathroom to the bedroom. When he was dressed up he walked out to the living room where the two sons were playing with their toy lorry. When they saw him they left their toy and ran to him shouting, daddy – daddy grapping him from all sides. He took the younger of the two, Owot, and kissed him, the boy returned the kiss. He bent down and kissed Otto, and he also returned the kiss. He carried Owot and held Otto by the hand as they walked to the dining room where Jane had set their breakfast waiting.

"What a beautiful table" he said.

"Thank you darling," she replied and took Owot from him. He gave the boy to her and turned to help Otto up on his chair. When they had all sat, Otto who sat next to his father did most of the talking while the rest of them listened and laughed. Then, when breakfast was nearly finished something dropped into the memory of Otto and he unplugged the fuse.

"Daddy."

"Yes Son."

"You know, when you were away uncle came to see us."

"Sure!"

"Yes." Jane nearly fainted when she heard the boy talk. She sat like a thief just about to be caught. She didn't know whether to knock the boy dead before he finished the story or ask him to keep quiet. But she knew interfering with the story of Otto in anyway may look like telling her husband that I went to bed with him. So she let the boy prattled on.

"Which Uncle son?"

"Mukasa. He said and went on. "He brought us sweets and biscuits."

"Did you say thank to your Uncle when he gave you the sweet and biscuits?"

"Yes daddy."

"You must always say thank you to people who give you gifts. Ok?"

"Yes daddy and Uncle sat with mummy on that big chair, he said pointing to the big chair in the living room. Odongkara could not help a laugh. The boys also laughed not knowing that they were giving their mother away.

"Don't you know that your Uncle is the brother of your mummy?" he said with a thick voice.

"Yes. But you know daddy, Uncle put his hand around the neck of mummy and they kissed."

"Okay Otto, it's all right. There is nothing wrong with that." he said, when he saw his wife in tears. Thank God Otto recalled his story when breakfast was virtually finished otherwise the beautiful table ornaments with all sorts of edibles would have been a waste. Odongkara got up caught his wife by the shoulder and kissed her on the cheek.

"Why do you worry over trifle darling?" He whispered in her ear.

"He is lying. Well, I told you Mukasa came here yesterday. I agree we sat together on the same chair, but he did not touch me nor did we kiss each other." She denied, sobbing, her shoulders heaving up and down as if they would fly away from her body. Odongkara controlled laughter. He would have busted into one thanderous one if he weren't playing his cards.

"I know he is, that is why I laughed it off. Don't worry darling come on keep those tears out of your face. I don't like seeing them you know I am likely to go out again as I have said and I don't want to leave you in an awful state like this. You must be happy and cheerful okay?"

"Yes" she answered in a sobbing voice. "So stop those tears".

"I will."

Odongkara took Owot from her bosom and took Otto by the arm and walked with them to the sitting room. He sat with them on the long piece of the settees. Jane was in the kitchen feeling a bit relieved that he has not taken the information given to him by Otto seriously. But she knew who her husband is. A very patient man who take things easy. He does not rush into things. As a result, people believe he is a man who can never be annoyed. Even if you insult him he laughs at you. You spoil his property, he forgives you, but whenever he lost patience he acted and did it to the extreme. So that all those who collided with him lived to remember the occasion for the rest of their lives.

In the living room, Odongkara decided to fish out more from Otto.

"Is this where your mummy sat with Uncle?" He asked as they came to sit down on the long settee.

"Yes daddy. Mummy sat here and uncle sat here," he said patting on the cushion.

"And they kissed?" "Yes daddy"

"What did mummy do after that?"

"Mummy said he should not have done it while we looked on, she said we would remember and tell you."

"What did uncle say?"

"He patted mummy on the back and said you won't be coming soon and by the time you came home we would have forgotten everything, because we are too young to keep anything long in our memory."

"Then what did they do?"

"They forced us to sleep and put off the light everywhere." "Did you sleep well?"

"No, Owot was scared of the darkness and he began to cry and uncle came and said he would not give him sweets again if he kept on crying."

"Did Owot keep quiet?" "Yes daddy."

"And you slept." "Yes daddy."

Odongkara sighed and began to drum his palm on the cushion staring blankly infront of him. He sat between the children resting his back on the sofa set. He didn't know what to do; he recalled the advice of his father.

My son I am telling you the truth and you are ignoring my advice. You're going to be disappointed in future and you will remember my words. You've left the girl with character and not much beauty and rushed after beauty, but no character so the headache will be yours do not turn to me. You're an intelligent son but you've failed to choose a wife for yourself. He looked at Otto and turned his head warily on the back rest of the sofa and looked at Owot and nearly wept. *I have engendered your existence. And I will make you happy at all cost.* Odongkara thought.

He got up from the chair with the children in his arms and walked with them back to the kitchen where Jane was drying the utensils with a cloth.

"Darling I must be going." I am sure Mukasa and the groups are now waiting for me."

"Daddy, where are you going again?" Otto asked "To the Office."

"Will you come back?" "Yes son."

"You'll have lunch here won't you?" Jane asked. Odongkara didn't talk but winked an eye to avoid arousing the interest of the boys. He kissed them good-bye starting with their mother.

"Shall I return the handkerchief of Mukasa to him?" He asked his wife,

"Please do." He took the handkerchief put it in his pocket and walked out to the garage and took the car out.

Now-now- now. I have a problem in my hand. What am I going to do? I have all the proofs that my wife is messing with Mukasa. One, the information by Ojuko's wife, she got them kissing in my house. Two, the Police Constable Kitimbo guarding the beach told me he found my wife and Mukasa lying naked at the beach where they thought no one could see them. The children were left with Mary. She was deceived that the two were going to Kampala and would be back after one day. This handkerchief and above all the story from Otto. Children always tell what they have seen. Never lie. Never. I am going to give this man a scare. I really want to scare him out of his senses. If he does not leave my wife alone, I will let him go behind bars for the rest of his life. I don't care for his family. After all, old as he is, he's not caring for my happiness. This looks terrible. I don't know how he's going to take it when I give him back his handkerchief. I am going to give it to him before we start the meeting in the presence of everyone and I will tell him that my wife found it in the bedroom and she has asked me to let you have it. I won't show any sign of annoyance or anger. If he comes to my wife again after this then I know he is determined to destroy my marriage then I'll strike him before he achieves his goal. On the other hand if she, besides what I have already collected about her goes her way, then I know she is seeking a divorce. There must be a way to forget her. I know it will be tough going, but given time, she will be someone to recall because of the children with me. There must be a solution to this problem. I don't know how it will end. I pray the two come to their senses and stop. Odongkara thought resentfully as he drove to the Police Station.

Chapter 2

Odongkara drove his *Citreon* UVX 225 and stopped at the gate of the police headquarters. He hooted once before a policeman on guard at the gate emerged. He flung his greener gun with the black leather strap over his shoulder and walked to the gate. He unlocked and opened the double shutter gate widely on both side and stood aside to let Odongkara in. The Constable saluted him and Odongkara waved back to him and drove to the parking lot reserved for him, written in bold capital white letters the *detective superintendent of police*. He switched off the engine, rolled the windows up on both doors, pulled out the keys from the ignition and walked out of the car. He swept his eyes at the lines of cars already packed in their reserved parking lots and noticed that all were in except him. As he glanced at the row of cars, he noticed that there was what looked like dried blood stained on the front wheel of Mukasa's official car. *What has the son of the bitch run down?*

Odongkara thought and walked round the car to see if there was more blood on the other wheels. The rear wheel, behind the blood stained front wheel, had some blood too. The other two wheels didn't have any blood stain. He became interested in the car more than the meeting. *What could he have killed? It can't be a human being could it? If it was, I am sure he would have made some effort to clean the car.* Odongkara thought and squatted down to examine the blood stain. More of it was on the inside of the front wheel. *I must take this blood for our laboratory examination. I would like to know what animal was killed by this man. That means the laboratory*

The Director Murdered

results should not be sent to Joe as they always did or he might become suspicious and get clever.

Two, I will stop him from using this car while I am still out. How am I going to do this?

Odongkara continued to think as he took out his handkerchief from the pocket of his trousers and carefully scraped the blood from the inside of the front and the rear wheels of the car and tie the scraping in different knots. As he scraped the blood, he kept on thinking of the best way to stop Mukasa from using the car. *I think if we are proceeding to Kitgum today, I will ask him to let us take the car with us. While there, I will order the car to be parked until I am sure of the blood result from the laboratory. We shall use the Land Rover in Kitgum police post for all other duties. I will tell him that the Land Rover here is in bad mechanical condition, getting old and it's slow. Since the victim in Kitgum is a VIP he may want us to move fast and get at the scene of the crime as soon as possible. Should I find out that the blood on the car is human, then it might not be necessary to pin him down with his infidelity with my wife. This could be enough gallows for him.*

When he let Odongkara in, and closed the gate, the Police Constable paced across the gate twice before he went back to the small hut build at the side of the gate for the guards, removed the gun from his shoulder and inclined it against the wall and sat on the high stool put near one of the tiny window used for monitoring the movements around. It was when Odongkara noticed the blood stain on the wheels of Mukasa's car that the Police on guard looked his way. He saw him walked towards the car and stood akimbo staring down at the front wheel. He saw him walked round the car, and came back where he had started. He saw him squatting down. From there he could not see whatever he was doing on the car. Later he got up and tied knots on a handkerchief he had in his hand and slipped it in the pocket of his jacket. He saw him flicked sand from his hands and walked towards the Office looking sad and irked.

What is up? The constable thought. *I must go and find out what this man has been doing there.*

Odongkara was aware that he was watching him as he worked on. *If he is going to be a reliable officer, then he is going to come here and try to find out why I have behaved like this otherwise he will let it that way. Anyway I am not bothered with whatever he will do. All I know is, I have a person who saw me behave strangely here. I am sure if I bring everything into light he will remember it.*

As soon as Odongkara disappeared behind the door, the police constable took his gun flanged it over his shoulder and began to pace up and down near the gate and slowly walked to were the lines of cars were parked. Stealthily he walked between the cars but could not see anything of interest immediately. *What has he been doing here?* He asked himself and moved in front of the police peugeot UP 128 being used by Mukasa. At first he couldn't make out any meaningful thing at a distance with his novice eyes in police. Later when he got nearer to the car he saw some dark dried substance. He moved nearer and saw it. He guessed that, that was the work Odongkara had been at. He shrugged and walked back to the gate to open for their police Land Rovers coming in. He closed the gate again and went and sat on his stool with his gun across his thigh and began to think of Odongkara.

This man is absolute. His eyes are trained to see everything that can be seen. Look, how did he see that blood stain on the wheels of the car? I am sure all those bunch in the office do not know a damm about the blood, might be Mukasa himself doesn't. From what I guess, they are going to get surprise. I heard someone was killed yesterday on Keyo road by a hit and run car. The occupant of the car was alleged to be a lady with two children. I don't know if this is the case. I have never known Mukasa letting the official car to his wife. There is always a beginning for a fault. He might have let the car to his wife yesterday for the first time and she messed immediately. That will be very sad indeed.

Odongkara walked up the flight of the steps and got to the second floor. The office of the DSP Odongkara and that of O/C C.I.D Mukasa were situated at the extreme end of the second floor. Odongkara's Office, was opposit that of the CID/OCP. Flung on both side, of about a meter wide aisle, were various offices. When he got to the door to his office, he stopped and opened the door and went in. He walked round the clients' sofa sets and went and sat on his swinging office chair behind his desk. He took a file on a murder case he had just been investigating and read through his finding as if he wanted to revise what he wrote before their discussion of the new case in their hand. As he read, he found himself thinking about the handkerchief of Mukasa in his pocket. He didn't know whether he behaved decently by bringing the handkerchief along with him.

I shouldn't have brought it with me. I must have gone out of my mind a little. But she's my wife why should he interfere with our happy marriage. I have the right to stop anyone interfering with our marriage. I know women are silly. But is this the right way of solving this problem? Should I be direct to him and ask him to stop fooling around with my wife or should I make him guess I know he is? What about this handkerchief now? Throw it away or take it to him? Okay, Now I know what I will do, I will take the handkerchief to him and say I got it along the corridor."

He got up put the file he was reading in the cabinet and locked it before he walked out of the office with his brief case in his hand. He pulled the handkerchief of Mukasa out of his pocket and held it in his left hand. He walked to the office of Mukasa and rapped on the door, opened it and walked in.

Mukasa, a short stocky man turning in his early sixty with big broad nose, large eyes and a bald head having fringe of grey hair at the temple sat behind his desk, which was directly opposite the door. He was crushing the burnt end of his cigarette in an ashtray when Odongkara walked in. The rest of the panel was seated on the clients' sofas discussing the radio message from Kitgum police post.

"Why do you think they did it if they are the one?" Odongkara found the police photographer asking.

"Good morning gentlemen and Happy New Year to you all."

"Good morning Sir and Happy New Year to you too." And they sprang up on their feet and stiffened in salute. Only Mukasa remained seated as the second in command entered the office.

"Sit down gentlemen. I am sorry I am late. I had a hell of problems with my car. I don't know what happened. It's firing like a stern gun. I came cruising with it like a tortoise and it brought me to this handkerchief. I got it on one of the steps down stairs. Does any of you claim it? It's an expensive new one. I was tempted to hoard it." Mukasa knew where he forgot the handkerchief and also knew Odongkara knew it is his and he didn't find it on one of the steps, but in his house. He fidgeted. He saw stars. He didn't know whether to accept that it is his or deny it. If it had been anyone else, but not Odongkara, Mukasa would have denied knowledge of the handkerchief. None of the panel in the office showed any sign of claiming it except, Mukasa who fumbled and touched his pocket and said,

"It's mine."

"Oh, so it is?" Odongkara said and gave it to him grinning.

Mukasa rose up a little from his seat to receive the handkerchief with a trembling hand.

"Thank you very much."

"You are welcome, but don't drop it again. I won't be able to pick it up for you the second time. Some lucky guy might help himself with it." Odongkara said and sat on a sofa opposite the finger print expert. Mukasa understood the sarcasm in his talk. He knew, the clear warning sounded to him was stern and serious. He found himself getting hot and small beads of sweat doted on the top of his nose. The bald was glistened with sweat. Odongkara saw that he had scared the pig off his wit. To avoid him wetting his shirt with sweat he changed the topic.

"Now where do we go from here? It looks we won't have a good year." Odongkara said.

"It has started rough, we hope it cools down." Mukasa endeavoured to speak and continued. "Constable Mugambi got this radio call from our police post in Kitgum at 23.00 hours." He said, and slipped the chit to Odongkara and continued, "the murder cases in the district are becoming alarming. Soon we will not be able to cope up with them. I think in some obvious cases for instance this one, we have just received from Kitgum, and we might just go and confirmed the evidence and closed the chapter on it."

When Mukasa was introducing the topic, Odongkara was half listening because he was reading and internalising the radio

The Director Murdered

message. *To OC Provincial Police Headquarter Gulu. Attention of the DSP Gulu is also drawn on the same. A murder has been accomplished in Kitgum Medical Research Center. The victim, the Director of the institute, Dr. Gunya was shot at point blank range in his house at about 22.00 hours. In addition, at about the same time, the main store of Medical Research Centre was burglarised.* When he finished reading the radio message he sighed and slid down on the sofa. He rubbed his nose and looked at Mukasa who had just finished his introductory comment.

"Why do you say this case is straight forward Joe?"

"Well you came in late last night. The news was on, on every foreign radio like BBC that he was gunned down by the notorious BDM. I guess you know where the Medical Research Centre is, in Kitgum?"

"Very well."

"You saw the type of fortification erected by the British. With all the barb wires atop the walls. I think only desperate people like the BDM could dare go and instill the insecurity in such a secured place. The place looked heaven to me"

"Your thought could be right Joe. But you know Joe one secret of life to me is some of the things we think are impossible are actually the very possible that criminals maneuver to their advantages. Iam going to give you two examples to illustrate my point. The first one are those fortresses you are talking about are actually high ways for thugs around town especially those working within the fortress."

"Really?" Mukase exclaimed.

"Yes." Odongkara said and continue.

"They looted cartoons and cartoons of drugs over those walls and maneuver their way between the barbwires like snakes among thorny bushes. Yet they leave neither clue nor a mark to show their entrance and exit. It was only in the late 60s that some were caught right on top of the walls among the barbwires with cartoons of drugs they were looting, then it became certain that the high way, through which the drugs were migrating, from the stores, to the outside wall was over the walls and between the barbwire. Could anyone imagine that Joe? The security at the main gate and all other gates were heavier than those you see at the President's gate, but yet the drugs went missing from the same store not through the gates but over the walls."

"The second example is what you know well. The Berlin wall. That wall divides the two Germanys. East and West. That, I saw myself. Its barbwires finishing on top of walls are much higher than what you see in Kitgum and are more deadly. The soldiers patrolle the whole length of the walls on both side like army ants, but yet always you hear some person has polevaulted the wall smartly into the West. How they do it in spite of the wall, the barbwires and above all the vigilant, soldiers leave anyone puzzled."

"So to comment a little on what you have just said, I seem to think we could stir up something of interest in Kitgum. Right now if we just look at the message sent to us I see these classified events. One, Dr. Gunya has been shot dead and this man as you know is the cousin of the President. Alright?" Mukasa and the other nodded their heads approvingly.

"Well yesterday we celebrated the People Revolution Day which brought the President into power. There could be connection between these two events, which seem to confirm the claim of the BDM on the BBC and other foreign mass media? If not, then what? If it is the BDM then, why the burglary in the store of the Medical Research Institute? Since the BDM started their movement they have not been reported to have burgled into any home or any government premises. If anything, they always destroy the government vital installations and significant big people who are at the moment at the helm of this country. You recall the assassination of the Minister of Finance. A very talented young man was gunned down in his own house. The guards at the gate and everyone in the house were there. But how the gunman entered the house and shot the Minister in his bedroom foxed even the best CID we have in the country today. The BDM claimed responsibility for the murder but what did we fine when we investigated the crime? They were the very guards who blew the whistles about the crime that became the culprits."

"What I would like you to appreciate here gentlemen, is let us not take for granted what we hear or see. This case at hand at the moment, could turn out to be the most exciting to begin the New Year with. So let us pack and go and see what we could stir up. If we find it a cake in a plate, then that saves us the trouble. We shall come back soon to enjoy with our families but bear in minds that criminals are tricksters." Odongkara warned.

"You are right Sir", the Police finger print expert, Lwanga agreed with him. "I have been thinking about the link between the burglary in the Institute store and the murder. The best I can think of are: Firstly, If it is the BDM in action then they are short of drugs now, and the Medical Research Centre, is the best place to go for medicine. Secondly the murder of Dr. Gunya was accidental. Probably he happened to pass that way when they were pulling the store down. He might have recognized them and to avoid publicity and identification they followed him to his house and fixed him. Otherwise, I don't see any other way the burglary could be linked with the murder of Dr. Gunya. Another question is how did they get in?" Lwanga asked

"Yes, those are some of the question you will be asking and answering when you are on the ground. We should get going this morning by ten oclck and we should be at the site of the murder by noon. Peter, you will go with this team." Mukasa instructed, ignoring the question of Lwanga.

The panel to go with Odongkara consisted of, Odongkara himself the Detective Inspector Police (D/IP) Police photographer Opiyo and working together with him, was Assistant Inspector Police (D/AIP) Lwanga, the finger prints expert, and the government pathologist Dr. Kizza.

"Which vehicle are we going to use? The Land Rover is still in the garage for service." Odongkara interjected.

"I had instructed them to make it ready for you this morning before nine oclock." Mukasa said.

"It could be the repair is major and may not be ready soon. In any case it is not safe to take a vehicle from the garage on such a long journey and on a rough road to Kitgum." Odongkara put in sarcastically.

"You said your citroen is not good at the moment?" Mukasa asked.

"It's no use at the moment for an emergency like this one. The best home for it is in the garage to see her doctor as soon as possible. She's choking. It was alright yesterday as we came back. In fact I had a nice sleep in it when we were returning? Wasn't it?"Odongkara asked DSP Opiyo.

"You are right. It started this morning. She might have inhaled something on the way. The road to Palabek wasn't good full of pot holes." Opiyo commented.

"I guess Joe will take care of her for me." Odongkara said

"I will do that. This leaves us with no option but for you to take my official car the peugeot. When I fixed your citroen, I will use her instead."Mukasa agreed.

"You're welcome, but don't bang her. She is comfortable, but tricky." Odongkara said with a triumphant joke and they laughed.

"I won't. I will treat her gently". Mukasa said.

"Shall we quickly go and kiss our wives happy New Year and good bye before we leave," Odongkara joked again. They all laugh and were almost on their feet to rush to their homes when a knock sounded on the door.

"Come in." Mukasa invited whoever was knocking on the door. The police driver, a short stout man with dense beard entered the room. He was in his overall. He had not button the shirt and his hairy chest stuck out in the open. He walked in and saluted them.

"Sir …"

"Will you button your shirt up before you begin to talk? Learn to be smart in front of your bosses. We are not interested in your hairy chest."Odongkara interrupted him.

"I am sorry Sir;" the driver said and quickly sealed up his hairy chest.

"Now what is the problem?"

"The vehicle not ready?" Odongkara asked affirmatively "No Sir"

"What is wrong?"

"The gearbox is completely wrecked. The first and second gears do not engage. I manage to bring it back with the third and forth gears only."

"That is not our problem," Odongkara said. Turning to Opiyo, Lwanga, and Dr. Kizza, he said, "let's go and wind up at home." The problem of the Land Rover is for those who are staying behind. Odongkara ordered and they walked out.

On his way out Odongkara passed through his office and put a call to John Mugondi the Laboratory Technician in charge of the government forensic Laboratory.

"Hello this is Mugondi's house." The daughter of Mugondi, Judy, answered the call.

"Who is talking?" Odongkara asked.

"Judy the daughter of Mugondi." "Judy, is daddy home?"

"Yes Sir."

"Could I speak to him?" "Who are you?" Judy asked

"Peter Odongkara. Tell him I want to talk to him urgently." "Yes Sir." she retorted and put the receiver on the table and went to call her father.

John was dressing up to go the Laboratory to check on some of his experiments he had set the previous day. Judy came and rap on the door to his bed room.

"Who is it?" "Judy."

"What do you want Judy?"

"Mr. Peter Odongkara wants to speak to you." "Where is he? Give him seat."

"He's on the line waiting for you."

"I am coming straight away," he said, and walked out of the bed room buttoning his shirt. He came and picked up the receiver and said.

"Hello Sir, good morning and Happy New Year." "Good morning John, and Happy New Year to you too." "When did you come back?"

"Last night at about 23.00 hours and we are going out again now."

"Oh dear. I thought you would. To Kitgum, isn't it?" "Yes, how did you know?" Odongkara asked.

"I heard about the case from Mukasa in the Club last night. I am sorry you will not enjoy your New Year at home with your family."

"Thanks for the sympathy. But John, I want to see you in person urgently."

"Now?"

"Now."

"Where are you talking from?"

"From my office, but I don't want you here." "Where then can I meet you?"

"I'll come to yourLaboratory."

"That's all right. I was on my way to the Laboratory." "Were you?"

"Yes."

"Fine. I'll be with you in a minute, Odongkara said and hung up.

John Mugondi hung up too and got up from where he was sitting.

"Darling." he called his wife who was in the dining hall laying the table for breakfast with her daughters Judy and Anne.

"Yes honey."

"I am going to the laboratory and … "But breakfast is ready" she protested.

"I am meeting the D/ASP Odongkara there now." "Okay. Will you be back soon?"

"I think I should finish up with whatever I wanted to do there before I come back," John said.

He walked out into the garage, pull out his fiat 127 and drove off to the laboratory. When he got there, he was just opening the door to the laboratory when he saw the police peugeot modle 504 UP 128 pulling up behind his car. Odongkara parked and walked out and nearly ran to the laboratory.

"Hello John," he said extending his hand for a handshake. "Hello Peter, The year has started badly for us I don't know how it will end."

"Bad beginning makes good ending," Odongkara said as he pulled out His handkerchief knotted in two places.

"Here is a piece of puzzle for you. I would like you to handle it very carefully. I have here in these two knots scrapping of sample of blood. I hope I took it well enough to satisfy the test. You'll excuse me if not. I am a non-technical man of course." He said and shrugged. Another thing about the blood is we do not know whether it's human or animal. We would like you to confirm that. If it is human, then do all the relevant tests on it as far as your facilities can allow. Things like ABO Blood group Rhesus blood group etc. You know what to do better than I do. If it's animal then tell us what animal species, if you can. Now the tricky part of it is, please, for goodness sake, do not give this result to anyone other than the one talking to you now. This is of paramount importance.

"Not even to Mukasa?" John asked.

"He should be the last to know the result. I am betting with him over this blood for something great. So if you give him the result, he might play me a trick and I'll lose." he laughed and patted John on the back. Here are your specimens. Test the two specimens separately. You can label them as you like the first specimen you can label it one or 'A' and this is the second one which you could label two or 'B'.

"Are you not taking the handkerchief with you?"

"It is not important, you can keep the handkerchief until I come back to collect the result." Odongkara replied and began to walk out.

John turned and walked into the laboratory with the specimens in his hand. He examined it meditatively. *What does this mean? Odongkara always has lots of puzzle for anyone. An unknown blood. Could be human or animal, he said and he wants the result in his hand not Mukasa. Why? They are betting over this blood. If the result goes to him he would get wise and play him tricks. What are these tricks he's talking about? He always talks in parables. I know what he said is not what is in the air. What I know is he knows everything about these blood samples. It is here for laboratory proofs to enable him speak without doubts. How does this tie up with Mukasa? Why should he be the last to know the result, yet officially all such cases have to go to Mukasa's office first before him. No other specimen has been as urgent like this one which he had to bring himself. Normally Corporal Oteng brought the specimens. I will keep my ears and my eyes open. I am sure something of interest will stir up within the station very soon."* John thought as he set up the Radial imunie diffusion test in the agarose gel, a method used to identify blood from different animal species. He used anti human globulin serum against the blood sample. For the negative controlled he used goat serum and for the positive control he used human serum. When he finished setting the immune diffusion he washed a portion of the blood in saline and tried to do human blood grouping.

The sharp reaction of the cells with the standard human sera Group B left him with no doubt that the blood was human. He went further to determined the Rhesus blood group which he found to be RhD Positive. He was excited at the preliminary findings and he wanted to ring Odongkara to give him the results. But when he looked at his watch, the time was half past 10 o'clock Odongkara and his team were on their way to Kitgum. *Well, he said he would come for the results here. There is no need to panic. The blood samples A and B seems to be from the same human blood presumably from the same person or people of the same family or even any other persons who are in the same blood grouping. I will see the ouchterlony immunediffusion result tomorrow just to confirm that these samples are from human.* Mugondi thought and walked to wash his hands in the sink.

Chapter 3

Immediately he finished working on Odongkara's samples, Mugondi was called for an emergency to do some blood group on a child who was killed by a hit and run car on Key road. He went, sampled the blood and, came back to the laboratory and worked on the sample instantly. He washed the blood grouping template and left it drying near the sink. As he wrote the report on the request form he noted that the blood group of the child was the same with samples Odongkara brought earlier.

Hey wait a minute! Mugondi exclaimed. Is this a coincident? Didn't I do blood grouping on that sample Odongkara brought and the blood group was also B RhD positive? What does this mean? Could Odongkara be working on this as well? Double murder cases in his hand to solve! This child was run down yesterday evening by a car whose occupant was described to be a lady with two children. Could it be that he was tipped about the culprit. Why does he want to exclude Mukasa in the case at the moment? May be he wants to ...

A telephone ringing in his office brought him to attention. He walked to the office and lifted the receiver glued it on his ear.

"Hello, government laboratory, can I help you?"

"Your breakfast, its ice cold, are you coming home for it or not?" He heard the demanding voice of his wife.

"I am sorry darling, it's difficult to come home and come back here again. I would like to finish everything before I come. I had finished the work of Odongkara but I was called to do an emergeny which I have also completed. I am now checking on some of the work I set yesterday. It shouldn't take me long. I'll be home let's say, at eleven thirty. I am sorry darling, don't throw the breakfast away I will come and gormandise it. You've in fact started off my hunger. I wasn't feeling hungry but your call has started my digestive enzymes and I feel I must eat something."

"Come home then."

"Okay I am coming," he said and hung up.

Now, now what is next? He whispered and walked to the laboratory. He read the cultural results and set up their sensitivity. Read the ouchterlony tests he set the previous day. When all were done, he disinfected his bench and put everything away before he went and washed his hands again. He walked to his office and took off his laboratory coat and hang it on the nail driven onto the door of his office for the purpose, closed the office and passed through the laboratory and out. He locked the door and walked to his fiat 127 and drove home.

When he was in Kampala Odongkara used to go fishing in Lake Victoria every Saturday. He always went with his packed lunch and he would sit at the lakeside from morning till 18.00 hours in the evening. He always caught quiet a lot. However, he developed much interest in fishing not because of the catch he always got. If anything, he would have done a lot better by not going to the river to fish. He mainly likes fishing because it was near the water that he always fitted the zigzag puzzle of some of the crimes he investigated.

He always went alone and sat alone at the bank of the lake and did more thinking than fishing as he watched the fish bite on his bait and dive with it under water.

That fun of jerking the fish out of the water, the lapping of the water on the bank caused by the waves, and the cool breeze blowing on his detective face, seemed to bring him brighter ideas to solve the equations of murder cases.

Since he read the radio message from Kitgum, Odongkara believed that, the claim by the BDM should be investigated. Because there were a number of false claims made by the movement in the past, which were broadcasted over local and foreign Radio stations like the BBC. Things which the never did, they went ahead and claimed responsibilities and these massmedia amplified the propaganda on their behalf. The BDM wants the world to appreciate their existence. So they claimed any accident, which happened in the Country. Once a bus over-turned, over river Achwa they claimed it was the movement which did it and the BBC was at their service to receive and broadcast the false claims. With these experiences, although the world has now been made to believe that the BDM was responsible for the murder of Dr. Gunya, he, Odongkara, had his skepticism about the news. He knew he would have to dig very deep into the murder before he accepted it was BDM who murdered Dr. Gunya. Because he knew there was going to be a lot of thinking, he decided to take his fishing kits he had just purchased from Kisumu with him. At 9.00 o'clock, the three drove off from the provincial police headquarters. Odongkara purposely decided to drive the the official car of Mukasa. He drove the car he knew had a case to answer, with all due care because he wanted to preserve the dry blood on the wheels of the car as much as he could. He wasn't sure if any other person had noticed the blood stain. *Anyway, whatever the case, the blood is already in the laboratory,* he thought as he drove the car in the gate of the hospital to go for Dr. Kizza the pathologist. He brought the car to a stop in front of the administration block of the hospital. "Okay, you wait right here." He said and got out and walked to the office of Dr. Kizza. He knocked and entered the office.

"Hello, you've come."Dr. Kizza welcome him and got up from the chair.

"Yes, we are on the move, we want to go and talk, think, and ask questions." Odongkara said sitting on a chair next to the table of Dr. Kizza.

"I will return tomorrow?"Dr. Kizza. announced his plan affirmatively.

"Even tonight. After examining him and confirming he is dead and done your magic on the carcass, I don't see why you should stick around with us. I suspect the murder could have been committed by utterly different person or persons who have nothing to do with BDM, we may stay away a little longer."

"You don't seem to believe that the BDM exist and they could commit a murder?"Dr. Kizza asked

"No, not that, but I have my doubt about them anyway. You know, of all the murder cases we have been investigating only about one percent is genuinely committed by the BDM. There are many bogus ill minded, failures in life thugs, who are being used by some power hungry men, to commit all these crimes. I am getting worried because of the fact that the BDM wants to be known, the thieves, robbers and all other villains have found ways of camouflaging themselves behind the BDM. What does it cost you to stick a knife into a person, blow a car off, burgle into a house and write a note to BBC that the BDM is at it again. Well for them, the news monger, truth or falsehood doesn't matter, the microphone is there. It's a matter of talking in it and the satellite completes the lies in your radio. I always hear the news with heartache. For instance, last week you heard the BDM claimed over the BBC that they blew off the bridge over Acwa River. Did you hear that?"

"I did." Dr. Kizza agreed as he packed his post mortem kits in the box and walked across the room to take his laboratory dust coat hanging on the door. He folded it and stuck it in the brief case.

"Now is there any sense in that? You and I are going to pass over that bridge now. Not a grain of cement was tempered with. With such lies, you and I, who live in this country, especially, a police detective like me, should take it for granted any crime committed and claimed in the name of the BDM? I always think otherwise. I am getting convinced that there are groups of armed thugs who are using the BDM as scapegoats in this murder of Dr. Gunya. I am going to dig and dig into this until I find out who is behind."

"I know with your determination, you will," Dr. Kizza said and snapped the brief case shut, put the keys in his pocket and looked around him. I am ready. Shall we go?"

"Okay," Odongkara replied and stood up and walked out first and Dr. Kizza followed him.

"Sir." Dr. Kizza called his attention. "Yes, Doctor."

"I have made arrangement to go in the hospital Land Rover to enable me to come back without interfering with your work tomorrow."

"You did."

"Yes it's there packed with the driver waiting for me."

"Oh well, that is fine. I was banking on our vehicle in Kitgum police post to bring you back."

"They could all be in the garage". Dr. Kizza joked.

"No, I checked with them, they are all in perfect condition."

"What do we do then?"

"If you must go with this Land Rover then you are welcome, but otherwise, you are assured of transport back tomorrow or even this evening if you will have finished with your job."

"The driver has already been paid his night allowance and I can't alter it now. I will take the vehicle from here."

"Well, no objection. You take it."

When they got to where Odongkara left Lwanga and Opiyo, they got out of the car to meet Dr, Kizza. After the the usual exchange, Odongkara explain to them the road map.

"This is how we are going to move. We shall have our lunch in Onyong 'nyong Hotel. You know where it is? The Hotel on the bank of river Aswa. That is another attractive nest for gossiping and rumor mongering. I am going to start work there. You might go ahead to Kitgum after lunch leaving me there depending on what I will stir up. If nothing surface, then we could go together. So, you with your Hospital Land Rover could give us a good camouflage. You can put it just in the parking ground opposite the bar. I will park a little off, before the hotel and we shall walk it to join you. By any luck no one will spot us. We shall all be Doctors if anyone will want introduction, otherwise, there is no need introducing anyone. I know you Doctors have friends everywhere. People who come to your garages for repair and panel beating. They always do not forget your kind." Is this okay with everyone? The three looked at each other and Lwang said, "it fine with us if you say it."

The time was 9.35 a.m when they left the hospital gate. "Gentlemen," Odongkara started to talk, bringing two men Opiyo and Lwanga to attention. Opiyo who sat infront in the codriver seat turned and looked at him while Lwanga sat forward from the back seat and rested his forearms on top of the backrest of Opiyo seat so that he got what the boss had to say.

"I was telling you and Doctor Kizza that we are going to have our lunch in Onyong 'nyong Hotel. I guess if we spend a bit of time there and keep our ears and eyes open, we might see or hear something of interest that will keep us talking on our way to Kitgum. Dr Kizzz will park his Land Rover in the parking ground opposite the bar and we shall park a little off before we reach the hotel. The writing on our vehicle Uganda Police and the registration number plate are scaring to many people, especially, to those who hate us. They might not be free to talk, or might even disappear if they see us out of the car. This might jeopardize our work right from the start. So we will be on the lookout for that. I always come over such an errand in my private car, partly because it gives me complete blanket cover and secondly, I get allowance for it." he said and they all laughed. "Anyway, when we get to the hotel, we shall sit with Doctor Kizza. If some of his friends should come to meet him who do not know us, we are all Doctors going to Kitgum to study an epidemic outbreak of cholera announced last week. As I said, I have twice got very useful information from Onyong 'nyong hotel, a rumor center there. We leave our car at my girl friend's flat and shall walk to the hotel to join Dr. Kizza."Odongkara said and smiled

"You have one here?" Lwanga asked.

I have them everywhere I go. I find them very interesting especially when you mixed boozing with eroticism. They almost show you their pussy and once a woman does that to you, you can ask her anything she knows, she will blurt them all out for you. Men are a bit difficult. You can't make them talk before you buy plenty of booze for them. My girl friend you are going to meet here is quite an informer. If there is any news we should know, we shall hear. She moves and sees and hears. However there isn't much to see on her. She is a heap of meat that is all there is in her."Odongkara said and they all laugh again.

When they got to her flat, Helen wasn't at home. All the same, they left their car at the backyard of her flat and walked to the hotel only about one hundred meters away.

"She might be rolling herself on some man's bosom in the hotel to mark the New Year Day" Odongkara said as they walked to the hotel.

Dr. Kizza had arrived in the Hotel. He was seated at a six seater table in the open air bar under a huge umbrella of grass. His Land Rover was parked in the parking ground opposite the bar. His driver was seated alone under a tree on the low walls built around the parking ground sipping his beer.

They waved to him, and he waved back, as they walked straight to where Doctor Kizza, had already set the flag waving.

"Hello Doctor, How's it?" Odongkara asked. "Fine! I am already doing it" Dr. Kizza replied.

"Well, that is the best way of waiting. Anyone you know around."

"Haven't seen one. May be in the inner bar." "Let me go and see. You guys what do you take?"

"Nile Lager." Opiyo said

"Club Lager." Lwanga said

"I will stock you in a minute." he said and walked to the bar.

As he predicted, Helen was in the bar seated between two men boozing. Her hoarse voice pierced the humid air in the bar insinuatingly. Odongkara heard the grating laughter and knew she was in. He glanced in her direction as he entered the bar, and it didn't take him long to spot her. When she saw him, she jumped up with excitement, her face beaming with smile as she walked to meet and hug him at the counter. They shook hands affectionately.

"Good afternoon and Happy New Year" Odongkara said "Good afternoon and Happy New Year to you too." Helen retorted.

"How was it, all these days?" Odongkara asked. "I've been doing well dear."

"You really look it". Odongkara replied and she gave him her grating laughter. Odongkara looked away to the bar man who was serving him his order.

"Let's go outside and I introduce you to my work mates?" "Before we go outside, I should introduce you to my friends." Helen said.

"Not necessary, Helen dear" Odongkara rejected.

Helen went to the two men with whom she was sitting and excused herself to go and meet the friends of Odongkara sitting in the outside bar. They went and the bar man followed them with a crate of beer containing a mixture of Nile, Club and Bell beer lagers.

"Gentlemen, meet Helen Angwec, Secretary to District Commissioner Kitgum. Doctor Kizza, Lwanga and Opiyo are my friends I've brought them here to celebrate the New Year Day with you." He introduced them indicating them by a wave of the hand.

"What do you have for them here?" Odongkara said. They exchanged handshakes with her and she sat down on a chair next to Odongkara.

"We don't have much for the visitors to this town these days, except insecurity. We have plenty of that here these days. People feel a bit secure during the day but at night you can hardly sleep. Gunshots and burglary into houses are part of us. When you escape a night, you pray God you should escape the next."

"That is bad, if you are going to welcome us with gun shots and hoodlum running after our lives." Opiyo said.

"What are the authorities of this place trying to do to contain the situation?"

"That, I can't tell you, not because I don't want to, but because I don't know anything about it," she said folding her arms over her huge breasts.

"That is one of the oaths Secretaries take before they become Secretaries of big men like DC et cetra. Never to let a cat out of any bag", Odongkara said and laughed. They all laughed. Helen eyeballed him, and didn't say any word.

"Even if I was the one, I think I would be careful under such situation." Opiyo remarked.

"Now, Helen, this I think is something which is not a state secret. Who are the people behind it? Very many times we hear claims over the radio stations that almost every obloquy happening in this town is being claimed by BDM. Is it true that they are responsible for everything?" Odongkara asked.

"You seem to think I know each and everything happening in this town."

The Director Murdered

"No, I am asking about the general hearsay from day to day." "What you said is what I hear every day." Helen said and kept quiet. Odongkara was disappointed at the precision she was answering the question. He knew it was not the time to yank all the information from her.

"Okay, Helen, thank you very much for the information you gave us. We shall be careful tonight not to think of nightclubs less we stop some straying bullets. May be if I have time I will come to see you. Will you be at home?"

"Yes, of course, you will find me home. Where else do you imagine a gutless girl like me can go when the armed thugs will be firing everywhere?"

"No date." "None at all."

"Those guys!" Odongkara said and winked his eyes towards the inner bar referring to the men who sat with her before he got in to buy the beer.

"Forget them. They aren't anything to me. They are mere work mates as I told you."

"I was taking care of my jaw bones. I didn't want them smashed by those powerful fists." Odongkara remarked and added, "before I forget Helen, I must apologize on behalf of my colleagues for violating your compound."

"You mean you checked on me in my flat?"

"Not only that, but we left our car in you compound." "You did, that's alright" she said indifferently.

"I thought you were all in that Land Rover" she added.

"How did you know the Land Rover belongs to us?" Odongkara asked.

"They are Drs. Kizza, Lwanga and Opiyo could be some kind of Hospital men. And that Land Rover UM, Uganda Medical or whatever it's is new to this town."

"And me?" asked Odongkara

"You are a news monger!" she said and they all laughed.

"You know the entire vehicle in this town?" Opiyo put in lightly "The common ones", Helen said.

Odongkara looked at his wristwatch, the time was 12.30p.m. "We must eat our lunch and start off to town."

"How is the accommodation these days?"Odongkara asked Helen.

"Nearly all the Hotels are fully booked. People seemed to feel secure in hotels than in their homes so they prefer to spend money and save lives."

"You think we shall not get any room in town?" "You might."

"Well, if we fail to secure rooms, you flat is roomy enough to accommodate all of us, and won't you do that and for once feel secured among men?"

"You will be most welcome," Helen replied.

CHAPTER 4

Odongkara was thinking of contacting Mukasa in Gulu using the walkie talkie when his, in his pocket, buzzed. He took it out and said.

"Hello Joe."

"Hello Peter, where are you now?"

"We have just arrived in Kitgum police post." The time was 13.00 hours when Odongkara and his team got to Kitgum. Kitgum police post was a small one in contrast to the town, which was growing in size and crimes. There were about forty uniformed policemen. The Officer in-charge of the station was an Assistant Inspector of Police AIP. There was no CID branch in the station. So, they depended on the staff of Gulu provincial police headquarters' members for criminal investigation.

"Have you spotted out anything of interest yet?" Mukasa asked. "Not yet Joe. We stopped in Onyong'nyong Hotel the center of rumor mongering, but we could not get much. All we picked was that the guns have found their ways into the hands of hoodlums around towns here, and they are doing all sorts of evil things with them. Nearly every night someone has to bleed to death, houses are burgled in, and properties looted. It looks a world of complete unrest. Big shots in town here have abandoned their bungalows and have taken refuge in hotels in spite of their cost. They find it safer in the hotels than in their homes. Our men here look too few to cope up with the situation. We might need the help from Captain Dramadri from the army in Gulu because of the deteriorating security in this town."

"You're right Peter. I have in fact contacted him on that already this morning. He said he has heard about the worsening insecurity in Kitgum town. People don't sleep at night because of gun shots and fear that their houses could be burgled into anytime."

"The hoodlums here have taken the law into their hands. They kill, they rob, and they burn down houses and shops. Only last night, two beautiful shops were burnt down here Joe".

"Which ones Peter?"

"The fire is still smoldering in Pop in shop opposite B.P. Filling Station on King George Avenue. Everything has gone down to ash in both Pop in shop and Baby shop."

"There are two Baby shops. The one near Park Hotel?"

"Yes, that one near Bata next to Park Hotel. The smoke from the shop is still itching our eyes."

"Any death?"

"No. A few were roasted, and they are recovering in the Hospital. The place is hot from the look of things Joe. I am taking Doctor Kizza, Lwanga and Opiyo straight away to Kitgum Medical Institute. We should move the body of Dr. Gunya to the Mortuary for post mortem by 14.00 hours. I'll give you the preliminary findings before sun set."

"A little more about those shops." "What about them Joe?"

"Are the owners safe? I mean not among those roasted." "They are as clean as you are. Those are the guys who are in their homes during the day but sleep in the hotels at night." "Have they talked to our men yet Peter?"

"They have except the owner of the Baby Shop who is nowhere to be seen with all the members of his family. But one interesting thing is that when our men went to the Baby Shop, they found some automatic machine guns, a dozen hand grenades and 0.38 mm automatic pistols about six of them, so we don't know why those weapons were there?"

"You know Peter, I hear that some of those big belly dicks in Kitgum are collaborating with the so called BDM, could it be that guy in the Baby Shop is one of them?"

Peter sighed in the walkie talkie microphone and said, "I don't know. There is a possibility Joe, that he is collaborating with them

The Director Murdered

but he could be acting alone. I think we are going to follow him very closely. I want to see how he will divert from the Institute drama. He could be linked with it. If we enmesh him, he will yap all he has in the gut." Odongkara said and was about to hang up when Mukasa came on again.

"So this is all I can wire to Kampala because they have just called to find out what we have done so far. Secondly I …

"Let them not forget that this is a criminal case and we need time to investigate it, Odongkara snapped in. "It's not just a matter of coming to Kitgum, picking the information, and transmit it back to them. Whoever we are looking for is not an idiot. He's trying his best to conceal all information we want including himself. Anyway, we shall let you have the doctor's result and some of the obvious information when we get at the scene. What is the second problem Joe?"

"You heard about the hit and run car accident on Keyo Road yesterday."

Mukasa said affirmatively.

"I did Joe. Any more to it?" Odongkara asked. "Yes. And it sounds ridiculous to me."

"Why Joe?" Odongkara said raising his eyebrows.

"You remember it was reported that the hit and run car was being driven by a woman with two children?"

"Yes, that is right. I remember it."

"Now it has turned out that the hit and run car is our UP125."
"Don't tell me that Joe. How comes?"

"I don't know."

"Have you talked to your wife about it?"

I haven't talked to her since yesterday after 16.00 hours after tea."

"You mean she is not at home?"

"She's but you know, immediately after tea yesterday, I went to the club playing darts and remained there until 20.00 hours when I got the call from the station about this murder case. I came back to the office and sat up to about 24.00 hours. I went back home and found that they were all in bed. I didn't bother her. I went in bed and slept. This morning I woke up a little earlier, at about six a.m. and came away to office. I have been here since morning Peter. My lunch was at the canteen this afternoon. When I came back to the Office at 13.00 hours, a boy came to the station, he's about nineteen or twenty. He is tall, slender built with dark complexion. He is at Layebi collage secondary school boy doing his East African Certificate, Ordinary Level this year. This chap has developed a unique hobby. He always sits near the road from midday until late in the evening recording the plate number of cars. And- and, you know what? one of the numbers of the cars he recorded before he went back home last night wasUP 125 and that is our Peugeot 504, which the witness claimed ran down that child."

"Find out Joe if your wife went out in the car. I guess you were using your own car in the evening? Is that right?"

"Yes, I was."

"You didn't lend the police car to any lady?"

"No, Peter. I have never done that. You know it yourself." That it's either you or me driving the car."

"Did you leave the keys for the peugeot at home when you went out?"

"Yes, I did."

"Is it possible that your wife might have driven out that way in the car?"

"I don't know. That sounds the most likely thing. But she has never done that."

"There is always a beginning Joe!" "Then what might have possessed her?"

"My advice is, Joe, have a time off and find out from her if she was the one who used the car, I mean UP 125 last evening and caused the accident." Odongkara said knowing that the old man was in shit. He knew the Peugeot UP 125 was certainly involved in some accident. Now, with the information by an eye witness, that boy who actually, saw and recorded down the plate number of the car involved in the accident, Odongkara was left with hearing the laboratory results only to confirm that some unknown woman knocked the child on Keyo road in the police vehicle UP 125.

I am sure laboratory test must have been carried out on the dead child to determine his blood group. We shall need the result to compare and contrast the blood groups of the child and that on the car which knocked him dead. Odongkara thought as he shut his walkie-talkie.

Shall I ring John up and find out what result he has for me? No. I have some work here at the moment that one could wait. He thought and he imagined Mukasa sweating in the dock in the court. Even if I don't pin him down because of his adultery with my wife, he is already sunk to his chin. First, his wife ran down a human being and made away. She didn't even bother to confess to the police that she has committed a crime. The husband now tells me that he doesn't know a dam thing about it? Who is going to listen to such excuses? A CID police officer in-charge of the Province, his wife with whom he sleeps on the same bed commits a crime and he tells me he could not talk to her all these time because he was too busy, is the greatest joke of the New Year. Since morning, up to now he hasn't gone back home! This man is not an expert in concealing a crime. In an attempt to conceal one, he opens up his guard and everyone, even a child sees his tricks. Secondly, he gave his official car to his wife to use and he pretends he doesn't know.

I would have sympathized with him but how could he play with my wife like that. I am glad I am not the one who is going to ruin him. He has ruined himself."

What Mukasa told Odongkara was right to some extent, but he was careful not to mention that in the first part of the evening he was with Jane the wife of Odongkara. What happened was this Mukasa knew that Odongkara was to return from his trip that day. In the evening at 16.00 hrs he put a call to Odongkara's house to check if his wife was in and what she was doing.

"Hello." She answered the call of Mukasa.

"What's ready?" He asked well aware that she had recognized the voice. Therefore, there was no need to mention names in case anyone was hearing on the line.

"Everything is ready." "Sure!"

"Yes."

"Are you alone?" "With the children."

"You are expecting him tonight, aren't you?"

"You should know that better. He rang me up yesterday and said he might come back tonight. Didn't he tell you?"

"That's why I am telling you that he comes in tonight. And …" "And what?"

"Tea at your home?" "I am busy." "Preparing for him?" "Yes of course"

"I won't stay long."

"Go home to your wife."

"You don't need to tell me that. I should have gone straight to her if I didn't prepare for you."

"Don't joke old man."

"I am very serious as a matter of fact."

"I sometimes don't understand you. Do you know who you are? And who I am? If you do, you wouldn't be talking like that. Are you testing me to find out how silly I am?"

"No Darling I think sometimes I get mad about you."

"I don't want to hear that any more. I had fun with you and may be we should stick to our family now. It will serve us a lot of unnecessary predicament. We have been lucky many times but one of these bad days we could get caught in the actual act then I don't know what I will do."

"That will never happen. We shall be careful."

"You are an old baby mister. Weren't we nearly caught doing it on the beach? We were got naked in the water. We were got kissing in our room here when you wanted us to have it on the chair what would have happened if I accepted? I am getting worried about my safety with you. I am asking you from today to start forgetting about me. I am very suspicious my husband now knows I am cheating him. And that is derogatory to me, a mother of two sons.

"Can I come for tea?" Mukasa asked ignoring her comment. "Go and have tea at your house."

"I could, but I have some letter for him I was intending to drop at your place before I go home."

"That you can do."

"Fine. I will be with you in a minute." "To bring the letter!"

"Yes of course." He said and cradled the receiver disappointedly.

"No skins off my nose," she put the receiver on the set, shrugged and went back in the kitchen.

Mukasa sat in the office staring blankly in front of him not believing what has happened. I can't take this as a final answer. I must go to her place. It's still 16.00 hours only I have plenty of hours with her before 18.00 hours. The time her husband said he would be in. Mukasa left the office and drove to his home first, parked the police official car in the garage and went in the house. He changed into a white T-shirt, a white khaki pair of shorts and white shocks completed with a white canvas pair of boots.

"You're going to the club?" His wife asked.

"Yes." he said and picked up the box of darts and walked out of the house.

"Tea is nearly ready won, t you wait?" His wife told him.

"Do you mind me going? A friend is waiting for me. Mukasa lied."

"If you are in a hurry I'll keep yours in the flask."

"Thank you very much darling." He said and went to the garage where he kept their Volvo UVS 663 pulled it out and drove in front of the house and hooted once. His wife came and stood at the door.

"I am going dear" he said putting his head out of the window.

"Go and enjoy yourself." His wife said.

"Thank you." he said and drove away. Mukasa drove straight to Odongkara's home. Jane was washing her sons preparing them for night sleep. She heard the hooting of the car and came out excited thinking it was her husband. She jerked the door opened and saw a stocky bald gray haired man with protruding eyes, and a fat nose, standing at the door. She nearly slammed the door on his face but she held it.

"Hello," he said and mounted up the steps at the door. "Where are the letters?" She demanded.

"What is the aggression for?" He asked and walked right up to the top of the steps.

"Let's go in." he said and held her by the waist and pushed her in.

She flicked off his hands from her waist and looked at him exasperated.

"Take it easy baby. I know you are …"

"Where is the letter? The children are up. I don't want any nonsense."

As she talked Otto darted from the bathroom and came out running. Mummy, mummy, and stopped short when he saw them standing on the floor glaring at each other like two wrestlers aiming at the neck of the opponent. The mother turned to him, took his hand in hers and walked him back to the bathroom to wash. Mukasa sighed, sat down on the chair, blew his nose and held the handkerchief in his hand. Jane finished washing the children and walked with them out, dressed.

"Say hello to uncle," Jane said to Otto. Otto came and greeted him and he picked him up on his laps. He hugged him and kissed him on the head. Old Mukasa had the trick of enticing women. He was as patient as death if he wants one.

Jane came and sat on the same chair but kept space between them carrying baby Owot in her bosom. They sat talking about this and that until it was 19.00 hours.

Mukasa waited, there was no sign of Odongkara returning home from his trip. The old man started his tricks. In the process he left his handkerchief on the arm of the chair and forgot all about it. It was when Mukasa was in Odongkara's house that his wife Mary got a call from a family friend, Onekalit. Onekalit, a rancher, lived about five miles on Keyo road. On his ranch, Onekalit had poultry of chickens, turkey, ducks, geese, herd of cattle, pigs, goats and sheep. Together with Komakec, they supplied the town with meat, milk and eggs. They had specific consumers.

Mukasa's and Odongkara's families happened to be the consumers of Onekalit's produce because of the proximity of his ranch to their homes. Komakech, the father of Odongkara, had his farm north of Gulu town about twenty miles away. He served half of the town with his produce and Onekalit served the other southern half of the town.

"Hello, good evening can I help you?"

"Hello Mary, Onekalit called her by the name as he recognized her voice on the line.

"Oh, Onekalit that is you, how are you? Are you apologising for the delay in sending us the milk today?" She said and giggled in the mouthpiece.

"Yes madam, my truck broke down last evening and we have been trying to put it right since morning. We expected it to be all right this afternoon but it isn't. I am now at a fixed. I don't know what to do for you people tonight. Some people have already come to collect theirs from here. I was even going to bring you some nice meat of turkey this morning for your New Years' Day tomorrow, won't you come and take one?"

"Yes of course I need one" Mary said with excitement of a housewife who wants to treat her family on a nice dish on a New Year Day.

"Will you come for it before they are finished or send my brother Mukasa to come for it immediately if you are busy in your Ministry of Home Affairs Office", he joked. She laughed and said

"I am busy, but I think I will call in for a few minutes. My husband has gone to the club and he's with friends now, I don't think it is wise to bother him with such duty now."

"That is why I think you are the finest lady I have ever seen. Mine would have dug me out among Kings and charged me with duties." Onekalit said and laughed.

"I hope the turkeys left are still good. They might have selected all the good ones and …"

"No madam, it's the contrary. The better and more expensive ones are still untouched while the cheaper, well, poorer if you like to call them so, have already gone. To avoid disappointment, come immediately and make your pick so that the New Year Day tomorrow will be a good surprise to my brother Mukasa. Turkey is fantastic blessed meat to eat on such a day. Beef, of course, is for those who see meat once in a year. You who eat beef often need a more tasty palatable meal like turkey for a New Year. Hum!"

"I am coming" She said.

"I will be waiting for you. So long", He said and cradled the receiver.

Now what do I do. He has gone away with our car and left the official car behind. Should I take this to him and exchange before I go

to Onekalit. Five mile is not far, a matter of ten minutes' drive, I will be back. She thought as she changed her dress to go and pick up their milk and buy the turkey. She picked her basket and called her daughter and the son to accompany her to Onekalit's ranch. They went driving in the UP 125 Peugeot 504. They got to the Onekalit and found him serving, with apology, his usual consumers whom he personally served every morning with milk and any other produce.

"I don't want you to move out of your homes on the big day tomorrow searching for milk," he assured them. Mary came last. She didn't want to push her way to be served before the others. So she went to the house chatting with Robbina, the wife of Onekalit.

When everyone else was served, and left, Mary walked out with her children to pick their turkey and the Milk. They got them and soon were on their way home. There was a bungalow standing about twenty meters away from the main road. When Mary was going to Onekalit's home she saw children in the home were playing with balls near the road. On their return trip Mary was driving the speedometer needle pointing at 80 kilometer per hour to catch up with time for supper. As she approached that home, one of the children chasing his ball ran head on to the speeding car of Mary and was thrown in front of the car. She drove over him and left minced meat of the boy behind. Hysterically, she sped on. She was mesmerized at the feel of the body of the child under the car. The crushing of the bones under the wheels of the car left her no woman, but a mad old woman. She cried as she drove away. She didn't know how she got home. She didn't know how she brought the car under control. When she got home, she forgot about herself. She forgot about the children, and the husband. She thought of nothing, but a gallows. She ran and threw herself on her bed and cried bitterly. The rest of the children who remained home were all awe stricken. They were stunned at the way their mother came home crying, but, their young brother and sister told them what happened. They all began to cry in sympathy with their mother, especially, when they thought of her being hang for murder.

Their elder brother wanted to contact his father in the club and break him the sad news, but the receptionist in the club told him that his father was not in the club and he hadn't been around since the club was opened.

"Isn't that strange? Daddy left home with darts box at about 16.00 hours saying he was coming to the club!" The boy insisted.

"I am sorry your father has not shown up here. He could be in the junior officers club. But why? I doubt very much. Anyway, try to ring there. Any message for him when he shows up?"

"No thanks." The boy said and cradled the receiver. The receptionist shrugged as the indicator light went off on the switchboard. He could be laying some chick some place, who knows. 16.00 hours up to now he hasn't reached the club, it's strange unless he is with some friends outside the club, but then why give the club as a place for contact. The receptionist tried to enquire if he was in the junior club.

His counterpart laughed at him and said, "Why do you think Mukasa could be here?"

"For a change may be."

"Well, he's not here and I don't think it is proper to try to find him here. Try other places in towns."

It was at about 22.00 hours that Mukasa appeared in the club looking gay and happy.

"Who is going to challenge me in darts?" He asked and walked to the officers who had played darts since 18.00 hours when the club opened. They were tired and wanted rest.

"We are tired now. Where have you been all this time?"

"I was in town." Mukasa lied.

When he left Odongkara's home he drove to the club after he had kissed Jane good night. As he drove away from the avenue to Odongkara's home towards the Senior Police Officers club, in his driving mirror he saw a car behind him pulling to a stop at Odongkara's home the indicator light indicating that it was going in. The characteristic head lamps of the Citroen were unmistakable. He saw it branch off to Odongkara's home. He knew he had come back.

How lucky I am, he thought as he drove away. I think she is right one of these days I might be caught in this childish game and I will remorse too late, he thought as he drove to the club.

Odongkara got home, parked his car in front of the house and hooted once. She heard the hooting of their car and walked out of the bathroom where she was washing the remains of Mukasa. She wrapped herself in a towel and walked to the door to open for her husband.

"Hello darling you are welcome home?" she said and opened the door wide.

"Thank you very much," Odongkara said and walked out of the car carrying his briefcase and slammed the door behind him. He mounted the step at the door and walked in the house.

"You are bathing late tonight?" Odongkara put in lightly. "Mukasa was here, he kept me talking and I could not leave him alone. He has just left in fact. Did you meet on the way?"

"No I saw his car driving away as I came in. Did he want to see me?"

"He said he had come to check on you, yes. And he brought some of your mails."

"Did he leave any message?" "No."

Umm. Odongkara said wondering why Mukasa should sit in his house late at night during his absence. He had never personally delivered his mails at home. If he had not heard of any rumor about his adultery with his wife, he wouldn't have been suspicious, but with the rumors in the air he had heard, he became very suspicious that something must have happened between the two.

Why the late bath after he has gone. Well, could be presentiment or over anxiety that I am having. She could have done nothing wrong, he thought as he walked out to put the car in the garage. He came back and found his wife out of the bathroom.

Mukasa had just sat down with his first beer when the receptionist at the switch board walked to him. He bowed down and said, "excuse me Sir, your son rang here an hour ago asking for you. He said the matter was urgent. I asked him to leave the message with me so that if you showed up I could let you have it. He said it wasn't necessary. I don't know if you've seen them already."

"No, I haven't." Why should they want me urgently at home? A visitor, he said and sipped the beer from the glass. "Okay thank you very much, I will see them."

"I think the champion has rested enough to challenge me." Mukasa addressed himself to Opiyo who had lost interest in the game tonight. Mukasa, before switching over from uniformed Police to CID police, was an exquisite shot man. He always won trophies in shooting competition and at one time in 1963 he was the best in the East Africa Police shooting competition held in Kampala.

With that accuracy in shooting, dart was his favourite game. No matter how drunk he was, he always won. He got his way up the ladder in the police service, not because of his brain, but his ostentation in maneuvering the gun.

With persistent plea for an opponent for the game tonight Opiyo, reluctantly accepted his challenge. The two men got up and chose their referee. They had just gone half way through the game when the telephone rang at the switch board.

"Hello Senior Police Club here," the receptionist said. "Police headquarters. Could I speak to Mukasa if he's there?"

"Hold on the line," the receptionist said, got up and walked to Mukasa who was throwing his darts missile on the darts board.

"Excuse me Sir," the receptionist said standing at attention. "Yes please. Is my son on the line again?"

"No, not him. It's the police headquarters in need of you."
"Police headquarters! What do they want me for at this time? I hope it is not another murder coming in," he said and threw the last missile in his hand on the board. The referee recorded his score. He plucked off the missiles and walked to attend the phone leaving Opiyo, throwing the missiles on the dart board.

"Hello, Mukasa here."

"Good evening sir". The police Constable at the desk in the station greeted him.

"Good evening. What is up". Mukasa asked. "Two cases have just come up for you Sir!" "All for me?"

"Yes Sir"

"You are sure there is nothing for Orwotho?"

"He has already handled his part Sir, so it leaves your wing open. In fact, I tried to contact you in the earlier part of the evening in your house but didn't get you. Your son told me that you were not at home and you weren't in the club because he was also trying to find you. I tried the club again but the receptionist at the switch board confirmed to me that you weren't there."

"In any case sir, this is just to make you aware of what happened on Keyo road." The police Constable at the desk said and went on.

"When the parents of the child, ran down by the unknow lady driver reported the case to the station at 18.25 hours, the superintendant of Police Orwotho was in the Office. He immediately dispatched his men accompanied by the wailing parents of the child to go and identify the site of the crime and make necessary inquiries. Four uniformed men went and were back with the body of the child in the police car. The body is now lying in the police mortuary. Orwotho said that John Mugondi will sample the blood from the dead child tomorrow and carry out relevant laboratory investigations."

"At present Orwotho has deployed policemen at road blocks along all the roads leading out of town. They are scrutinizing every car with their searching torches. They are trying to sport the car which got involved in the hit and run of tonight. I think the more imperative case for you Sir is the second one. The Police Constable said and continued. "We have also just got a radio message from Kitgum."

"What time."

"It was at 22.00 hours. That there was a burglary in the Medical Research Institute main store and the Director of the Institute was shot dead in his home by an unknown gun man."

"Don't tell me!" Mukasa exclaimed in astonishment. "Yes Sir that is the message we got."

"Dr. Gunya? I don't believe it. Dr. Gunya shot dead?" He said almost shouting.

"Well that is it."

"Okay, I will be in the station straight away now. But, without Peter in, we can't do much tonight!" Mukasa explained.

The Director Murdered

"And by the way Sir, another message has just been received that two shops are burning in Kitgum now. The firemen can't go nearer because there are lots of shooting around the place."

"What the hell is happening there? How are they ending the year? With violence! Silly idiots. Instead of celebrating the New Year Day tomorrow happily, they are pulling their limbs apart. This is the trouble with us Africans. We know we are the most backward continent in the whole world. We can't make a needle by ourselves, not even able to feed ourselves and here you get the rapacious power hungry men destroying everything we are trying to build. Destroy roads, schools, hospitals, shops with the Whiteman's gun and bombs. It's sad! What is happening in Kitgum is yet another evil the African independent countries are going through. Kill your brother to get his power, his money." Mukasa complained and cradled the receiver angrily and walked to Opiyo looking sad and annoyed.

"What is up big man?"

"Kitgum Town is assaulted with all crimes!"

"Is it?" Opiyo asked indifferently as he threw his missile on the darts board.

"Yes it is. The Medical Research Centre main store has been burgled in, the Director of the Institute has been gunned down by an unknown gun man and two shops in town are ablaze now. The fire men are unable to get any nearer to quench the fire, because there is shooting on all sides around the burning shops.

"Umm." Opiyo said. I don't know why Dr. Gunya should be shot." he added.

"Enemies of the nation. People who are brain washed can commit any crime. It looks we are going to have a bad start tomorrow. I don't know if Peter has returned. He has been running around too much. I thought he should rest a little this week, but the Devils have done it again. He will have to lead you to Kitgum tomorrow I am afraid. There is no way out. I am going to the station now and see what I can organize for tomorrow programme. It's imperative. You know who Dr. Gunya was?"

"I do." Opiyo retorted curtly, turn and walked to the group of police officer seated boozing their beer. Mukasa followed him, wished them good night after he had told them the news and walked out of the club and drove straight to the office.

Being the last day of the New Year, the club was kept open throughout the night. Because of that, the officers sat up late into the night to have a two years drinking spree. It was great fun to drink in the last seconds of the old year and the first second of the New Year. A legend which has been going on for years in the Police headquarters among the senior and junior officers.

When Mukasa got to the office, he received the recorded Radio Message from Kitgum. He read it and put it in the pending tray. *Not much can be done without Peter. Unless he returns tonight. If he does tomorrow he will have to go with Dr. Kizza, Opiyo and Lwanga* he thought and took a compiled police report on the child ran down by hit and run vehicle.

The report said that the driver who was driving the car must have been over speeding and was driving on the wrong lane on the road. Because the home in which the children were playing was on the right. And it was not possible for the child to have run into the left bumper of the car and be hauled on the right hand side of the road where the body was found smashed by the right wheels of the car. There was a very high probability that the driver would have avoided the accident if she was driving on the left. Their suspicion was vindicated by the eye witnesses who saw the car run down the child. The police remark stated that the hunt for the car which caused the accident was being intensified along all roads. All cars are being scrutinized critically for blood stain.

Mukasa read the report and put it in the pending tray on top of the Radio message from Kitgum. He sighed and stretched his legs under his table. He rubbed his eyes and yawned. He looked at his watch and noticed that he was in the new year and the time was 1:00 am.

Oh my God! I must go home to sleep. He got out and climbed into the car and drove out of the gate. As he crossed the main road, the headlamp of his car picked up a lady walking alone.

What could a lady be doing on the road alone at this time of the night? He thought as he pulled the car to a stop near her. Immediately he stopped, the lady disappeared under the shrubs growing at the road side. He didn't bother to get out of the car. He shrugged and drove on. *Let her enjoy her New Year Day though it's against the law for unaccompanied lady to walk alone at this hour of the night.* He thought as he drove away leaving her behind. When he looked in the driving mirror, he saw the same lady on the street under the streetlight running after him. *What is wrong with this woman? Has she committed a crime from which she is running?* The thought made him fidget and he felt a chill along his spine. *I must get her and ask what is worrying her in this New Year.* He drove fast in front and park in a dark corner, put off the light of the car and ran back crouching, following the lines of shops. Some night watchmen guarding the shops got up startled from their sleep thinking he was a thief but he whispered to them "Police, don't make noise!"

The lady came running like a devil out of hell looking behind time and again as she ran. The pat-pat sound of her bare feet plodding on the ground, amplified by the still night, echoed by the shops, could be heard far away.

Mukasa came and laid ambush for her just at the end of the line of shops. He saw the lady slowing down but walking briskly towards him.

Has she seen me? He thought. *I don't think so otherwise she would have turned back.* He saw the lady come walking straight at him. He didn't know what to do spring on her like a lion and hold her or frightened her to stop at gunpoint. He had no gun, but he knew at night like that anybody's knees would buckle at the sight of a stick and the word Police. *Okay I will say, police if you run I will shoot to kill.* This may save me the trouble of chasing in the night. The lady turned and saw him at a good escaping distance. She screamed and sprang into a serious run. Mukasa followed. Mukasa chased her under the streetlight. She knew if she kept within the town, she was going to be caught with the aid of the patrol policemen or the night watch men. It seemed she knew her path and where she was going. She ran off into the dark. Mukasa knew the lady must be a criminal, *if not, why the flee.* He put in some more effort to chase the lady.

As she fled along the marram path, she hit her toe on the stone and tumbled and fell. Mukasa was on her. He grasped her by the waist. She struggled up and shook his grip away from her waist. She started to run but Mukasa kicked her legs and she fell down on her back. He came and grasped her by the arms and felt the rigidity of her bones, which told him that it could be a man disguised in a lady's dress. She jerked her arms and Mukasa lost grip and staggered away like a drunk who has run into a stone. He stabilized himself and charged her. She hit him hard on the face with the type of blows of a man. It then occurred to him that he must fight her as a man and not as a woman if he didn't want to go home humiliated. He put in more effort, got the arm of the lady and tried to twist it on her back. It was like twisting a steel bar. *Hay are you a woman or a man?* Mukasa thought as they fought. He gave a slap across her face, which sounded like a calabash crush under foot. She screamed. The scream was typical of a woman. She rushed forward and clawed him with her long finger nails on the neck and bit him on the chest. Mukasa felt a burning pain on his neck and chest. She tried to claw on the face. He fell back and she missed. There was a space between them. She made a quick jump, ran wild into a tree which stood near them. She fell on her back soaring her limbs in the air as if she fell from the sky. Mukasa ran forward wondering about the woman with this rare type of strength. She picked up a stone she found lying near them and tried to split the scalp of Mukasa with it, but he held her arm before the stone landed on his bald head. She jerked her wrist and as she did, Mukasa lost the grip of the wrist and the stone banged on his ribs. His lungs wobbled inside his chest. He was nauseous. He spat out salty saliva which he mistook for bloody spittle from his lungs. As they fought, a car drove along the road following the Bank Street where Mukasa left his car. She heard it and jumped away and started running wildly into the dark. Mukasa stood looking after her, only her frock flickering in the dark indicated her position. Mukasa dared not follow her. He walked away humiliated.

I've never found a woman as strong as this. She fought like a man. She must have committed a crime somewhere. Why is she running away like a fugitive late at night like this? If I got her, even if she wasn't a criminal, I would have charged her with vagrancy. A lady to walk alone at this hour of the night is most odd. Mukasa thought as he walked back to his car. He didn't know whether to tell the story to his friends or not. In the end he decided to keep quiet about it. As he entered his car, he saw a small paper held on the screen by the wiper. He ducked out a little and pulled the note and read it. *It read. You will get shot one of these days if you aren't killed. Keep clear of town at these hours of the night BDM.* Mukasa read the note, put it in his pocket and drove away.

He got to his house at 2 o'clock. Every member of his family was dead asleep. He parked the car in its place and walked straight to their bedroom. He found his wife who had cried the whole evening fast asleep. He entered the bed and slept.

Mukasa left for office before any member of his family had woken at 6 oclock in the morning, after breakfast which he prepared himself. He drove in his official car unaware of the accident it caused the previous evening. He drove to the police station and park the car on the parking lot reserved for him, locked the door and walked to his office.

After drawing programme for the day Mukasa look at his watch and the time was 7.30 a.m

It's now good enough to ring. I must find out if Odongkara came back last night. The car which went to his home after me last night could be someone else. If he did, then I am glad we should embark on this Kitgum case immediately. This Keyo hit and run woman could wait. Unless the car is located, there is not much we can do about it. He thought and dialed the house of Odongkara. That was when he got remorseful Jane awake and busy in the kitchen, she attended to him.

Mukasa had just cradled the receiver of his telephone after talking to Odongkara when he got a telephone call from his son.

"Hello, Mukasa here." "Good morning dad."

"Good morning son what do you want?" he barked at his son as if it was a crime for him to ring him in the office. "What is bothering you? You have been ringing me everywhere yesterday and …"

"But daddy, mummy …"

"What is wrong with mummy? If she isn't well let her go the hospital. I am too busy to come home to attend to her."

"She is crying daddy since yesterday evening!"

"Hear me son. What you do is ask her what the matter is. If she is sick and she is unable to drive to hospital you drive her, okay? I am really too busy to come home now. Perhaps after I have discussed some of the problems here with my colleagues."

"It's imperative daddy, that you come home immediately!" "Don't be silly. Is she dying? I left her sleeping well what has happened again."

"No daddy! it can't be discussed on the line like this daddy." "I'll come." Mukasa said and cradled the receiver.

What the hell is she calling me for? He complained as his mind wondered into his past. He said she is crying since yesterday evening. Did she see me with Jane, followed, and spied on me through some spy-hole? If not then what is she crying for? Women, no matter how old they are, are very selfish with their men. They yell their tops open when they suspect you are cheating. I am sure there is no other reason why she should call me home either she saw me or someone told her that I was with Jane last night and she is trying to prove from me whether I did it. If this is so, then I have got obloquy over me in front of my grown up kids. What do I do? Go home and talk it over? Or wait until late at night? But she will spend the New Year Day unhappy. Mukasa thought remorsefully.

Oyoo the man whose child was knocked by Mary lived about four miles in a trading from center off Gulu town on Keyo road in a bungalow inherited from his father. He was married with four sons and two daughters. Oyoo worked as Superintendent of Works in Gulu Municipal Council. During his leisure hours, he goes hunting for games and birds. The rifle gun he used for hunting was also inherited from his father.

That Sunday evening, when his child was run down by Mary, he had gone out hunting wild game and birds for meat for the New Year Day. Oyoo was a stingy miser. He always felt awful whenever he spent as much as a shilling on an item he could have got from his sweat. His miserliness was described by his friends as horrible. Most of the things in life were unnecessary for Oyoo. His children,

The Director Murdered

although should have been playing with the best toys in town, always got some made for them from the workshop of their father. Their Cookeries and cutleries were those cheap types you find in the huts of peasants farmers in villages. He dressed in simple dress and so did the rest of the family as he controlled the family's account. The furniture in the house, although his wife made all efforts to make them look nice, were those he inherited with the house. He had never replaced any, nor repaired any tear. His best means of transport was a Hercules bicycle, although he would have easily afforded a car. Because of his tremendous love for money, he was nicknamed by his friend *"Minister of Finance"*. In short, they called him Minister Oyo. That evening when his son was knocked down by the car, the five year old son was running after a toy ball, made for them by their father out of banana fibers, his sister had thrown towards the road. He did not hear the sound of Mary's car speeding back to town driving on the right hand side of the road. He ran head on with the car and was thrown about five to six feet in front of the car, which later came and rolled over him mincing him to a pudding.

Oyoo returned from his hunting at 18.35 hours. He found his wife wailing for their dead son. He was dumb founded. He threw down the guinea fowls he had brought, disappointed.

"What happened?" He asked his wife. "He was knocked by a car."

"Did you note down the plate number of the car?" Oyoo asked "I was in the kitchen, but the children said it was a blue Peugeot modle 504."

"Did you note the number?" He turned and asked the elder son who stood near them.

"No." the boy replied." How he wished he had a car, he would have gone chasing the car even if it was going to be a goose chase. But with the Heckle bicycle, he could not do much. He smacked his lips and paced the compound, lost in thought. The only thing he could do was to ride with his wife to the police station and report the matter immediately.

With his wife on the pillion of the bicycle, they set off for the Police headquarters to give in their account of the accident.

There were three eyes witnesses who claimed they actually saw the vehicle knock and ran over the boy. The three voluntarily reported to the police station to record their account of the accident.

They gave their statement separately to Superintendent of Police Orwotho. Lam the immediate neigbour of Oyoo was the first to make statement to Orwotho. Lam a local Motor Vehicle mechanic in town was a good friend of Mukasa because Mukasa always repaired his vehicle at his garage and more often Mary took their private Volvo to his garage whenever it was faulty. On that fateful day Lam was returning home from his garage when he saw Mary crashed the son of Oyoo.

"You said you saw the car and recognized it at a distance that it was the official Police car of Mukasa?"

"Yes sir."

"What made you so sure that, the car you saw was no other car than that of Mukasa?"

"Because, one; The blue colour, two; The plate number UP 125 and Three; a dent on the rear bumper and lastly; His wife was behind the steering wheel.

"Do you know his wife well?" "Yes I do."

"How well do you know her?"

"I don't understand what you mean by that question."

"I mean, as you now claim she is the one who knocked down that child and yet we don't have any report from her, can you describe her to an artist so that he can draw her picture which would help the Police to locate her if she wasn't known to us?"

"I think I could do that." "You think? You are not sure."

"If you mean the general appearance which you and I see, then I can give you."

"Will you try and I hear."

"Mrs. Mukasa name is Mary. She is about one and half meters tall and weighs between 75 to 80 kilograms. She is brown in complexion, with long fat neck having a ring of flesh at the back of the neck. She has an oval face with thick nose, with broad nostrils man like than female, bulging eyes with a growth of warts on the chin. That is all I know about her."

The Director Murdered

Orwotho sighed complacently, shrugged and said well, "thank you very much Lam, we shall look into the information you gave us. *Why is she hiding if she's the one?* Orwotho thought aloud.

"I don't know." Lam replied.

"Sorry, I did mean it for you to hear." he said and wrote down the information of Lam.

Will you let me talk to the girl; her name is … "Alok."

"Yes Alok."

"Hello girlie, how are you? Sit down." he said giving her a smile to encourage her to talk and not be afraid.

"You are Alok aren't you?" "Yes Sir."

"How old are you?"

"I am eleven years old." "Are you at school?"

"Yes, I am in Primary seven at Pece Primary School." "That's good, Alok."

"Will you pass your examination?" Orwotho ask to lead her away a little from the very subject and put her in the mood to talk.

"I think I will."

"What was your class position last December?" "I was number one."

"That's fantastic. If you keep it up, I agree with you that you will pass your Primary Seven examination in Grade one.

Now Alok, where were you coming from yesterday when you saw the car knock down that boy?"

"I was coming from town." "Walking?"

"Yes Sir."

"How far were you from the scene, I mean, where the car knocked the boy."

"I was near Sir."

"I know you were near. I guess last year at school you learned some measurement of distance in meters et cetra didn't you?"

"Yes Sir."

"Well, can you roughly estimate the distance which was between you and the car?" Alok kept quiet.

"Let us put it this way, you stand up and come here." Alok went to him. "Look out of the window, from the gate up to the steps leading to this office is about thirty meters, were you that far?"

"Yes Sir."

"Okay, that is done. I know you are not familiar with the different makes of cars? But you should know if the vehicle was a pickup, a car or a lorry which hit the child"

"It was a blue car."

"Did you notice any other thing you would like to tell me about the car?" Alok kept quiet for a moment, but later said, "I only saw two letters UP on the plate number before I jumped away into the grass."

"Why did you run into the grass? Did you fear the car would knock you also?"

"Yes Sir."

"Why?"

"Because I was walking on the left hand side of the road and the car was driving straight on at me. I thought the driver was drunk, because the car was on the wrong side of the road. So the best I did was to jump into the grass."

"Sorry" Orwotho said, and added "You did well caring for your life Alok."

"Did you see who was driving the car?" "Yes."

Was it a woman or a man?" "A lady."

"Was she alone?"

"No, two children sat at the back."

"Okay, Alok, thank you very much for your information, you can go home and if we shall need you again, we shall send for you.

Meanwhile, have a nice happy New Year and work hard at school next year."

"Thank you sir." Alok saide and got up to walk out.

As you go out, call for me Olweny please.

"Yes sir." Alok said and walked out closing the door behind her.

She's an intelligent girl, very courageous, and talks like an adult. Orwotho thought as he wrote the final information she had given him.

Olweny knocked on the door and walked in with his register and greeted him.

"Good morning Sir."

"Good morning Olweny. How are you?" "I am fine Sir, thank you."

"How is the New Year?"

"It's has started badly in our village. "How?"

"This car accident." Orwotho felt impressed right from the start with personality of Olweny and the eloquence with which he spoke.

"I am sorry for that Olweny."

"Thank you Sir. Your condolence is welcome."

"Olweny, I want to know a little about yourself and the car accident you have just mentioned."

"I will tell you anything I know, which you want to know." "What is your name in full?"

"Samuel Olweny, people call me Sam." "Okay, Sam, how old are you?"

"I am fifteen years old." "You are at school?" "Yes Sir".

"Where are you studying?"

"I am at St. Joseph College Layibi" "What year?"

"I am in senior three this year."

"What are you best subjects at school. Do you like Arts or Sciences?"

"I like Sciences, but don't like some Art subjects, for instance, History because it is things of the past?"

"You do not like to know about the past?"

"I do, but they are not very useful in our modern daily life." "What do you intend to be in future?"

"An Engineer."

"There are many categories of Engineers, do you know that?" "Yes, I do."

"So which one would you like to be?" "Motor car engineer."

"I see. Is that why you keep records of vehicles which pass along Keyo Road?"

"Yes sir."

"Why are you doing that?"

"I just want to know which type of motor cars dominate Keyo road, and how often they move along that road."

"How near the road do you always sit when you record the number of the cars?"

"At the bank of the road Sir."

"You always see the plate number very clearly." "Yes Sir."

"What other information do you record about the vehicles beside the make and the plate number?"

"I also record the time vehicle has past." "I see. You have a wrist watch."

Tell me Sam, the number of cars you recorded yesterday between 17.00 to 19.00 hours.

Olweny read for him the number of the vehicles which included UP 125 Peugeot 504 which passed going towards Keyo at 17.45 hours and came back at 18.15 hours.

"Who was driving the car? A man or a lady?"

"A lady. She sat alone in the front seat and two children sat behind."

"Can I have a look at your register Sam?" He asked extending his hand to receive the book.

"Yes Sir." Sam said, got up and handed the book to Orwotho. He flipped through the pages and reached page dated December 31st and read through. He saw that the numbers were clearly written without cancellation.

"May I keep this register for today? I want to study it and get a photo copy of this page. You could record your vehicles on a piece of paper today and transfer them in your register tomorrow. Will that be okay Sam?"

"I am busy today and shall stay home with my parents to celebrate the New Year Day with them."

"That is fine Sam. Thanks a lot. That means I won't inconvenience you in any way when I keep this book? You can go home and have a nice New Year and my regards to your parents."

"Thank Sir", Sam said and walked out of the office closing the door behind him.

Orwotho got up from the chair and stretched himself.

The Director Murdered

This is interesting. What is wrong with Mukasa? He is concealing a criminal in his home. I don't know what he will say when this news flares up. May be he knows what he is up to. What foxes me is why he let the vehicle out of the station. Does he think he is going to capitalized on the absence of the vehicle from the station to justify the guilt of his wife? Is he going to use it as an alibi? But he must realize that the crime was committed yesterday when the vehicle was still here and its only today that the vehicle went out. When I deliver my investigation report to him today, I will demand the car to be returned immediately before all the evidences that might be on it are destroyed. The car is very highly suspected and there seems to be enough proof on it that it was involved in the crime. All we still need is to detect the blood on it that will match that of the dead child, the old man is sunk. If I were him, I would have reported the matter to avoid charge of concealment of a criminal and probably get a lighter sentence of abuse of office. Now he has two charges on him to answer. Murder concealment and abuse of office. I pity him. He must have a very strong reason to acquit him of all the two charges. Orwotho thought as he compiled the statement of the three eye witnesses he interviewed in the morning.

"I don't understand what is happening Joe. The reports of today seem to involve us in yesterday's hit and run out car?"

"What do you mean?"

"You read what I have got from the three witnesses I interviewed this morning." Orwotho said and gave him the written statements of the eyes witnesses. Mukasa literally snatched the papers from his hand. He read through it with trembling hands his eyes bulging out as he read each subsequently word. He became nervous as more and more adrenalin seeped into his blood circulation. The gray hair fringing his bald head briskly stood on end like the prickles of the porcupine spines ready to act in defense. Orwotho sat and watch him with amazement. He read it including the register of Sam.

"What about this?" He asked referring to the register of Sam. "There is a young boy, Samuel Olweny, he is generally known as Sam as you saw in the report. He is interested in knowing the common vehicles that use Keyo road. So, at his leisure time, not everyday, goes and sits along the road and records the numbers of the cars, the make, and the time that the car passed to and from town," Orwotho endeavored to explain and he wondered why Mukasa didn't see that fact he elaborated in the report.

"I thought I included that bit in the report?" Orwotho asked. Mukasa didn't answer, but put the papers down and stared at Orwotho as if he was not sure who he was.

"Do you believe these?"Mukasa asked in a silly frightened voice. "We have to prove that, Joe. That our vehicle is not involved. Because of this suspicion Joe, I think you contact Odongkara and let him send back the Peugeot immediately today. And tell him he should in the presence of one Police officer in Kitgum, examine the car thoroughly and make notes of all what they will see and the car should be delivered here before sun set. If nothing will be found that the car was involved in the hit and run crime of last night, then we could send it back, otherwise, we shall impound it here for witness and we shall find out who was driving the car. Fingers are pointing at Mrs. Mukasa, but I still regard these as allegation, no truth" Orwotho said.

"I just don't believe it. My wife never drove my official car. She never would do it. I can almost swear she didn't do it?"

"There is always a beginning for a fault Joe. She could have tried and she mess it up first time."

"And where could she have been going at that time of the evening? She is such a coward that she wouldn't go out in the evening. She fears darkness. I tell you she does."

"Probably that's why she caused the accident. She was rushing back home to avoid darkness getting her on the way out of home and , in so doing, she hit the child and still the scare of darkness chasing her, coupled with the fear that if she stopped the relative of the child would take revenge, she sped away up to her safe house."
"Okay, Orwotho let us not have a preliminary inquiry here. I am going home now to find from her what happened."

'What! You-you mean since last night you haven't talked to your wife?

How strange Joe."

"No, I haven't Mukasa answered with a quiet guilty voice. I have spent most of my hours in this office since we received that news from Kitgum yesterday. I am getting calls from Kampala nearly every ten minutes enquiring into the case. So to be frank with you, I haven't talked much to any member of my family. Only my son telephoned me this morning asking me to go home because my wife wasn't feeling fine. I think that could be it."

"Okay Joe, I am sorry about the event." Orwotho said slapping both hands on his thighs, got up, straightened his uniform and walked out.

Chapter 5

Odongkara put off the walkie talkie, sighed, looked at Paul the O/C of Kitgum police post and sniggered.

"What is up there?" Paul asked.

"It looks as if the wife of the boss is in shit." "What happened?"

"They are suspecting her to be the woman behind the steering wheel of the hit and run car which crushed a young boy on Keyo road yesterday evening?"

"She didn't report to the police station." "Seems she didn't."

"That is sad. And Mukasa knows about it?"

"Well, he could be acting, but he first told me that he doesn't." "How? He doesn't? That is a homework for you Sir."

"That, I almost got the answer now. I only need few bits of confirmation and push the answer to them. I know criminals are tricksters but not Mukasa. He is going to leave the entire clues which will track him to his lair, his wife the culprit we are looking for in that hit and run car. I am not hitting low at him, but that is my impression about him. That case is no hair off my skin." Odongkara said and looked at his wristwatch.

"We must get cracking on this task here. I know I am going to eat peppers here before I get anywhere nearer to the solution of these problems. Please, get your uniformed men ready for any emergency. I am suspecting trouble and a big one too. If it's the BDM involved, the moment they sense my presence here, they are going to make life difficult for us, especially, me. They will make me feel I am in hell, and therefore, must leave forthwith. You see what I mean." Odongkara said addressing himself to the Paul.

"But Sir, here we know that wrong elements are actually erroneously associating themselves with the BDM. They commit crime and give the credit to the BDM and they, the BDM, vehemently claim the events on foreign mass media that they are responsible."

"They want publicity."

"Yes they do, to give the world the impression that they are very active, and to deter all foreign aid, investments and loans from getting into our hands." Paul said. Paul a tall huge man with a lot of muscle in the biceps and the chest, which formed balls of meat making him look as tough as a gorilla. He always demonstrated his toughness in javelin and discus throwing in which he was the national and the East African champion. His ability to manhandled and roughen prisoners was not new among the Police officers, so that in events of roughness, he was always alerted and he did it fine. He was generally known as the '*Rock*', a nickname given to him when he one day mollified a mad man who was thought to be untouchable. His long fat fingers had the grip of a vice so that whenever he held his victims with them, he stagnated them as they writhed in his hand yapping for mercy. The glowing brown eyes against the black face made him look fierce and vicious.

"We are going to leave the Peugeot we came in, in your garage. It's a bit faulty and I would rather say no one uses it." Odongkara lied got up, and walked out of the office. Paul followed him closing the door behind him.

The police driver at Kitgum police post drove their Land Rover packed with the Paul and about four armed uniformed police officers. Odongkara with his team from Gulu police headquarter drove in front of them in the Ministry of Health Land Rover in which Dr. Kizza came. Dr. Kizza sat in front with the driver while the three detectives sat behind. It took them five minutes to drive from the police post to Medical Research Institute.

The Medical Research Institute stood at the foot of Kitgum hill on the bank of Lake Anyma about three miles from the center of Kitgum Town. The Institute was fortified with high bricked walls completed with four lines of barbwires on top, spaced about a foot from each other running all round the entire perimeter wall of the Institute. The main gate stood to the East of the walls. The huge gate was closed by metallic double shutters made of vertical steel rods with pointed sharp ends. The double gate shutters were locked together with a huge lock.

They got to the main gate of the Medical Research Institute and stopped. The guard at the gate came to open for them. He had recognized Paul and their Land Rover. He unlocked the gate and pulled the double shutters open to let them in. Paul had been to the Institute earlier in the morning to post some uniformed men to guard the house of the Director, the scene of the crime. They drove in the compound. The guard waved to them and they waved to him as he swung the gate shutters closed behind them. They drove along the path to the main administration block, parked and walked out to the office leaving the armed uniformed policemen in the compound near the two Land Rovers.

The Deputy Director of the Medical Research Institute, Rhajabu, was expecting them anytime in the afternoon. He was in his office waiting for them. A Muslim, Hajji Rhajabu, dark in complexion, two meters tall weighing about 180 kg, had a cunning simple, quiet temperament. His thick nose and lips gave him the typical look of a Nubian. However, Hajji Rhajabu was a pragmatic Muslim who practiced his belief with all the zeal of Allah. He never drank alcohol as all Muslim. A few people in the Institute wanted him to be Director of the Institute because of his quiet nature.

Dr. Gunya a disciplinarian was a tough and very strict on late coming on duty. The penalty for every late coming was a loss of a day's salary or wage, but he was generally kind and parental.

The team lead by Poul entered the office and Hajji stood up to welcome them.

"This is Hajji Rhajabu the Deputy Director of Medical Research Institute. Hajji, will you meet Odongkara our Detective Assistant Superintendent in the province."Poul introduced them.

"How do you do!" Odongkara said and extended his hand for a hand shake "How do you do" Hajji Rhajabu replied.

"This is Dr. Kizza our Government Pathologist."Paul continued with his introduction and the two men shook hands grinning at each other like two boxers shaking their gloves before their duel.

"Opiyo is our Detective Assistant Police and a photographer, and Lwanga is our Detective Assistant Inspector of Police and fingerprints expert."

"Nice to meet you." Lwanga said and shook hands with Hajji. "Sit down gentlemen." Hajji invited them.

As Hajji lowered himself in the chair, Odongkara impatiently said, "let's go to Dr. Gunya's house we are getting late. The earlier we see the body and move it to the hospital for him to perform his magic on the carcass the better. Iam not used to putrefying odor I may vomit my intestines out if we go there too late. That is if he is dead anyway."Odongkara said and they all sniggered.

"After we remove the body to the police mortuary in town, I would like to talk to a few people before we go to rest."

"Who are these Sir?"So that I may alert them?"Hajji asked.

"I feel I should talk to you, as the Deputy Director of this place and now the incharge. Next I want to talk to the night guards who were on duty yesterday evening, the store keeper and possibly, the servant of Gunya. Any other person I should interview I will let you know. Let's first go to the home of Dr. Gunya and Dr. Kizza flogs him to wake up. If he can't then he should find out why and what has caused him to sleep too long." Odongkara said and they walked out of the office.

The house of Dr. Gunya was at the end of the senior staff quarters. In his compound Dr. Gunya had a beautiful flower garden where he had planted many tribes of lovely flowers. He personally took charge of the flowers. He loved them much. He gave them the rest of his free time on Saturday and Sunday if he wasn't in the laboratory working. He planted trees all over his compound so that the place was cool and nice for resting in the hot dry season. He had ordered some wooden flat forms from a local carpenter and placed them in the shade of the trees for relaxation in the open air during the hot dry season. It was there that he and Rose Mary his girl friend spent most of their free hours inhaling the sweet scent from the flowers.

Odongkara preferred to walk to Dr. Gunya's so that he could see set up within that walking distance. The path through the senior staff quarters was tarred and the sides were lined up with pine trees trimmed at a height of a meters. The houses were lined on both sides of the path. Those with even numbers on the right, while the odd numbers stood on the left. The homes were separated from each other by pine trees fencing kept at the same height like the one along the sides of the path. The home for Hajji Rhajabu was on left and one block away before that of Dr. Guny.

The uniformed policemen who were left posted in the morning by Poul to guard the house of Dr. Gunya, had been doing some searches around the house to detect anything of interest. They checked every inch of the ground in the flower garden around the shrubs of hibiscus and row of flowers planted in the compound.

When Odongkara and his men arrived at the scene of the murder, the two police constables were seated on the forms Dr. Gunya had put in the tree shades. They stood up on seeing them and stiffened to salute.

"Anything of interest?" Poul asked.

"A few Sir." One of the constables answered.

"Okay, get to work Opiyo and Lwanga." Odongkara ordered.

Leaving Poul talking to his staff.

The two understood what he meant. They could not tamper with the door until it was free of valuable finger prints. Quickly, they rushed to the door, put down their gadgets and Lwanga opened his powder pack, began to dust the door handle, the glass at the door, and the window. Some prints were detected which Opiyo snapped shot. When they were doing this work, Odongkara went round the house checking every inch of the wall and the window. When he came to the window of the toilet at the back of the house, he noticed that the putty around the glass was scraped off. He stood there and examined the mark. It was new. *Well, there could be something of interest here. It looks the assassin was trying to go in through this window* he thought and continued to walk round the house scrutinizing every inch of the place. He came to the front window with the curtain drawn off. He saw the two sharp round holes through the glass. He sighed and moved nearer. They are bullet holes. *The gun must have been fired from here.* On the ground below, there were no obvious signs of any intruder, but the grass which was kept low and smart indicated that some heavy boots or shoes trodden on them some hours ago. *Whoever, committed the crime was very careful not to leave any clues behind.* Odongkara walked back to join the team at the door.

"All ready?"He asked.

"We have finished this part of the world." Lwanga said "Any luck?"

"There are few prints yes. One for a man and the other for two different ladies."

"That's fine we shall sort that later." "Can I open the door?"Hajji asked.

"Yes, so that we go and wake him up. He has slept too long. Dr. Kizza has the *juju* for that."Odongkara joked. "If I fail?" Dr. Kizza asked.

"Then you'll cut him to wake him." Odongkara continued with his joke as they entered the living room of Dr. Gunya.

Dr. Gunya had spent most of his money furnishing his house, dressing himself aristocratically and drinking. Executive sofa sets looking as solid as rocks, and the cushions as soft as cotton lint, stood against the walls with their florid embroider casing, made the rooms look bright and elegant. The carpet on the floor was thick enough for one to lose shoes in. A bookself with all the medical books you care to name, stood like the Medical School Library, stretching the whole length of the shorter walls and stood as high as the ceiling. A reading table was stuck on one wall with a lamp shade hanging above. On the same table a telephone body sat with the receiver laid hanging above the floor. Below it was the body of Dr. Gunya laying in a dried blood.

A thick curtain drawn to one side of the wall separated the living room from the dining hall where a six seater table stood with its six high back rest chairs, making that wing of the house looks like a state lodge. A refrigerator, a safe for cutleries and a cocktail cupboard were spaced up in the dining hall.

Dr. Gunya was attending to a telephone when he was shot in the chest. There were two gun wounds on his chest which penetrated though to his back. He fell on his back hitting his head on floor as if he was thrown from above, his legs and arms spread outwards.

"Yes, Dr. Kizza. This part is yours? Odongkara said. Is he dead or sleeping?"

Dr. Kizza quietly moved to the body of Dr. Gunya, ignoring Odongkare question, took the arm of Dr. Gunya in his hand and felt for the pulses. He was cold and stiffen no pulse was detectable. The eyes stared emptily in the air without any expression which indicated that he was taken unaware when he was shot at.

"He is about fifteen hours dead." Dr, Kizza replied.

"Well, we'll remove his body to our mortuary in town. You go and work on him but get his print before you take him out. We are going to look around here before we go to Hajji's home and the Institute to chat with a few people."

All left the house of Dr. Gunya except Odongkara, Lwanga, Opiyo and Paul.

"Gentlemen, let's sit down for a while. Let's talk and plan our strategies before we start messing up clues. I consider this case the one most challenging crime to be investigated. This place as you have seen is another heaven on earth. It's quite safe. So safe that you would almost think it is impossible for anyone to come to the Institute without passing through the gate. With that, it makes me think that any insecurity like this one is the responsibility of the people who know this place well, and who are these? They are the people who work and live here. But I warned you criminals are tricksters. They commit a crime, which makes an innocent man a suspect number one. The Institute store was burglarized. There were gunshots at Hajji's house, no one was shot at nor was anything taken from his home. The guards at the gate were all beaten up except one. Dr. Gunya was shot dead. Was it the BDM? or who did it?

We have to establish a fact beyond doubt that armed people from outside came into the Institute last night and committed these three offences."

As he talked, the walkie talkie in his pocket came alive; he opened it and spoke in it.

"Hello Joe, what is up?"

"Hello Peter, how are you there?"

"We are boozing ourselves, celebrating the New Year day in Rock Hotel with all the beautiful chicks around us", Odongkara said ironically.

"I know you aren't Peter, what have you stirred up at the moment?"

"Not much Joe, we are in Dr. Gunya's house. We have just done the preliminary and elementary detective. Dr. Kizza has confirmed the body of Dr. Gunya, a carcass, and he has gone to scatter it to ascertain the cause of the death. The bachelor had spent all his dough in decorating his house. It reminds me of the house of the British Prime Minister. The sofa sets and the carpets are very kingly Joe. His car is a Jaguar. Anyone who drives a Jagcar at this time of inflation must be a millionaire."

"Peter, what do I tell Kampala?" Mukasa changed the topic suddenly.

"Tell them we are at work. Those who committed the crime are in hiding and we are digging for them and it is not an easy job as they seem to think. Let them be patient. Yes, Joe I will ring you soon for more information when I chat with some of these people here. I have arranged interviews with a cross section of them. We hope it will be useful." Odongkara said and nearly closed up.

"I am in shit my brother Peter, I need your advice." "What is that Joe?"

'My wife."

"What about her?" "She did it."

"Sorry to hear that", Odongkara said feelingly. "Thank Peter."

"That is bad Joe. And why did she not report to the Police station?"

"She said she was too frightened and scared to think of any other thing, but death. She wanted to talk to me first before any other person."

"Well she was right and where were you hiding the whole of last evening?" Odongkara pinched him.

"I was in the club and …"

"But I gathered that your son couldn't reach you because you were not there?"

"That is not an important point now Peter. All I want now is, the superintendant of Police here would like you to return the Peugeot 504 here immediately before sun set and before you send the car here, he wants you to give your remark concerning the car, that is, if there are some clues of interest on it and this should be done in the presence of Poul and the two of you should sign the document and you send a driver from the station together with an escort with the report on the car to us here. We are going to reexamine the car here and compare the two results. This is from Orwotho."

My wife has already messed me up, what do I do? Should she go and report or we continue to conceal her?"

"If I were you Joe, I would let her report and use the same excuse she used to you. In this way, as a lady, especially as your wife, she could be considered for pardon, but still face the charge of manslaughter."

"Peter you sound happy about everything." "Why? I am stating facts."

"I am sorry Peter. I am thinking of maintaining the present stand that my wife was with your wife during the time of the accident and another woman, not my wife, was in the car."

"And whose wife is that?"

"A woman who took the car during our absence."

"It sounds a childish plan to conceal a crime Joe. Can't you think of anything better?"

"That is why I call you. I want your help."

"I have already told you the best thing to do if I were in your position."

"Expose her to the law!"

"That is what I said. Don't deceive yourself that if we provide her with an alibi you will go away with it and don't forget that beside the three who testified before Orwotho, many other people are still in the background who saw your wife out at that time in the car. They will swear to that Joe and if you maintain your stand, it will be a sad state of affairs later."

"And who are these?"

"Where did your wife go by the way?" Odongkara asked.

"To collect the milk and buy the turkey at Onekalit's." "And you think no one saw her there?"

"I don't know."

"Oh well Joe, am very sorry, be kind to yourself and try to do what I have suggested. Let me know of any development, if any. Meanwhile, I am going to make observation on the car and send it immediately, with our comments at this end. We are also going to get you involved in the Kitgum drama. It is a hot line. We haven't touched anything on the incidence of the smoldering shops in town. How do we know they aren't connected?" Odongkara concluded switch off and turned to the three men.

"Yes, gentlemen, as I was saying, let us use our brain for the first time ever since we started our profession of criminology. I bet this one is going to be very challenging indeed. We have to prove that the three crimes, perhaps, the fourth one, the burning shops in town, are the work of one body or entirely separate bodies but coincidentally the time were approximately the same.

This particular murder could be the work of someone within. Why the hoodlum just fired several shots at Hajji door and vanished without taking a needle from his house? And in the store, they just broke in and left everything as they were? What was the point of coming out at all? Why take the risk of braking into a guarded place like this without a motive? I don't understand. In addition to this, it could be some of those incompetent research officers who he dismissed, or it could be that the BDM claim is correct or it could be the work of anyone who was after him for a reason which is not related to any of the categories of the people I have just mentioned. I think, if we are to stir up anything, we should work along these lines I have mentioned. So now, you Opiyo and Lwanga are going to start from the living room here. Pull the house in bits. Leave nothing unsearched. When you are satisfied you have done a thorough work in here, go out round the house and do the same. While you tear the house apart, Paul and I will go and interview some of the institute staff. We shall meet later, perhaps at 16.00

hours, to compare the result." Odongkara turned to Paul and asked, "you said you have already taken the cartridges for identification?"

"Yes Sir, it went by air this morning, we are expecting the radio message result this afternoon."

"That is fine. It leaves us with very little to search outside." "Then we shall go round the Institute to find out where they passed from if they really came over the walls and between the barbwires. If they did, then I guess it must be near those mango trees using a rope. I tell you, human beings are impossible beast to deal with. We are like large body of fast flowing water which you can't stop. This is what a human being is, you build walls with barbwires atop to keep him out of a place, he comes in with anti barbwire suit and slithered through, like a serpent and goes out smart and clean. Shall we get to work then", Odongkara said and left Opiyo and Lwanga in the house of Dr. Gunya; while the two of them walked following Hajji to the Institute to meet the people he wanted to interview. They had been alerted by Hajji Rhajabu and were all waiting for him in the Institute boardroom.

"Let's start with you Rhajabu. We just want to talk to you so that we know where to start work. We are not suspecting any of you, but with your information, we could be put on the track of the culprit or culprits. I know the country and more so each one of you in the institute is greatly affected by the event of last night in one way or another."

"You have already been introduced to me by Paul, but I want you now to introduce yourself to me according to Ugandan law.

You are …" Odongkara said and left the question afloat. "Hajji Rhajabu."

"What are you in the Institute here?"

"I am Principle Research Officer and Head of Biochemistry Department. Administratively, I am the Deputy Director of the Institute."

"How old are you Hajji?" "Forty five."

"You are married?" "Yes I am."

"How many wives?" "One Sir"

"Any child?"

"Two boys and a girl."

"Okay Hajji. What do you know about what happened here last night?"

Hajji sighed rubbed the dark callus on his forehead, formed from the way he prayed by knocking his forehead on the ground, each time he praied and adjusted his buttocks on the chair. He cleared his throat and said.

"It was at 21.05 hours when I left my laboratory. I walked home and got to my house 21.10. When I got home, I went and had a bath before I joined my family at table for supper.

"Is that the time you normally eat you supper?" "Always between 21.00 hours and 22.00 hours. Yes." "What happened after supper yesterday?"

"We sat talking for about twenty minutes I felt tire, excused myself, and went to sleep. I had laid down for about 45 minutes when I heard alarm and the whistle sounding in the Institute. I thought it was very odd indeed. At first, I thought the night guards were fighting among themselves. My family was still chatting in the living room. When they heard the alarms and the whistle spreading, they put off the light in the sitting room and went to their rooms, put off all the lights except the security light at the front door. The alarm and whistle died down after sometime. We were all quiet in our rooms but very attentive. Then we heard someone running along the path in front of our house. My wife was frightened and scared. She hysterically fell on me and said they were coming to our house. I got up and asked her to keep quiet as I surreptitiously stole my way to the window to see what was happening. Then what I saw beat my imagination. I saw two men walking right to my door, each of them carrying a gun in his hands ready to fire. I did not understand why I was being attacked. I withdrew from the window and let the curtain fall back. Then I heard a knock on the door. It was one of those savage knock you get from a drunken friend once in a while. I was mesmerized. I thought I fainted. But my wife on sensing trouble, sent out a shrilly scream which jarred my ear drums, waking me up from the mesmerism I was undergoing. The children in their bedroom thought we were wiped out. They all rushed into our bedroom screaming like little trains. The men at the door opened fire, and fired into the ceiling of the veranda.

After a while, they ran away. We heard their footsteps fading. We were left almost dead, clinging onto each other for protection. I must admit, I did not scream, probably because I was hypnotized by the appearance of the gunmen."

"How did the men look like?" Odongkara asked. "They were in civilian dress, with high black boots. They all had hats on, and wore them sloping in front of their heads hiding their faces. All I saw about their faces was that they had some beards."

"When they fired shots at your house and ran away after you screamed, I mean, your family screamed, did you probably hear which way they ran?"

"No. We didn't. I was too frightened, and in any case, the thumping of our hearts muffled the sound of their footsteps."

"Then what happened Hajji?"

"We were quiet for some time, all of us in our bedroom. We had started to gain our nerves when we heard the car of Dr. Gunya drive past to his home. He was driving fast, not his usual speed, he used whenever he returned from his outing."

"How did you know it was Dr. Gunya driving?" "From the sound of his car."

"You are very familiar with the sound of his car?" "Fairly, the only Jaguar around."

"No other car in the whole of Kitgum town sounds like his? Someone else with a Jaguar like his could have been coming to see him?"

Hajji kept quiet and rubbed his nose with his hand.

"Well, that is noted. Dr. Gunya drove past your home at high speed and then …?" Odongkara asked.

"I thought he was probably being chased." Hajji took over from Odongkara and went on. "There was a period of stillness which you always experience after violent commotion. The whole world felt like a vacuum. Then about thirty minutes after that, we were startled by the sudden blast of guns. It sounded just next to our house and that was at Dr. Gunya's house. We even heard some stray bullets whizzing in the air. We resumed the screaming and making alarm. I stole my way to the telephone and tried to ring the police, but there wasn't any dialing tone, only engaged tone was on. That was when I realized the attackers must have done their homework before they came in to finish us up. I crawled back to my family and then we heard the same footsteps running back towards the Institute. I think everyone else within the Institute was frightened stiff."

"Let's get some points right here Hajji" Odongkara put in. "How many times did they fire the shot at Dr. Gunya?"

"I didn't count."

"Again why did you decide to ring the police after the shot were fired at Dr. Gunya and not before that?" Hajji kept quiet

"Okay Hajji. From your house you could hear the sound of the straying bullets?"

"Yes – yes, I heard something like it."

"You are not sure whether it was a bullet or wind blowing through a cracks on you window glass?"

"I think it was a bullet sound."

"Let us assumed it was the sound of a bullet zipping in the air over your houses.

"Then what happened?"

"It was quiet. We were expecting to hear another blast any moment, but nothing came until morning. Then today in the morning when we woke up, everyone was concerned about our safety and they all came to see us. We were found alive and well, but when we moved on to Dr. Gunya's house, we found the rear window curtain drawn and the window glass shattered by bullets as you saw, and when we peeped into the house we saw the body of Dr. Gunya sprawling on the floor the telephone receiver dangling by the code from the set on his reading table. It was when we were peeping in the house, that the two policemen came out from their hide out, and ordered us out of the place and warned us not to touch anything there. I didn't know how the police got the news because when I tried to ring them during the time of the murder, my line was not working. As a result, I couldn't contact even my neighbours for help.

"If you didn't ring the police, then who did immediately the murder was accomplished?' Paul asked.

"I don't know. And I don't think any of the member staff did because, how could they have known that Dr. Gunya was murdered?

I should have been the first to report the death as the immediate neighbour."

Odongkara stared at Hajji thoughtfully and asked.

"How would you have known that Dr. Gunya was murdered by the mere gun shot at his place? But similar shots were fired at your house and you are here talking to us." Hajji again kept quiet. As Odongkara wrote something in his book. He lifted up his head and continued with Hajji.

"Your phone is not working up to now?"

"No. Not only mine, but all of us who are on that line have our phones jammed."

"What about other lines are they working?" "I think so."

"Then why your line only?"

"May be they did that because they knew they were going to operate there."

"I see. That is an interesting point, we have to find out from your members of staff who have telephones in their houses, who rang the police station at 22.00 hours reporting the murder. And we should find out from the post office, what caused the jam in your line." Odongkara said and noted the point on a separate page from what he had been taking in short-hand on what Hajji was narrating. "Okay, any more you know about last night surprised visit to you here? I hope they don't come tonight again?" Odongkara joked. "I pray they don't, Hajji admitted."

"When the policemen dismissed us, we all dispersed sorrowfully to our houses mourning Dr. Gunya. It was hard to believe that it happened but there it was. In addition to the death of Dr. Gunya, the news started coming from the Institute that the Institute store had been burglarized and two of the three night guards at the gate were thoroughly beaten up, and the third one who was held at gun point by the arm gunmen was not even slapped. There, the whole events became a mystery to me. What foxed me most was this night guard who escaped unbeaten told us flabbergasting story in the presence of the police when they talked to us this morning he

The Director Murdered

was there", Hajji said and pointed at Paul. "May be he should tell you that bit himself and you hear from him, Hajji suggested."

"I am not asking him. I am talking to you Hajji. In any case the guard is on my list for interview." Odongkara said and scratched the corner of his mouth with the end of his pen. Allow me to ask you a few more questions before I wind up with you this afternoon.

"How do you think this armed men entered the Institute, as I seem to think they didn't come through the gate?"

"I cannot say for sure, but I am talking from the experience we occasionally have been having here. A few years back, before independence, group of men were caught with cartoons of drugs they had stolen from the store on top of the walls among the barbwires. Similarly I guess, these men came in over the walls using ropes. Otherwise I don't see how they could have come in any other way. We walked all around the walls this morning there are areas showing activities I have mentioned."

"Hum, I see." Odongkara said scribbling something in the book and leaned back on the chair chewing the fingernail of his thumb.

"How was the relationship between Dr. Gunya and the senior members of staff?"

"It was good. They liked him very much because he was very strict on everybody about punctuality and respect among the members of staff. I think there was a good understanding among us. I have no doubt about that."

"He never had any rough word or quarrel with anyone in the Institute of late?"

"Not that I know, he could have had some which I don't know. You knows, Dr. Gunya was a very respectable dignified man. I have known him for the last ten years in his position as the Director and me his Deputy, I have not even once seen him bark at anyone in the compound or at his working place. He always, called those he wanted to talk to in his office where the two would iron out their problems. He would warn you, first verbally, and then when you commit the same offence, he would warn you in writing quoting the date you discussed the same issue verbally. I think people liked him that way. "What about the rumour that you were preferred to him because of your quiet sympathetic nature? Many people in fact wanted you to be the Director of this place because of your affability, don't you think that someone quickened up that post for you?" Odongkara asked.

Hajji stared at him without saying a word. He sighed and said, "Who told you that? I don't believe it. I have never been an ambitious man. I am content with my work as principle research officer. I want to spend my time on the bench than in administration. In fact, I wanted to resign even this post of Deputy Director and remain just an ordinary Researcher. No – no, I must disassociate myself completely from that claim. If it is true that someone did it because he or she wants me in the chair, then I'm very sorry. Because, even if given, I won't take it." Hajji said adamantly and begun to weep.

"I am sorry Hajji; I just wanted to find out from you if you have also heard the same rumour." Odongkara said apologetically.

"I don't want to be the cause of loss of life of anyone. Never, Allah helps me keep away from earthly desire."

There was a pause between them, no one talked. They all watched and waited as Hajji Rhajabu stabilizes himself. He blew his nose in the handkerchief he was using for dabbing his tears, put it back in his pocket, and returned the stare of the two men who were seated side by side.

"I am sorry Sirs, I had to do it. I felt insulted and abused by the rumour you heard about me. It gave me the feeling that people are winking their eyes at me that I am behind this murder of Dr. Gunya, because I wanted his chair!"

"I don't think so at the moment, but if the rumour gains momentum, you could." Odongkara put in humorously.

"That is, deformation of my character and loss of my reputation." "Don't worry about that may be no one will talk about it again."

Odongkara said comfortingly and sighed.

"Hajji, if last night attack on you in particular was genuine, what do you think motivated it? I mean, why should people come and attack you? Have you been having rough time with people?"

"To begin with, I don't understand what you meant when you said that if the attack on me last night was genuine? I mean, let me say honestly before you now, in the name of Allah, that what happened in the Institute here last night was a surprise and indeed a great shock to me as it is to any other person. I had no preknowledge of what happened or am I associated with it in anyway. I know there have been very many incidences in the country at the moment where men in authority have been killed by their assistants because they wanted their chairs. They planned the murder and bought these gunmen to commit the murder while they sit and wait for the chair to fall vacant. But I would like you to get it clear from me Hajji, that I really had no pre-knowledge of what befell us last night. I repeat, I am innocent. I have no hand in this matter. As for the rest of the question you have asked, I simply can tell you that I don't know why my house was attacked. You will probably hear from the night guard that the men who came to the Institute compound last night, although the version of his statement made this morning was very contradictory, had a list of names of people they wanted to visit. And among the names, I was on top list. Because, besides my other duties mentioned to you, I am charged with security of the Institute. I recruit and discipline the night guards, and arrange their duty roster. Of course, there were other names mentioned which I prefer him to tell you. I also suspected that they visited me because I have buses and they thought I could be having plenty of money with me at home."

"But they didn't get at it?"

"That is why I don't understand their motive for attacking my place. At one time, I thought, because they seemed to have walked in over the wall, they most certainly didn't have vehicles so when they burgled into the store, they found that whatever they wanted to carry could not all go over the wall easily as a result, they wanted some transport and as they might have known me to be having buses in town and my Volkswagen pick up here within the Institute, they thought they could force the pick up out of me and use it for carrying their goods. But even this didn't work out right. Was it the scream and the alarms of my family that drove courage out of them? I don't know."

"What about among the members of staff, none of them have grudge against you?"

"No, not among these present one. But there was a Senior Research Officer in Pharmacology Department, he was an obstinate man. He was working with Miss Susan an English girl, who is heading the Department. We all know Susan as a nice young girl, dedicated to her work. She is always punctual and works until late after official working hours. But this man always came to the Department late, drunk, steaming alcohol, like the brewing pots, and start ordering Susan around to do his work, just because she was a white lady. He enjoyed the fun for sometimes and Susan, in spite of her position as the Principle Research Officer and the Head of Department, bore the insult for a long time. But one day he came drunk, and as he always did, not only ordered Susan to wash his tubes but also spewed on her as they argued near the sink. Susan thought she had born enough of his insults and humiliation. She rushed with her dress stinging like a pit latrine to Dr. Gunya.

Dr. Gunya was shocked silly. He couldn't believe he was seeing right. Anyway, we had a senior staff meeting about that and in the meeting; Susan revealed all what had been going on between them. She was backed up by all the laboratory staff in Pharmacology Department. Dr. Gunya and I went to the Ministry and seeked for his dismissal from the Institute. Before he left, he threatened to kill Susan, Dr. Gunya and myself. We reported the matter to the police. I hope he will bear me out."

Hajji said and pointed at Paul again.

"Yes we have the record of that report. But the man he is talking about was killed in a car crush." Paul pointed out.

"Yes he was." Hajji agreed. "I gave him as an example of someone who would have been a suspect if he was alive.

"No possibility that he had pass words onto someone else to do the work for him even if he is gone?"Odongkara asked.

"That, I don't know." Hajji replied.

Let us talk a little about your store. It's well known to everyone that your main store, stock medical drugs and medical equipments?"

"Yes."

"Well if that is true, it means there are lots to take away from the store but these men came and broke in the store and took nothing! Why do you think they did that?"

"You are right Sir. Beside the drugs and medical equipments, I have a feeling that other things they could have wanted to take from the store were the spare parts of the vehicles we advertised last week. The spares were in the store. You saw the scraps of these cars lying in the compound?" Hajji asked.

"Yes." Odongkara agreed.

"Those vehicles were here during the colonial days. Since independence the vehicles were grounded after they developed faults. The Institute, of course, with the financial crisis could not meet the cost of repairs. As a result, they were impounded. We feared that if they remain there with all the valuable parts, some of these dishonest men could help themselves to them, moreover, parts like the tyres would rot if left in damp places all the time. So we picked every part working and kept them in the store.

"Our financial position has not improved much since then, so we asked the Ministry headquarters if we could sell off the vehicles and make money out of them. It was agreed. And last week on Monday, Dr. Gunya advertised these vehicles not to the nation as a whole but to the Institute workers only. I could be wrong. I am guessing that words could have got out from the people working here that those vehicles were on sale and of course, knowing where the spares are they could have arranged to get them free and then buy the body later cheaply. And that seemed to explain why they call at my place. To avail transport to carry the spares as I said before."

"Do you have anyone in mind who could have organized such a racket?"

"I don't, but there is a possibility, funny things like these happened in the past. For instance last year in October, we advertised the sale of a speed boat engine. We had been using the engine in the Bilharzia survey on River Aswa. We got another engine, which was more powerful so we decided to sell off the smaller one to any member of staff of the Institute. People applied and when their applications were being sorted out, one of the members of staff came in over the wall using a rope and took the engine out. He was suspected. His home was searched and the machine was found buried behind the house in newly planted potatoes garden. He is now in prison. There are other examples I could give which might make you begin to think in my line." Hajji said. Odongkara yawned and looked at Hajji suspiciously thinking. *Criminals are trickster. How can I trust he is drawing me away from him and pointing at a wrong direction for me to follow? A goose chase that is what he wants to tell me when he, the criminal is sitting with me here looking at me right in the face?*

"Okay Hajji, thank you very much, if we shall want to talk to you again, we'll get in touch with you. I want to talk to this night guard who escaped unbeaten. Seems he has some exciting news for me. Will you call him in please?" Odongkara said and Hajji walked out of the boardroom where the interview was taking place. He reported to the policeman guarding those to be interviewed that the night guard was next. The policeman beckoned at lanky swarthy middle aged man, looking pale and weary, as if he had just stopped his hunger strike. He wore on his head a white turban the Muslim wear for identity. The black callus on his flattened forehead which looked as if he was once swathed on the face, confirmed his Islamic belief. He stood up from the form on which they sat with their heads stooped down and dragged himself to the interview room and the door closed behind him.

CHAPTER 6

"This is a beautiful album." Opiyo said as he opened a photo album of Dr. Gunya he found on the bookshelf. The golden glazed, thick, cover of the album with the picture of a sparrow driving its beak in the red rosesy flower gave the album an exquisite beauty. The thicken pages of the album also glazed contained a number of photographs. On the first page of the album there were photos of two old couple in their fifties and below them was the photograph of Dr. Gunya in his academic gown. He looked very much like the old man and Opiyo guessed the old couples were his parents. Below his photograph on the first page, Dr. Gunya had stuck the photos of three beautiful girls. The first on the queue of the girls he wrote below it, Miss Rose Gown born in 1931 DIED IN 1953 under the second photo he wrote Miss Betty Atto born in 1929 died in 1958 and under the last photo he wrote Miss Victoria Acheng born in 1935 died 1962 and below the three photographs he wrote in capital Red letter, *'May the Almighty God rest their Souls in Peace'*.

They were real African beauty. He knew what chick to go for. Opiyo thought as he stared at the faces of the girls in the photographs. He yawned and wiped his face with his palm and sat back on the sofa he was sitting on. *I am tired he whispered to* himself. And turn and looked at a cocktail cupboard of Dr. Gunya stocked with all kinds of alcohol. *Help yourself on a tot. It will rejuvenate your tired nerves. That is the only answer.* Opiyo heard a voice talking within himself and crossed the room to the cocktail cupboard and carried out the half bottle of Dry Gin whisky, shot a mega tot in the glass he had taken from the utensil cabinet, threw the tot at the back of his throat, swallowed the liquid painfully gnashing his teeth and felt every cell on his body vibrating as the liquid diffused through his body.

"I am feeling fine now we could go on working here until tomorrow", Opiyo said. Lwanga who had already joined him laughed and said, "Don't overdo it."

"I know. It's back in its home." Opiyo said as he replaced the bottle of the whisky back and closed the cupboard.

"Which room haven't you checked? I have been through the bedroom and these two rooms.

Behind the first page on the top most corner, was a photo of a woman he knew. *This is the photo of the manageress of Rock Hotel. She must be the one. She is also one of his friends?* Opiyo thought and shrugged and flipped through the album seeing beautiful faces of young, and middle age girls whom he did not know. He was fond of beautiful girls. *They hide lots of explosive material behind those attractive faces* he continued to think as he browsed through the books in Dr. Gunya's library. Beside the album he didn't get any other book of interest. He took the album and put it on a table in the center of the room. He began to work on the carpet the chairs feeling and massaging every inch of the chair. He turned the cushions on the chairs and massaged them, lifted the carpet and checked below but he didn't detect anything of interest. He worked his way to the dining room. There was very little to see there, and so he opened the refrigerator. It was stocked with milk, meat, sausages, eggs line up at the door of the refrigerator. Tomatoes, cabbages, egg plants and some ripe bananas were the content of the refrigerator. The freezing compartment of the refrigerator was packed tight with beers. He restrained the temptation of helping himself on one. *This man lived an exotic life*. Opiyo thought and closed the door of the refrigerator and pushed it from its standing position to see behind it. He didn't see anything of interest. He moved on to the safe for the cutleries he opened it and peeped inside. It was pack with sets of plates, cups, spoons, forks, knives of different size and purposes. He carefully moved the safe from the wall and at the foot of it he saw two cartridges lying down. He took them and examined them they were blood streak on them. *These*

The Director Murdered

could be some of the cartridges notpicked this morning which actually went through him, may be some are lodged in his chest. Dr. Kizza will tell us.

He took the cartridges and put them on the table on which he left the album. He went on to the cocktail cupboard, and looked inside, he saw four bottle of Vat 69 three of chinzano two bottles of Uganda Waragi and half bottle of Dry Gin whisky all growing like the chess men on the chess board he looked at them and wonder why a single man like Dr. Gunya should stock so much drink in the house. *Is it because of these girls who could be having different choice of drink?* Opiyo thought as he closed the cocktail cupboard, checked below it and walked to the kitchen. There was not much to see in there.

The cooker stood next to the door with its knobs staring like keys buttons on a piano. He search everywhere in the kitchen but got nothing of interest.

"Hey Lwanga, Opiyo called out" "Yes Sir."

"Got anything of interest? I am bored of seeing beer and Whisky at this end.

"I have got this knife under his pillow and this 0.38 mm revolver pistol in the bedside locker." Lwanga said.

"It is very interesting, isn't it? We shall try for prints on them and see who handled them last." Lwanga said and carefully put the knife and the pistol on the coffee table in the sitting room. He dusted them. Some prints were seen on the butt of the gun and the hilt of the knife.

"I have found these." Opiyo said and placed the two cartridges and the photo album on the same table.

"The manageress photo is also displayed in the album."Opiyo said

"Which one?" Lwanga asked "The senior spinster in the Rock."

"Oh', that one". Lwanga said and looked at the photo of a fat lady Opiyo had displayed in the album. And turned his attention on the pistol he was working on.

"Has the gun been fired?" Opiyo asked when he saw that Lwanga was more concerned with the pistol than the photos.

"No, the barrel doesn't smell and the bullets are all intact."
"Odongkara is going to be mad today. I don't think he will sleep tonight."

"No. I am sure he is squeezing those he is interviewing out of words."

"What do you make out of these findings?" Opiyo asked Lwanga.

"My feeling is, it looks that Dr. Gunya knew that someone was after his life. He prepared himself waiting for the attacker and he bought this knife and the pistol for the purpose of self-defence. In spite of these, the attacker changed tactic and got him off guard and fired at him as he talked, may be, to some of his friends in the album."

"It doesn't sound off the line of ingenuity. But supposing it was him who was brewing a murder, say one of his girl friends? Why hide a knife under the pillow if it was intended for an external aggressor? Well the gun, there could be some justification that he could have been expecting an attack on him and in self-defence, he acquired a gun to use if necessary, but certainly the knife, unless he was a knife thrower."Opiyo commented.

"Well he has been abroad, he could have learnt the art of knife throwing from some of those thugs in Britain. You see, as Odongkara said, this case is very challenging. We have got to think fast and accurately. Everything looks possible. Your suggestion fits, and I think what I have said is not too bad a suspicion either. With the knife under the pillow there is a lot to it. Self defence with a knife under the pillow sounds possible only if that someone who was going to attack him was going to do it in the bed." Lwanga added

There was a silence among them as each was busy with his findings and Lwanga broke the silence again and said, "alternatively, one of his girls who was intending to murder him came with the knife, and findings she was unable to accomplish her plan, decided to hide the knife under the pillow with the intention of using it, later in the night when Dr. Gunya would not suspect her of any wrong doing?"

Opiyo sat up and looked at Lwanga meditatively and said, what caused Dr. Gunya's death is not going to be very far from job competition or women affairs. The BDM just don't come in at all."

"Then what about the group who burgled into the Medical Research Store, are they not the BDM?"Lwanga asked.

"Planned tricks! We have no proof whatsoever to that. If they wanted drugs, the research Institute store with very heavy security was not where to look for them. They would have done well by breaking into the hospital pharmacy or the series of pharmacies in town. I am highly suspicious that someone used the BDM as a scape goat in this murder of Dr. Gunya. Lets us first compile our findings of today together and see where we stand." Opiyo said and walked out to the living room of Dr. Gunya skipping over his dried blood, on the floor.

Lwanga followed him carrying the 0.38mm revolver pistol he found in the bedside locker and the knife found under the pillow.

"I think we should look round the house and see if we can spot out anything that hasn't been seen." Lwanga suggested. He opened the door leading to the garage and descended the one step bellow.

The living room of Dr. Gunya was directly connected to the garage so that when one parks the car and locked the main door of the garage, one walked straight to the living room. The black Jaguar stood in the garage with the driver front door ajar.

"We were forgetting this part of the building" Lwanga said. "And yet it looks pregnant with clues." Opiyo commented and walked to the front door.

"Let us dust them before we start work around the deserted de-lux." Lwanga said and put down his pack of powder. He started working at all the suspicious corners, where he thought he would detect finger prints. When he was satisfied that all was done, they opened the car and climbed in. They searched every nook in the car but came out with nothing of interest. They got out slammed the door closed and opened the bonnet of the car. There was nothing unusual. They walked to the rear of the car and opened the boot. In it there were, a toolbox containing the usual tools for the car, a spare tyre fully flated laid at the corner of the boot, a foot pump had its tube coiled on the body stuck next to spare tyre, an empty five litters jerry can of petrol laid slightly obscuring the funnel. One by one, they took them out of the boot, gave them a thorough search. On the floor of the boot, there was a large sheet of black rubber covering a white paper. Only a fraction of the paper showed. Lwanga saw it, took out the paper. It was an identity card issued by 'Food and Beverages', and the owner was a swarthy, long haired twentyfive year old, Salim Bin Rhajabu.

"Look what I have found." Lwanga said giving the card to Opiyo who was packing the tin tool. He got up and took the card from Lwanga.

'What is the name of …?' "Of who?"

"Sorry, the identity card belongs to 'Food and Beverages'. I was thinking it could be his servant's identity card." Opiyo corrected himself.

"Unless he is working in two places." "Possible?"

"Depending on how much he has to do here and at what time. These days people are very crafty, they register for jobs here and there. All they have to do is show themselves in all those places everyday for one or two hours, and at the month's end, they go round collecting their salaries from office to office."

"We shall find out who this Salim Bin Rhajabu is, and what connection he has with Dr. Gunya." The two men unbolted the garage door and walked out. They first followed closely to the house examining every inch of it. Beside the bullet holes on the hind glass and the scrapping on the putty of the glass at the toilet window, there was nothing of interest on the outside of the house. They walked and sat on the forms placed under the tree, each one carrying his findings dug out of the house. "Transport should be here in five minutes." Lwanga said as he looked at his watch. Opiyo glanced at his watch, unstrapped the camera from his neck and began to clean the lens with the cloth he always carried with him meditatively and asked, "Which shop got burnt down in town last night according to the Nation Daily News paper? , do you remember their names?"

The Director Murdered

"Pop in shop opposite the Post Office, and Baby shop next to Bata. What about them? You think they must have connection with this Institute's drama?" Lwanga replied.

"I am not sure, but it was reported that the Baby's shop had some arms in it and the owner has disappeared. What is his name? Do you remember?'

"No I don't. Those are homework for tomorrow. I don't know what the boss thinks. I am exhausted." Lwanga complained.

"When Odongkara has an unanswered question in his hand like this, I bet, you are going to be a corpse if you are already complaining of exhaustion."

"May be we should go back in and jar our nerve cells with his half drunk bottle of Dry Gin Whisky. After all, who is going to remove them now?"

"Why not? I think that will stimulate my thinking faculty. I think well when my gray matter cells are agitated by the liquid. Come on, pack your gadget and we go."

"It would be nicer out here, go get two glasses and the stuff here. Better in open air", Opiyo dictated and continued to wipe the back of his camera and shut it and put it in its brown leather case.

Dr. Kizza in the police mortuary finished opening up Dr. Gunya on the chest. He found that the heart, the liver and the lungs were fragments. They were completely shattered by the two slugs which ripped through his chest. He confirmed that the death of Dr. Gunya was the result of severe internal bleeding he had from the heart, liver and lungs when they were pulverized by the bullets. To him Dr. Gunya died before he fell down. When he finished compiling his report he looked at his watch. The time was only 14.00 hours. *I think I must go back to Gulu.* He thought as he packed up his files. Using the telephone in the police headquarter he put a call to Odongkara.

"Please, will you let me get the Institute?" he said to the operator at the switchboard. What is your extension Sir? The operator asked him.

"256". Dr. Kizza answered.

"Okay, call you back?" The operator said and Dr. Kizza cradled the receiver. In less than a minute, telephone in front of him rang.

He lifted the receiver and heard a voice of a lady saying,"Hello, good afternoon. This is the Medical Research Institute, can I help you?"

"Yes Madam. This is Dr. Kizza speaking from the police station could I talk to Odongkara? He should be somewhere in the Institute."

"Hold on the line Doctor." the lady said.

"I will,"Dr. Kizza said and heard the phone clicking on the other end indicating that she was trying to connect her to Odongkara. She tried Hajji Rhajabu's office first. She thought they could still be in his office.

The jarring telephone startled Hajji who had sat in his office thinking of what happened. He jumped and picked the receiver and talked in it.

"Hello, Hajji here, can I help you?"

"Yes Sir. Dr. Kizza at the Police station would like to talk to Odongkara."

"He is in the boardroom."

"Thank you Sir, I will connect him there." the lady said. Hajji cradled his receiver and resumed his meditation.

It was when the night guard was entering, that the telephone in front of them rang. Paul picked the receiver and said, "Hello, can I help you."

"I would like to talk to Odongkara." The lady at the switchboard said.

Paul swung the receiver to him and said, "It's yours."

"Not for another crime", Odongkara said receiving the receiver and sat back in his chair.

"Hold on for Dr. Kizza. "You are through to Odongkara Doctor."

"Thank you", Dr. Kizza said and heard the voice of Odongkara at the end of the line.

"Hello Doc. woken him up?"

"I have failed to awake your man. He had an engine knock. It needs a complete overhauling and you know no human money can buy that engine. It is irreparable and cannot be replaced. He's written off the road."

"Disposable car?"

"If you like to call it. Anyway, Sir, I have opened him up. The heart, the liver and the lungs were just fibbers and pieces of meat. They were shattered completely by the bullets. I guess he must have died before he fell down."

"That was bad. I will track down the person concerned until I get him. I am now beginning to see strange things which might put us on the track of the person we want. So what is your intention now, are you going back?"

"That is what I want to do." Doctor Kizza replied. "Fine. Will you do us one favour?"

"And that is?"

Take back the Peugeot UP 125 to Gulu Police Station. "Why? How will you come back?"

"We are still staying here longer. By the time we finish, another transport will have availed itself. But that is not the main reason why you are taking it back."

"Why then?"

"The car is having a case to answer. It is going to be a silent witness of either a complainant or a defendant?"

"I don't understand you?"

"You don't have to Doctor. Briefly, the car seems to have been involved in an accident. It is as innocent as innocence, but someone who dragged her to commit a crime is guilty. So she is just going to stand a dumb blue beauty. She won't say a word, but the mud she carried on her will talk for her. Anyway Doctor, we are going to be there in about forty five minutes time and I will give you a chit to take with you back to Gulu. You will be escorted by one Police officer from here to make sure you don't force her to have a bath on the way." Odongkara said. He cradled the receiver and stared at the night guard, a swarthy nervous man, standing in front of him.

"Sit down."

"You are also Hajji who?" Odongkara asked.

"I am Shaban Bin Juma."

"How old is Shaban Bin Juma?" Odongkara asked. "I am thirty five years old Sir."

"Are you married?" "Yes."

"How many wives." "Seven wives."

You! Seven wives!" Odongkara said astonished that a night guard could afford to marry and maintain seven wives.

"I see congratulations." Odongkara said sarcastically and they all laughed.

"How many children do you have?"

"Twenty five." Odongkara laughed and threw his pen on the table and look at the man the way you would look at a magician swallowing a live snake.

"I don't want to disbelieve you. How many more children would you like to have Shaban?"

"As many as Allah can give me."

"Okay Shaban. What do you do in the Institute here?" "I am a night guard Sir?"

"You work only at night?"

"No Sir. I sometimes work during the day." "What schedule were you on last night?" "I was on night Sir."

"Well, what do you know about last night's event in the Institute? I think you were lucky to escape unnoticed by the armed men who came here, because the rest of your friends are in the hospital now." Odongkara said.

Saban adjusted himself on the seat and rubbed the black callus on his forehead as if to generate wisdom in his head and cleared his throat.

He began, "We didn't quite see how the men came in but we guessed they must have come over the walls behind those mango trees. We had just returned from our routine surveillance around the walls from within and sat at the main gate talking. The three of us who were on duty. We had hardly sat for thirty minutes, when we saw six armed men in uniform walking towards us from the direction of the main building. We were scared and frightened."

"What type of uniform were they wearing?" "The National Army uniform."

"Umm", Odongkara murmured and said, "go on with story."

"We were frightened because we didn't know what to do to challenge them." The best we thought we could do was to run away because our clubs, bows and arrows could not compete with the type of guns they were carrying."

"What type of gun were they carrying?" "The automatic rifles."

"Are you very familiar with different types of guns so that you could identify them at night?"

"Not quite so."

"How did you know that the guns they were carrying were automatic rifles? They could have been the ordinary rifles or any other gun?" Saban kept quiet.

"So you are not sure of the type of guns those men were carrying."

"No."

"What initiated you to guess they were carrying automatic rifle and no other gun?"

"Because they were army men." "Where they?"

"Yes Sir." Odongkara sighed sat back and looked at the man without saying a word and began to write.

"Do all army men carry automatic rifles?" "That was what I thought."

"You thought wrongly Saban." Odongkara corrected.

He felt that the man knew all what happened and he was only acting, which, if confused with tricky questions, he would forget the trend or the steps he had probably been trained to talk and might just blurt out the secret.

"Did you recognize any of them?" "No Sir".

"Then why are you convincing me that they are army men." "Because of their uniform Sir."

"So if I get hold of a National Army uniform now, and put it on, I automatically become an army man?"

"No Sir."

Then why do you assume the men who came were no other persons disguised in the National Army uniform?"

Shaban began to sweat, the callus in the forehead glittered with sweat. He took the turban from his head and held it in his hand. The bald head with fringe of grey air was damp with sweat.

"Are you alright Shaban?" Odongkara asked. "Yes, I am alright sir."

"So can we proceed with our story? The six armed uniformed army men came towards you with automatic rifles. This is so far the summary of our talk is that right?"

"Yes Sir".

"Okay, go on from there."

"We tried to escape, but were shocked to find that both sides of the wall near us were washed with the armed uniformed men. They ordered us to lie down with our faces on the ground. Then all the men converged on us. We laid down at their feet feeling dead. Then one of them took a paper from his pocket and opened it."

"How many were they in all?" Odongkara asked. "They were fifteen."

"Fifteen all in the National Army Uniform!" "Yes Sir."

"You counted them and saw one of them take a paper from his pocket and opened it with the back of your head because I understand from you that you were ordered to be lie down with your face down."

Shaban only licked his lips and didn't talk regretting why he was born.

"Yes, one of them took the paper, Opened it and what did he do with the paper?" Odongkara asked.

"The paper contained a list of names of some of the officers they wanted to see last night."

'Did he read the names out to you?" "Yes Sir".

"Who were these?"

Dr. Gunya was on the top list, Hajji Rhajabu, Miss Susan, Miss Shoemaker, Dr. Ruliabandi and Mr. Otyeno, the head of the Askaris in the Institute here.

"Those were all?" "Yes Sir".

"What happened afterwards?"

"He asked one of my friends who was nearest to him to lead them to their homes. But he refused, saying he was only recruited a week ago and therefore, didn't know the homes of those officers. He then asked another friend who was next, he also said they were recruited together. They suspected that I was going to say the same and I heard one of them say "They are lying, let's teach them a lesson that it's no good lying to us." I thought they were going to shoot us so I screamed out that I would take them. So they started on my friends. They beat them with the butt of their guns, kicked them with shoes, and left them nearly dead at the gate.

"What language were they using?" "Swahilli."

"Okay, they beat your friends, and you?"

"One of them grasped me by the collar of my shirt and stood me up, slapped me hard on the face and said, "you take us to these people." Then we started the march, six of them behind me with their guns ready to fire on my back."

"Where did the rest of them go?"

"Four remained at the gate with my battered friends. They didn't want them to cause trouble."

"Now, Shaban let's get the number of these men right. You at first said they were fifteen is that right?

"Yes Sir".

"If my arithmetic is still viable, six plus four is ten. Where did the other five go?" Saban saw stars. He knew he was sliding too fast. He tried to talk, but no words came. His lips parted and remained with the gap, like a fish dying out of water.

"Okay lets go on, you marched to the officers' home."

"Yes sir." We walked past the homes of Susan and Miss Shoemaker and went to the home of Hajji Rajabu. I went and knock on his door."

"Let's get this part right again Shaban," Odongkara said and sat up.

"Why did you pass the homes of Susan and Miss Shoemaker and went to Rajabus' home? Yet the names of these two ladies were also on the death list?"

"I thought I should start with the furthest home first, and come up later."

"I see! You are very wise. But if your intention was to start with the furthest and work your way backward, then you should have started with Dr. Gunya because his home is last in that line. Am I wrong?"

"No."

"Then why did you start in the middle? You hate Rajabu that is why you took the men to his house first. You wanted him to be killed first, so that the other could take precaution before they were visited. Is that right?"

"No Sir. They said they were not going to kill them." "What did they want from them?"

"They didn't tell me."

"Who killed Dr. Gunya then?"

"The gun men did Sir." Odongkara gave an angry stare at Shaban and said

"Yet we all know the gun men killed Dr. Gunya and they assured you they were not going to kill anyone."

"I do not know why they did it."

"When you were at Hajji's home, you went and knocked on the door. Was there light at the door?" I mean, security light at the door, was it on?"

"Yes the security light at the front of the door was on." "Could you see each other clearly?"

"Yes Sir."

"So if we brought those army men now you could identify them?"

"I am not sure because they were slanting their caps forward covering most of their faces." Odongkara sighed and said, "go on Shaban." You knocked on the door and what did Rhajabu do? Did he open for you?"

"No he did not but his wife began to scream?"

"How did you know it was his wife screaming and not any other lady, a visitor perhaps who was more scared than any of them?"

"Because it was the voice of a lady." Odongkara sneered at him and asked him "How about the children and Rajabu did they also scream?"

"No. Only his wife." "What happened next?"

"The men fired shots on the roof. I fell down and in the commotion, crawled away into the dark. They didn't notice me go. I crawled under the fence and hid there until I saw them leave the home of Rajabu."

"Shaban, Iam sometime slow in understanding clever people. The men shot in the ceiling board of Rajabu, is that right? You

The Director Murdered

the guide a very important man in their operation melts away and leaves them without one? Does not mean much to me. Anyway congratulation you survived to give us clues."

"Which way did they go?" Odongkara continued with questions after noting in his book.

"They went towards Dr. Gunya's home."

"Then what happened after that? You should be telling me all these Shaban, without me asking you many questions. These events happened in your presence. The whole thing from the beginning up to the end. So please, get your points together and tell us what happened." Odongkara said emotionally.

"I remained under the fence and after a period I heard gun shot at Dr. Gunya's home. I thought they did the same as at Rajabus' home. But in his case they shot at him." Odongkara took a deep breath in and out and said now we have reached where Dr. Gunya is shot at, tell us how you knew that the gunmen actually shot at Dr. Gunya and not fired the shots at the verandah as they did at Rajabus' home?"

Saban kept quiet.

"Just a few more questions before you leave Shaban. When you led your men to their target, you said at Rajabu's home you escaped. True, anyone who has escaped from an episode like that would think twice about going back immediately. It's said that it is a foolish fish which get caught in the same bait twice. Now how long was it from the time the men left Rajabus' place and went to Dr. Gunyas' home when you heard the shots?"

"It was about 5-10 minutes."

"Did you hear anything else before the gun shot?" "I thought I heard a telephone ring."

"You did."

"Yes."

"In Dr. Gunya's house?"

"I guess so. I was rather messed up. I could hear things but was unable to point the direction of the noise."

"No sound of moving vehicles?" "No."

"Okay, Shaban thank you very much. You can go and tell the police officer outside that I want to talk to the store keeper next.

What do you make out of these Paul? He is mixed up. He wasn't coherent at all in his talk, was he?"

"No he wasn't; and I am surprised, what he told us this morning is very different from what he said now."

"I wonder why his observation doesn't conform to that of the Hajji. To him the men who broke in were all in uniform and ..."

A knock sounded on the door. A dwarfish, flat head man entered into the boardroom, his large bulging chameleon like eyes searching them suspiciously avoiding danger. The dense growth of beard and moustache made him look one of the pygmies you occasionally see on Kinshasa Street. He had fat, short, hairy arms with fingers which look as if they were once homes for leprosy. He walked in, greeted them and stood in front of them about a foot taller than the table.

They replied his greeting and wave him to a seat. He sat down and cupped his fingers on his knees. He looked a ten year old boy. As they stared at each other with amusement, the telephone on the table rang again. This time, Odongkara snatched the receiver and glued it onto the pinna of his ear. "Hello, can we help you?"

"May I talk to Odongkara?" He heard the same voice of the telephone operator.

"Speaking baby!" Odongkara said and grinned.

He heard the girl's giggle insinuatingly at the other end of the line. Odongkara felt enchanted by the giggle. He felt he must hear more of that possibly at night, and no other time. With all the boring interviews with the people he called suspects, he needed a more recreational evening with such a doll. Moreover, with her on the switch board of the Institute, if he handles her with ecstasy, she might be willing to blurt some of the telephone conversation she over heard going on, if the culprits he was searching for were in the Institute.

"Hey baby, what is your name?" You have known mine and every detail about me. I am always a jealous man, I don't want to be known one sided, if you know me I must also know you."

"I am Miss Betty Aweko."

"You are *missing* Beauty Aweko? Where do you live beauty?"
"But Sir, there is a man on the line he wants to talk to you." "Let

him wait, I am bored with official transaction. Answer my question. Where do you live?' Odongkara insisted

"I live with my sister in town, next to Rock Hotel." "Plot number?"

"26B."

"Can I meet you at say....What time are you free by the way, beauty?"

"I am never free."

"Take the hell away. You can't tell me that you two ladies living in the same house are always busy from dawn to dusk. Well, if you mean you are busy before supper, then I see you ... at say, after supper or any time even after 24 hours. Will that be okay?"

"But sir, you haven't seen me, how do you start calling me beauty?"

"Your voice told me all about your appearance, you are a beauty." "You are wrong. I am blind and lame. I move on a wheel chair, a complete ball of a human being. You won't stand my sight if you saw me."

Odongkara got a wave of anger rising in him. He knew that most of the telephone operators are the disabled, handicapped people. He felt like throwing the receiver back onto the cradle, but of course, he knew he had already blundered. If she was really what she told him, he must behave humanly and with lots of sympathies.

"Okay Miss Beauty, I don't care how you look. I will want to see you tonight. So tell me the time I will pick you up."

"Well sir, not to keep the gentleman on the line waiting and because you have accepted your embarrassment tonight, you come and you push me in my wheel chair wherever you want to take the hag of a woman."

"What time? I will come equipped for the push." Odongkara said and found his anger receding as he convinced himself that the girl couldn't be what she had told him. *Such a sweet voice to be lame? No. Even if she is, I will go and pick her take her to a lonely place and try to find out how much she knows about the people of the Institute, especially Hajji and Dr. Gunya. I am suspicious about Hajji now. He seems to be an accessory of this murder.*

"Come at 6.00 pm." "That is a bit early baby."

"Ha-ha I've got you. You now fear being seen pushing my wheel chair in the day isn't it?"

"No, not at all. I am giving this excuse because I might still be compiling my report and I don't want to keep you waiting. I don't mind pushing your wheel chair in the afternoon through the town and into Rock Hotel to eat with you." he said and heard her giggle again."

"Shall we make it at 8.00 pm? I am sure by that time I will have finished everything, will that be all right with you beauty?"

"It is okay Sir, see you then at 8.00pm. Can I put you through now to your caller?"

"Please do."

"You are through to Odongkara." he heard her say. "Hello, Lwanga here."

"Ho Lwanga, what is up? What have you stirred up there?" "A few things which we think might interest you."And …

"Interest me! You sound illogical. I am not the alone in the chase. You, me and everyone else should be interested in anything anyone of us will dig out here. We are here on a teamwork and not individual interest."

"I am sorry Sir, my apologies for the statement." "It's okay Lwanga, but watch your words next time." "I will sir."

"What is the problem now?"

"We have searched all places here thoroughly and have come up with some items, we shall discuss later. What we want to know from you is, do we leave this place now?"

"And go where? Are you bored of that place? Check in his refrigerator and the cocktail cupboard and help yourselves to anything that will make the place and the New Year day livelier. Go walk in the flower garden and smell the roses. Okay?" Odongkara said and cradled the receiver. Lwanga sat with the receiver pinned on his ear and stared at Opiyo who was enjoying himself enormously with the whisky.

"What does he say?"Opiyo asked

"The baboon wants us to stay here. He said we should check in the refrigerator and the cocktail cupboard and help ourselves to anything that would make this place exciting. So go ahead and empty bottles. There is meat there, cooked sausages are all teaming up in the refrigerator waiting for teeth to masticate them." Lwanga said and gulped the whisky in his glass.

"He's indubitably an impeccable CID officer. He loves his work and wants each and everyone who accompanies him on a trip to do the same." Opiyo commented.

"I understand, but I don't have to be barked at."

"Work hard so that you may bark at someone sometime in future boy!"

Lwanga kept quiet. He walked towards the refrigerator, opened it, took one huge cold sausage, bit it nearly half way and began to munch, walking with it towards Opiyo.

"You have aroused my appetite, you idiot, get me one." Opiyo said.

Lwanga walked back and carried the whole tray packed with cooked sausages and put it on the table in front of Opiyo.

"You must be a carnivore. Are you going to gormandize this entire heap?"

"I wanted one to go with the Gin."

"Taste it first and see if you won't push your hand back in the tray."

"I am not ready to take orders walking to and fro, from the refrigerator for more sausages."

When Odongkara finished talking to Lwanga, He turned and looked at the store keeper sitting in front of them and said. "I am sorry to keep you waiting." Odongkara apologized to the store keeper who sat on the chair his feet just touching the floor. "Let's get started."

"What are your names?" "I am Fred Masiko." "Fred, how old are you?" "Twenty nine Sir." "Married?"

"Yes Sir."

"How many wives?" "One, with two children."

"You'd better marry more wives and get more children like Shaban." Odongkara teased him.

"I haven't enough income to support a school of children and a team of wives like him."

"That is a wise idea Fred. What are you in the Institute here?"
"I am a senior storekeeper Sir."

"Well, Fred, I am interested in knowing from you what you know about what happened here last night, especially, your workplace which has been invaded."

"I am going to give you precisely what I know", Fred said and Odongkara nodded his head approvingly at his eloquence of speech. "I woke up perturbed about the turmoil in the Institute last night. I thought it was a coup. I made sure I got up and tuned in for the first news, but there was no new news apart from the previous ones. However at 6.30 a.m, the driver of the taxi of Dr. Gunya came to collect the vehicle from my garage. "Dr. Gunya had a taxi?"

"Yes Sir, A Volkswagen mini bus. "That is news to us', Odongkara said.

"Yes he had A Volkswagen mini bus UVS 128."Paul confirmed "You are right Sir" Fred agreed.

"He was parking it in your garage?" "Yes Sir.'"

"You don't own a car?"

"How do I own one, when I am almost failing to feed my family, the best means of transport I can afford is perhaps a new pair of shoes." Fred said and they all laughed.

"Yes, the driver came, I opened the door for him and he announced to me that my work place has been burglarized and that the spare tyres of some of the Volkswagen mini buses advertised last week to the Institutes' members of staff were outside the store and that, some iron sheets, were scattered everywhere in the compound. I nearly ran out of the house to see what had happened had the driver not added,"and there was an attempt on the life of Hajji Rajabu, but Dr. Gunya was shot dead in his house."

"I couldn't believe the subtle news he was telling me. I thought I was dreaming, or having a nightmare perhaps. I got a tight feeling in my chest which crept in my throat and tried to strangle me."

"You see, we all come from different corners of Uganda, but Dr. Gunya was special to me. He had a special personality I admired which I haven't found in many Ugandan." Fred said and snorted through his nose as tears rolled down his cheeks.

The Director Murdered

"Take it easy Fred." We shall find him. I know I will. My hand is already on the plough and I promise you, I am not going to plough sand." Odongkara said comfortingly. "Tell us what happened next." But Fred kept quiet trying to stabilize himself snorting through his nose.

"Then instead of walking to the store," Fred began, "I walked straight to prove that Dr. Gunya was really assassinated. I found others were already there. But we were asked to leave the place by the police officers who were already there. They warned us not to go near the house."

"How many were you?"

"I can't remember the exact figure, but I think all the staff members were there except, Hajji and the family."

"When the Police sent you back what happened."

"We walked away back home and met some people going to Hajji's home."

"Do you think that is why Hajji didn't go with the rest of the staff to Dr. Gunya's home?"

Fred kept quiet and said "could be."

"Fred, according to your personal thinking, you have seen that your store was force opened and not a thing was taken from the store. At the gate the two guards were beaten up and are in hospital now. One of them escaped untouched. Hajji Rajabus' life was threatened and Dr. Gunya was assassinated. Now, why is this?"

"Sir, to my own personal feeling, I think there is something funny about this attack on us last night. I have been having a presentiment for a long time that something would burst up here and it has happened. The only clue I can give you to answer your question is if I were a CID officer, investigating this case I would concentrate my investigation in this Institute other than think of false information intended to lead me from the target of the crime," Fred said.

"Thank you Fred for your advice. It's well noted and kept", Odongkara said. "I am sure I will still be talking to you as you have given us all your cooperation to help in this matter. I am sure with your help, we will get this mess cleared up within this week. I am equally determined like you to expose the man who did this."

"I would like to warn you sir, that there are many guns in this Town. So watch your steps and be more careful with the ladies. They could turn out to be unpleasant chicks."

"Thank you again Fred. I will watch my movement", Odongkara said, *thinking that the warning could have been directed against Betty whom he heard him chat with. But for Betty, he was ready to risk.* He slowly slid his hand in his jacket to check his 0.38 automatic police pistol he had carried. He touched the warm butt and knew it was there. *As a CID officer, you have to risk your neck in many detrimental, lethal things in order to find facts otherwise, if you want it to come easy your way, you won't get a damn. He is warning me as a civilian. I appreciate it,* Odongkara thought and stretched himself.

"Okay, let me wind up my discussion of today with the servant of Dr. Gunya', Odongkara said and Fred Masiko jumped down from his chair and sulkily walked out of the boardroom nearly slopping out tears again.

He walked out closing the door behind him, and immediately, an old lanky, stooped man, winding up his forties, walked into the boardroom. He was the exact opposite of Masiko in physique. The overgrown limbs were lean and lanky. The flat stomach made him look too weak to lift even an empty sauce-pan of any size. The man entered the room, bowed to the two men, went and sat down on the client chair, scratched the kinky hair on his head which had started getting gray and stared at them expectantly.

Servants could be dangerously tricky. They could conspire into many things, especially those who do not stay together in the same premises with their master. Odongkara thought as he planned and framed up the questions for him. After going through the usual routine questions of name. Marital status and occupation, Odongkara asked Mzee Ongwen the servant of Dr. Gunya.

"How long have you been working for Dr. Gunya?" "Since 1960. That is about eleven years ago."

"Mzee, you were the servant of Dr. Gunya, there is what is known as the servants quarter in the same compound where you were supposed to stay. I gather that you were not living there, why was this?"

"I was coming from my home which is just a short walking distance away from the Institutes. It was not worthwhile to move my family from our home and come with them here. Instead, I preferred to walk to my place of work every day, and more over, as a married man, I could not sleep here and leave my family, especially my wife, alone at home. Finally, I like gardening and because of these facts, I stayed outside the Institute.

"Was Dr. Gunya nice to you? I heard he was a very harsh strict man, who scrapped people all the time and I imagined he was doing the same to you, and that people did not like him much in the Institute here? Hajji was more preferred by the workers. Am I wrong?"

"I will answer that question, as a previous group employee of the Institute and then as a servant of the late Dr. Gunya first. As far as I can remember, Sir, you are wrong. I started work here when I was only ten years old and now I am forty nine. I worked here in different jobs. As I told you, I was cutting grass around the Institute compound. I saw good and horrible Directors both white and black. I tell you, those who are telling you all the nonsense about Dr. Gunya should have worked here during the colonial days when a white man could call you a dog or a monkey. As a servant, I worked for many people here, especially the whites, most of whom have now left the country. I have seen inhuman men and women, people with huffy temper. What I am emphasizing to you is, I want you to appreciate that Dr. Gunya was the nicest man I have worked for in the last nine years in this Institute. He never scolded me or insulted me. In fact, he treated me with the respect a son bestows on a father. He addressed me with respect and kindness. No, it's not true. Dr. Gunya was not what you have been told. Well, as an administrator responsible for about one thousand people, you are bound to have people for you and people against you. Not all will like you and for the sake of good administration, you stick to good administration principle to establish the smooth running of the place. This is when the enemies of the one in the chair will stand up and say no this is not it, it has to go the opposite direction, and of course, they antagonized each other and you get the type of report you might have heard about Dr. Gunya."

"Among the members of staff of the Institute who was his best friend?" Who used to come to see him often at his home?"

"I think the person who comes to my mind immediately is Fred Masiko and his family. The two were together most of the time. I am sure the death of Dr. Gunya is a terrible blow to Fred. The rest of the senior members of staff used to come, but not quite often like Fred." "What about Hajji Rajabu, your immediate neighbour, did the two stay together often? Moreover, Hajji was his number two?"

"I think there was something fishy between the two. I think it all started about a year ago. You know, Dr. Gunya was a very smart man. He liked to keep everything about himself smart. I am surprise he wasn't a botanist. He loves plants and flowers. You have seen it for yourself in his compound. There was a time when the daughter of Hajji Rajabu, without the permission of Dr. Gunya, went to his flower garden and cut his flowers. Dr. Gunya was not at home. When he came, I asked him whether they had permission from him to cut the flowers. He said no! Of course, that annoyed him. He immediately rang Hajji to find out why his children behaved that way. Instead of apologizing, I learnt from Doctor Gunya later, that Rajabu asked him what he was going to do with all the flowers drying up in his garden. Dr. Gunya was angry and said, "But the flowers are mine and in my compound, I have the right to use them in any way I want." To make the matter worst he told me that Hajji said he was acting like that because he had no child. I think that wasn't a good remark to make, especially in Hajji's position. Since then, the two met, I think, in the office. None visited the other,

"I see!" Odongkara said nodding his head and asked,

"Mzee, you know just as much as I do, Dr. Gunya wasn't married and I guessed he might have been bringing some ladies at home. Some of them might have been regular visitors, and some occasional. Do you remember any time, recently, that he might have brought home a lady and had an open quarrel which you witnessed?"

"No. To the best of my knowledge, I don't. It's true he had been bringing ladies at home, but I think he was more regular with one lady whom I saw in the house very often, may I say, almost every

The Director Murdered

weekend. This lady is the manageress of Rock Hotel. The two were great friends. But they were, I don't know why, they could not live together. At one time I thought they were going to wed, and then things slug, but they kept close to each other all the same."

"Was there any disagreement which you noticed, that things were not moving fine with them."

"I don't think so. It looks like they were only getting bored of each other. I don't know. What I mean is, the lady was spending most of her evening with us during the period I suspected them to march to the altar, then all of a sudden, she reduced her visit to our place but each time they met, they looked happy."

"Were they hiding their feelings away from you, you think?"

"No. Dr. Gunya, I think, never learnt to hide his feelings. You remember Hajji's case about the flowers and many others I know, if he didn't like you he didn't like you. There was no way he could pretend. That is why I am convinced that there was nothing wrong between him and the lady."

"Mzee, this could be a very heavy question for you. But your opinion about it will be very useful as one, you are a long serviced man in this Institute both for the Institute and in some individual homes and two, you lived with Dr. Gunya for the last ten years. How do you account for the incident, which happened here last night? You think the men who broke in came over the walls as some people think? And why should they kill Dr. Gunya?"

"To start with, what happened last night has left all of us still asking questions as to why it happened. Because, if you follow the event, you find that there are very many things that leaves one puzzled. Let's start with the main store. The door was broken, the spare parts of the vehicle scattered, but none was taken. You move to the gate, all the night watchmen got beaten up, except one who lead the thugs to homes of selected senior members staff to be killed, and there he escaped from them later. I personally don't understand it. In one home there were gun shots, but not a bullet was fired into the house. But at Dr. Gunya's place, the bullet was aimed at him. I am an old man, but I think we should think hard to verify the different statements being made. As to what entrance and exit these men came through and left, I have no idea. They could have come over the walls. It had happened before, or they could have come through any of the easy way."

"What do you mean through any of the easy way?"

"What if they came in the Institute during the day through the gate and stayed on until that time of operation?" Mzee said. Odongkara nearly jumped out of his skin at the wisdom of the old man. He wondered why he didn't think of that possibility if the suspect is to be within the Institute. He felt angry and embarrassed, but all the same, he congratulated Mzee for his wisdom.

"As to why they should kill Dr. Gunya", Mzee went on, "there are many reasons one could think about and could not be too far away from the main target. He was a progressive man in his profession and someone might have been after his chair, two he had a beautiful car, which someone could have been after, three, he had just bought a new mini bus which someone could have been after too. The women we talked about could have been the cause. Or, he was just killed by a Frenzy lunatic murderer who enjoys pulling the trigger of his gun at any human being."

"I am very impressed by the information you've given us Mzee." I am going to digest all you've told us and will act accordingly."

Meanwhile, I would like to convey to you my sincere heartfelt condolence to you for his death. I know he must have been a good man to you."

"He was. I don't deny that fact, and I think I will never get another job, and be respected and treated as he did to me. I wish you could get the hooligan who killed him and bring him to book. I will be very grateful to you Sir."

"I'll try. I don't promise you that. Before all these, he must have planned a lot and now I have got to prove to him that I think better. If I don't, then I don't find him but if I think harder and better, I will find him. All I can tell you now is that I will try my best to think better than him."

"You can go home Mzee, but keep around. I might need you anytime and should be able to reach you easily.

"I will be at home until this matter is cleared and I know who shot Dr. Gunya."

Mzee said and got up, bowed to them, and walked out.

Chapter 7

The two men laid separately on the long settees in Dr. Gunya's living room their heads resting on the arms support of the chair feeling fine at the effect of the whisky. The empty tray of sausage, the empty bottle of whisky, and the glasses they had been drinking from including the items, they individually found in the house were sitting on the long coffee table in the middle of the living room. Opiyo was turning drunkenly on his chair when the telephone rang. He felt lazy and vertigo to get up. Lwanga, who was half asleep, woke up at the ringing of the telephone, yawned and rubbed his eyes. "Will you attend to that telephone you idiot? It's shattering my nerves, making me more drunk and sick", Opiyo ordered.

"You clown, who told you to take too much of the stuff? You said you needed only a sausage and you emptied the whole butchery." Lwanga replied, got up and walked to attend the telephone. He picked it and glued it to his ears.

"Hello, can I help you?" he talked in the mouthpiece while yawning.

"Bloody idiot, how dare you talk to me like that? I am not your contemporary. You big thick headed pig". He heard the voice of Odongkara fuming on line. "If you repeat that again, I'll wipe off that obstinacy from your head."

"I am sorry Sir."Lwanga said apologetically. Opiyo heard and turned his head and leered at Lwanga through his eyes lashes. He heard the voice of Odongkara booming in the receiver and knew Lwanga was being disciplined. He sneered at him amusingly, sat up from the sofa, put on his shoes, and began to fasten the laces while looking at Lwanga.

"Okay Lwanga", Odongkara said relaxing the seriousness of his voice on the phone. "Will you pack up your findings and get ready to leave as soon as the two police men arrive there."

"Yes Sir." Lwanga said slowly as he cradled his receiver and turned to Opiyo.

"Sorry for …" Opiyo had begun to talk.

"You ape, collect your findings and get ready to leave", Lwanga said with a sneer on his face.

"You fat nose pig, I didn't fire you myself. Why did he do it anyway? Was it because we didn't attend to the phone immediately?"

"No. Because I talked to him while yawning."

"Serves you right. How do you talk to a person four ranks higher than you as if you were talking to your houseboy?"

"How could I have known he was the one?"

"That is why you have to be respectful to all at all time and you'll never go wrong. Behave well towards every human being, at all time regardless to their status but if you have the primitive prejudiced ideas, that certain groups of people don't matter and you are the only person, then at times you fall in such a trap."

"Keep your advice in your pocket and give it to your son later." "Up to you." Opiyo said and took the photo album, the two empty cartridges, wrapped up in a piece of paper and slipped them into his pocket, strap the camera around his neck and, walked out on the verandah leaving Lwanga fastening the laces of his shoes. Lwanga collected the pistol and the knife, he found in the bed side locker wrapped them up in a newspaper taken from the rack below the coffee table, and his pack of powder and staggered out of the house following Opiyo who had already sat on the form outside under the tree waiting.

"Oh, I have had the new year day fine. Although I have celebrated it out of my house on a dead man's whisky and sausages." Lwanga said. Opiyo looked at him and chuckled but didn't comment.

The Director Murdered

"You guys steam whisky, have you been bathing in it?" Odongkara said as they climbed on the Land Rover which came to pick them to the police station.

"You told us to look aroundin the house for anything that could make the place lively and less boring", Opiyo answered.

"And that is what you got?" "Yes Sir".

"That's fine if you've enjoyed yourselves. I had a hectic time and I think the evening might be more hectic. The programme for the evening is going to run as follows. One, we are going to hand the Peugeot 504 we came in back to the station in Gulu. Dr. Kizza is going to take it back."

"Why?"Opiyo asked.

"I was talking to Mukasa at 14.00 hours this afternoon about the car. They suspect that the car was involved in the hit and run accident on Keyo road last evening. There are some witnesses who swore that they saw the car and it was the one which ran over that child."Odongkara explained.

"'I don't believe it. Mukasa was in the club last night?" Opiyo protested.

"The driver of the car was a lady with two children the witnesses said." Odongkara corrected.

"And Mukasa never let the car to his wife." Lwanga said. "That is what everybody thinks but, it looks as if she illegally took the car to go to Onekalit farm." Odongkara responded

"That will be sad if she is proved to be the driver."Opiyo remarked.

"Certainly it will", Odongkara agreed. Anyway we shall hear more in due course but as I was saying about the evening programme, we shall officially hand our car to Dr. Kizza to take it back to the station for further examination. Our second activity is, we shall go for coffee and thereafter compile all our reports together before I contact Joe in Gulu. I am sure those bastards in Kampala are sitting on needles now expecting some information from Gulu. After all these, we should go out to relax in some of those bars with our ears on the ground, our eyes open and noses on the tracks of every suspicious characters. I have already made an appointment with a chick I am going to pick at 8 p.m.

"Where did you get her?" Lwanga asked.

"Don't worry where I got her, you go find one in the bar tonight but be careful. This town seems to be packed with guns in the hands of lunatic murderers. I don't want to hit the head line in *NATION DAILY* tomorrow. Some of these ladies, I hear, are more lethal than the men. They carry not only guns but knives too." Odongkara said.

Time was 16.00 hours when Paul the O/C of Kitgum Police and Odongkara handed the car to Dr. Kizza with the sealed note to Orwotho. The note said: *We have made a thorough examination of the vehicle in question, UP 125 Peugeot 504 Saloon dark blue in colour. Here are our remarks.*

It appears that there are dried bloodstains on the left, front and the rear wheels and the rear bumper has a dent just near the plate number of the car otherwise, there is nothing more of interest on it.

Signed D/AIP Odongkara & O/C Kitgum Paul.

Dr. Kizza with an armed police constable drove off in the UP 125 Peugeot 504 while the driver for Gulu hospital drove in front of them alone in the Land Rover they came in, in the morning.

After their coffee, the four men met in the Police seminar room.

The time was 17.00 hours.

"Yes gentlemen, let's put our zig-zag puzzle together and see what pattern we can make of this case. From the interview we have had with the people directly associated with Dr. Gunya, I have now dropped out the suspicion that the BDM could have been responsible for the assassination. What I think we should dwell on, is the planned murder by a group of people. Here I do not want to bias your thinking. Our collective conclusion will be made after we have laid all our findings of this afternoon down and that will be used as the foundation of our search for the culprit. Let's get one and the rest will come our way. But one point I want to emphasize to you is, as we search for them, they are also searching for us and slipping away from us. Let's hear from you first before I read for you the various interviews we had with a cross-section of people working in the Institute. Shall we start with you Lwanga?" Odongkara said and sat back in his chair.

Lwanga got up, walked in front and pulled out a pistol from his pocket placed it on the table in front of Odongkara and Paul. Then he unwrapped a knife with a short black hilt with depression for the four fingers to provide better grip on the hilt and placed it on the table in front of the two officers. Odongkara took the pistol, examined it, opened it and noticed that not a bullet was fired. He closed it and put it back on the table. He took the knife and read the inscription on its blade saying, '*made in Great Britain-Smith Limited.*' He rewrapped it and put in on the table. Finally, he took the identity card which Lwanga had also put on the table in front of them and read the heading PROPERTY OF FOOD AND BEVERAGE and the name below was that of a 25 year old, Salim Bin Rajabu. Odongkara turned the card in his hand meditatively. *Is this yet another trick? Is the card thrown behind to lead us from our target or is it genuine card dropped behind by the murderer who is now regretting having dropped it behind. Well we shall find that out.* Odongkara thought as he placed the card on the table and stared at it. "Wait a minute." Odongkara spoke out and took the card in his hand again.

"What have you observed about your card, Lwanga?" He asked.

Lwanga took the card in his hand and read it, turned the back and read it.

He couldn't make out what he was up to. "I haven't noticed anything strange Sir." "Pass it on to Opiyo." Odongkara said.

Opiyo received the card and after what he thought was a thorough scrutiny, looked up at Odongkara and gave the same answer to that of Lwanga.

"I see. Have you any identity card on you?" "Yes Sir". They answered in chorus.

"Take them out, compare with this one and tell me what is missing."

The two men took out their identity cards, looked at them, and at the card they found in the boot of the car.

"I think it has no number." Lwanga said.

"You are damn right, Lwanga. A genuine identity card must at least have a number that is indubitable fact. So you see, someone is still putting up a guard to detour us from the target of our search. This still gives more emphasis on what I have just said. There is a fugitive on the run and we mustn't dig blindly or else he will shock us. Anyway, let's hear more from you, the card is not genuine. It's fake, but all the same, with this name, we shall try to trace the owner if he exsist ."

Lwanga, what do you have to say about your investigation in and around the house?"Lwanga sat up and paired his hands together, and began to talk as he drummed his thumb together.

"Perhaps I should start from the frame of the house" Lwanga said and explained to the two men how he and Opiyo performed search around the house and the entire compound of Dr. Gunya.

"We found that one of the glasses on the back window in the sitting room was completely smashed violently from outside, possibly, with the barrel of a gun. We dusted around the window for any fingerprints but there was none. We moved on to the main door, on the handle of the door, we detected three different prints. One was of a man but could be that of the deceased, but the other two were all belonging to two different ladies. We got to the main living room. The telephone receiver contained the prints like that of the man we found on the door of the deceased. The visitors' bathrooms, toilets and all other bedrooms did have anything of interest. However in his bed room there was a giant wardrobe packed with his suits of different colours and styles, neck ties, pairs of trousers, shirts, shoes and handkerchiefs name them, were just too many for one person. Elsewhere in the room there was nothing of interest except in the bedside locker and below the pillow on a double bed, I got the pistol and the knife. It was at that time that Opiyo came to join me. We dusted the knife and the pistol together and found that they both contained the finger prints of one of the ladies whose prints appeared at the door.

"Is that so?" Odongkara asked. "Yes, the same lady."

"That is fine." Odongkara remarked.

"When we were through with the interior of the house we walked out of the house through the garage where we search the car and dusted every handle on the vehicle and glasses. All the prints on the handles, especially on the driver's side, were that of the man found on the phone and on the door of the house. When we opened the boot and ransacked it, we found this numberless identity card." Lwanga said and they all laughed.

"So now you know?" Odongkara commented and added, "Is that all you have for us?"

"Then we walked out of the garage to look around the house we did, but we couldn't find anything of interest", Lwanga concluded his story.

"Umm, well done." Odongkara remarked and said, "you Opiyo what do we learn from you this evening?"

"Thanks." Opiyo began and sat forward on the chair.

"In fact Lwanga has made my life easy because he has already mentioned most points and lightly bowed to Lwanga and they both smile.

"I ransacked the sitting room and the dining hall and came out with these two items." He said and got up to place the photo album on the table. I thought it could be of help to us and behind the safe, I got these two empty cartridges part of the cartridges which were collected this morning and sent for identification, otherwise, I did a lot of snapping." Opiyo said and slid back in the chair he was sitting and rested his back on the back rest.

"Now it's my turn and Paul to brief you on our findings. I prefer to start with Paul.

"Paul." He said and turned to him, "will you give us all what your investigation collected for us since morning when these cases were reported to you. I mean the incidences in town and the Institute?"

"Yes Sir. Paul said and adjusted himself on his seat. "The two shops which got burnt down were, the Pop In Shop and the Baby's Shop", Paul started.

"Baby's shop was burnt down by petrol, which started off the fire. An exploded drum was found in the shop where the fire originated. There were automatic rifles, hand grenades and a large quantity of ammunitions found in the back store of the shop. All the firing, which was heard last night, was the ammunitions and the hand grenades exploding in the fire. The owner of the shop, Salim Rajab, has disappeared with all his family. Roadblocks have been set on all roads to enmesh him, but we have not been lucky yet. Search for him is still continuing. We hope by the end of the day or later in the week we will get him. And finally, all the ammunitions, the fire arms and the hand grenades collected from Salim Rajab have been sent to our barracks here for identification because last year on the 16th September, there was burglary into the armory of the army barracks here in Kitgum where a large quantity of ammunitions, fire arms and hand grenades were stolen. So we suspect that these are the one. We are waiting for the results." Paul said and concluded the police report on the shop. The other shop of Olwoc, the Pop-In -Shop, was burnt by fire transferred from Baby's shop because of their proximity. The owner is being held for questioning as a rutine police intervention.

"Well, there we are gentlemen. You see what pudding we are buried in?" a real mess. The enemies are not brainless. They knew they were going to be traced and before they did it, they did some thinking and now, as I said earlier on, we have got to prove to them that they are brainless." Odongkara said, smiled at them turned the file in front of him opened and added, "I will read our interview with the people in the Institute so that you can see what you can make out of it."

"I would advise you to take notes because you are going to meditate on them alone and see what we come out with. Odongkara said and read through the interview he had with the four men in the early afternoon.

"I am going to cable our findings to Joe right now so that we also know what is happening there."

The office of Hajji Rajabu, the Deputy Director of the Medical Research Institute, was next to the boardroom where Odongkara had been conducting his interviews. The two rooms were separated by a thin bricked wall so that when one talked in the boardroom especially in a loud voice, it was clearly and distinctly heard in Hajji's Office. When Odongkara finished interviewing him, Hajji walked to his office with numb legs. He felt dizzy he wasn't sure if he didn't give himself away. He felt like crying. The sobs he had in the board room in front of Odongkara was not a condolence for Dr. Gunya, but it was a remorse, a remorse in that he gave himself up during the interview. He saw it in Odongkaras' eyes, he saw it clearly that he wasn't convinced he was innocent. He was guilty, he was afraid, he regretted what he did, but there was no way of undoing it. The best way to go about it was to commit more crime and die after a handful of lives have sunk. He came and sat in his office looking confused and when the telephone rang in his office for Odongkara, his heart missed several beats because he thought Odongkara was calling him back for cross-examinations. How grateful he was to Allah, when he heard the telephone operator asking for Odongkara. He directed her brusquely to the boardroom, cradled his receiver, and sat staring blankly in front of him wondering what next. Resign from the Institute or continue to play his innocence and continue to knock off suspicious character that might show threat to his safety. As he heard Odongkara converse with Betty as if they had known each other in years, he realized that one time, his direct line was out of order and he used the general line through the switchboard to talk to Salim Rajabu, the son of his brother, about the plan to obtain the army uniform and the fire arms from the barracks. Although they spoke in Arabic, he was suspicious that Betty could have guessed their conversation and suspected that something was going bad between him and Dr, Gunya. The conversation he had with Salim Rajabu wasn't a healthy one.

He had heard Odongkara making appointment with her and the time was 8 p.m. Rajabu also heard how Fred and Muzee swore that they would help the police to find the assassin of Dr. Gunya. He knew they suspected him because the two knew that something was wrong between him and Dr. Gunya. Muzee had mentioned it to Odongkara and he heard it with a qualm in the stomach, which made him nauseous. He felt like burying a bullet into the head of the lanky old man. *We must act and act very fast. May be if I drive the boys myself I will succeed, but from the look of things, the accident in the shop has betrayed us. The guns and the cartridges are going to be identified as those which got missing from Kitgum barracks and the uniform will be those collected from Captain Dramadri. But the body of Captain Dramadri was never found since he disappeared two years ago. The explanation will be that Captain Dramadri was killed by us and we used the uniform to deceive the men on guard at the gate to collect the uniform from the store and to collect the arms, ammunition, and hand grenades so easily without any risk from the armory. We packed these weapons in Salim's shop in town. We even hoarded a drum of petrol in the house in-spite of the government's warning against hoarding fuel which has now caused us trouble,* Hajji thought retrospectively. *Dammit, Shall I throw all the blame on Salim now that he is on the run? I'll say I have no knowledge about a thing, and with my quiet temperament, I could fox them that I am innocent. But why should I let Salim go it alone I initiated it. He planned it for my own sake and he did it. Why do I cowardly reject him in the most needful hours when we should be fighting together? How will I feel to see him hung, shot by firing squad or decapitated because of me, and his ghost will haunt me forever? His blood will pour on my head and the heads of my children for generations. I am not giving him up. I will strive with him until the end. If it means death, we both go.* Hajji continued to think and lifted the receiver of the phone of his direct line glued it to his ears. The line was clear. He dialed the private number of the son of his elder brother, Salim bin Rajabu.

Salim was lying on his back cursing whoever caused the fire in the shop, which burnt off their shelter, and exposed them to the law. Salim had been carrying out criminal orders of his uncle, Hajji Rajabu, very successfully for years. Whatever Hajji wanted, Salim always brought it to him on a plate. Salim was the son of one of the seven wives of Ibrahim Rajabu the elder brother of Hajji Sadala and Hajji Rajabu. Hajji Mustafa Rajabu had two wives only. His second wife bore for him daughters only and in Muslim society, girls are not the gender to smile at. Because of that, Mustafa loved the mother of the three boys more. When their father was dying, all his will went to Ibrahim his elder son. Hajji Sadala and Hajji Rajabu were very young at school. Ibrahim inherited the shops, bakery, butchery and all the fleet of Lorries and pickups their father had. He was rich and acquired more riches with time. He married nearly any woman he made love to, so that his home were congested with the so-called wives. The mother of Salim Rajab happened to be the second wife in Ibrahim's chains of women. She unfortunately bore for Ibrahim only one son, Salim, and ceased to deliver. In

Islam, that seems to be worse than producing girls. Because of that, Salim's mother was neglected but kept in the home for sex. Had Ibrahim maintained cordial relationship with his brothers Sadala and Rhajabu and his son Salim, Salim would have not turned out into a cosmopolitan murderer. Ibrahim denied Sadala and Rhajabu access to the business their father left, to any of them. But the two didn't show any sign of claiming their prerogatives of the share of the business from their brother at the earlier ages. They knew they were still at school and must let him pay their requirement at school first, and when they were through, they would spring on him like a trap on a mouse. When the boys kept calm, Ibrahim knew everything was all right and kept on marrying, as his business expanded. Thanks to Allah, he was a gifted businessman. He could not even remember some of the wives and the children, but they knew him as their husband and father.

Salim grew up like one of those sons not known to Ibrahim. To Ibrahim, he was any boy in the district and his mother a mere woman for sexual lust. Salim and his mother knew that if they were to depend on Ibrahim for maintenance, they were dead. So Salim, without any education, began to sell some sambusas made by his mother, along the streets in town. Whenever he went to the grocery to buy wheat flour for his mother, he dipped for other commodities such as sugar packets, coffee, tins of cooking fats, et cetra. One time, Salim was caught in the act by one of the grocery attendant when he was putting cakes of bathing lux soap into his cassocks' pocket. The grocery attendant was standing behind him watching because he looked very suspicious to him.

When Salim looked around the grocery and saw that everyone was busy selecting putting whatever they wanted to buy in their trays before going with them to the cashier, he picked a packet of five lux soap and, slipped them into his cassocks' pocket and began to walk out. The grocery attendant went and intercepted him at the door. Salim froze when he saw the man he had seen standing behind him unconcerned a while ago demanding him to produce receipt for the soap in his pocket. He was dazed, he felt like crying but his throat was blocked, he wanted to urinate but there was no urine, his knees buckled and he felt the floor on which he stood agitating. He tried to talk but no words came out. He was angry with himself. He hated Ibrahim who brought him to the world with all its evils. Meekly and timidly, he produced from pocket the packet of soaps. At the police, station Salim admitted having stolen the soap. His family background was noted.

"This is not the first time children claiming to be sons of Ibrahim have been brought before us for mischievous banditry acts in this town. I am getting fed up with them. Nearly all those rift-rafts you see running about along the street at night in long white cassocks with the turbans on their heads are all the bastards of Ibrahim. He is not going to produce children like fleas who will be detrimental to the nation in future. They are spoilt kids in the true sense of the words. During the night they go stealing chicken, goats and foods from villages and bring them home, to their miserable mothers to cook. And in the day, you see them selling the meat on the street. We have to talk to Ibrahim himself. He must round up all his children and keep them or else he will be paying heavy fines for any offence that any of his bastards will commit." Paul the O/C of Kitgum police Said when Salim was brought to his office. Salim heard the comments of Paul. If he hadn't hated his father, then the hatred for him was born that day. He felt if he got a chance, he would kill him. Because he admitted his guilt, Salim was given five strokes of the cane at the Police Station and sent out yelling looking for love, the love he never got.

Salim grew up among hoodlums who, as Paul put it, were future problems for the nation. Salim practiced all rough games when he was young. In spite of his lame left leg, he was the strongest wrestler and Walter weight boxer in town. He learned even fighting with knives and sticks. They practiced swords fighting and you could be amused seeing how Salim sparred on his one good leg.

Salim never stopped shop lifting. He knew there were bad days when he would be caught, but he tried as much as he could to avoid it happening.

At the age of twelve, Salim was employed by an Indian as a baby sitter and houseboy. Salim did well with them for a few months but soon left them when the Indians insisted that he washed even their knickers. Salim didn't like the idea of washing huge knickers, which look like those of elephants. He tolerated for the first month, but at the end of the month when he was brought a blood stained knicker to wash among other dresses, he walked away quietly leaving all the dresses in water and never went back even for his wage he had worked for. He nevertheless went into that Indian's shop and stole a shirt and a pair of shoes on different days.

Once more, Salim came back onto the street selling shamusas and loitering in shops verandahs, stealing here and there. Two years later, Salim was employed by a white man, Gray John, a game ranger superintendant, as the houseboy. John liked Salim because of his strength. Occasionally, he went hunting with him and was surprised to see a lame young boy turning fifteen lifting meat he, John carried with difficulty. He took interest in him and kept him well. Salim thought he had a good master. He was faithful to John like a cat. He did everything right, the way he wanted them done. With that confidence, John thought it would be fair for him to let the boy know how to handle light firearms, in case of danger in the forest, Salim could come to his aid. John had two rifles, two short guns and two pistols. He taught Salim how to use the short guns. He got his hand at it within days, he could shoot targets. John admired the skill of Salim and that increased his liking for him.

At the age of seventeen, Salim lost his master in a motor accident and was left without employment. On the day of the accident, Salim stole one rifle, a shot gun and an automatic pistol of John and hid them under ground in a sack with all the ammunitions belonging to them. When the Police came to check on John's belongings, they found Salim who looked so sad about the loss of his master. He showed them all what belonged to John. The other rifle, the short gun, and the pistol. The Police noted down everything, locked the door and took the keys away from Salim. They didn't suspect him of any mischief. But when a staff from the British embassy from Kampala was sent to take the remains of John and to remove what belonged to him. He reported to the police before he was led to the house of John. Mr. Cook the staff from the Embassy had the list of what he was specifically concerned about. These were the two rifles two pistols, the short guns and a typewriter from the Embassy. When the list with the Police was compared, they found that one rifle, a short gun and pistol were missing together with the ammunitions. When Salim was contacted he said, on that day his master went out with one rifle and a Pistol.

"I saw him belt the pistol around his waist and the rifle he put in the front seat of the Jeep, before he went on duty."

"Did he always do that?"

"Not always, but only when he intended to go hunting after duty, he did that."

"It could be they were taken at the site of the accident." Salim said defensively.

"Possible." Cook said not convinced.

"Do you know anything about guns Salim?" Cook asked "I know guns yes."

"I mean, do you know how to shoot?"

"John showed me one day, yes how to cock and fire, but – but I never did it a lot."

"I remember him telling me one day that he has a houseboy who has tremendous skill in shooting, isn't it you?"

"Could be, because I remember the day he showed me to cock and fire, he asked me to try and aim at a goat he wanted to kill. I did and I shot the goat right on the head. It leapt and fell down dead. John was full of amazement and lifted me shoulder high. He couldn't believe that I had never handled a gun before. I don't know if that wasn't an accident that I shot the goat." Salim said.

"Did he allow you to handle the gun thereafter?"

"No Sir, he always locked them up in the cupboard in his bedroom."

"Did you find the cupboard locked when you came to take the inventory of John yesterday?" Cook asked Paul.

"Yes, the cupboard was locked." Paul retorted.

"I see, we must find the missing guns," Cook said and got up and began to serch the house together with Paul.

Salim went back on the street for the third time. This time he was nineteen years turning twenty. He looked fierce and belligerent. Looks of men who search for life invain. He looked frustrated, disappointed and angry. Salim would have probably forgotten the gun if it was not because of the birth of revolution in the country. Guns found their ways into the hands of everyone. Salim thought it was time to put the guns he had kept hidden for the last four years into use. Salim with his pistol became as deadly as death. He terrorized not only the civilian, but the Police and the army, so that he was known as Salim the lion.

It was at that time that his Uncle Hajji Rajabu and Hajji Sadala graduated from Britain, with degrees in Medicine and Economics respectively and came back home. The two brothers approached their eldest brother, Ibrahim, for the share of what their father left for them. But Ibrahim told them that their share was the education he gave them. He had nothing more to give them and moreover, when the two were languishing in Britain, he was struggling alone at home, to maintain the business and enlarge them both in size and the structural set up, which were totally new and not the old dilapidated buildings their father left them. So, he said, there was no way for them to claim any share in the business premises. However, he said, if his brother Hajji Sadala an economist wanted a job with him he would be most welcome and he promised a brotherly pay. Sadala didn't see it as an insult. He took up the job with his brother and didn't do badly. He was given brotherly salary and a big post of the General Manager Account of the shops, butcheries and hotels. He was content with his employment, and responsibilities. He preferred this employment to Government services. Hajji Rajabu, however, got a job with the Medical Research Institute in the Department of Medical Microbiology as the head of the Department and the Deputy Director, with Dr. Gunya as the Director. Hajji Rajabu wasn't happy with his brother Ibrahim rapacious selfish attitude. He wanted a share of their father's business. He became vehemently anxious to acquire the business from his brother and knew there was no other way to do it but to get rid of him. But how to go about it was the problem. His brother Ibrahim was a powerful wealthy man who was known to all men of the new revolution. They gave him all protection he wanted. Besides, he was allowed to carry guns. So, approaching him was like walking into a room with blasting bombs. Hajji Rajabu thought of Salim the son of his brother, he was hearing about everyday.

The Lion. He thought if he organized well with the lion, he would probably get away with it. The Lion was born when he was finishing his secondary education. He saw him when he was only seven. Since then, he hadn't seen him. Could he recognized him if he saw him? And where could he find such an elusive man who was always in hiding fearing for his life? Would he even stop to talk to him? May be if he went through his mother, he would get her to convince him to talk to him. I am sure he will be excited at the plan.

One evening, Hajji drove to the mother of Salim. She was alone at home. After discussing the day to day problems, Hajji enquired where Salim could be found. To Hajji, the mother of Salim was very open. She was able to talk to him without fear. She trusted and knew Hajji wouldn't turn out her son to the security.

"Do you want to see him?"

"Yes, I haven't seen him for a long time, don't you think I must know him and he knows me too?" Hajji persuaded the mother of Salim.

"I think you should doctor. He's a frustrated son. I understand why he's behaving like that. He hates his father and he wants to defame him with the bad behaviour. A wealthy man who has failed to educate his children. All the children doing evil things in town are his. They are frustrated doctor, they are desperately looking for their father and they cannot get at him. They are angry and I tell you, they are mad and could do anything that is bad to him. Tell them to do it and you will see them at it," the mother said to Hajji.

"I quite see your point, you are right. Children of that type behave like that. They are never at peace with themselves. At times, they do all those sort of things because they want to get killed. It's sad."

"When would you like to see him? He is always at home at midnight for few hours before he goes out at dawn."

"Where does he go?"

"I don't know Doctor?" she said and tear slopped from her eyes. "Umm", Hajji said and paused to think where he could meet

Salim. I can meet him tomorrow night in your home here? Hajji said.

"I will tell him tonight if he comes home that you would like to talk to him."

"I will be grateful." Hajji said.

The following day Hajji, returned at 9. p.m. sat with her until 12 mid-nights. Salim didn't show up. The time was crawling through to one a.m. there was no sign of Salim coming.

You never know with people these days. People have killed their own mother, because of money. If sons can kill their mothers, why can't the mothers do the same? My mother could have got fed up with me and now she wants millions because she wants to hand me over to the police. I will be careful. Why should Hajji want to see me now after all these years? I don't understand it. There could be a trick behind this. Tonight; I won't go to see her at 12 mid-nights. I will go at 2. a.m. Salim thought. At twelve mid-night Salim crept near their home and climbed a tree which stood near their compound to see if there would be any strange movement in the compound. He sat in the tree with his eyes focused on their hut. He couldn't see any car because Hajji came on a bicycle that evening and the bicycle was already parked in the hut. Time crawled by and at 2 a.m when Hajji and the mother of Salim were almost giving up hope that Salim would come again, when they heard a flimsy knock on the door. Hajji stirred and whisper to her, "It looks he's come."

"It's him. He always knocks like that. She whispered back, got up, walked to the door and unbolted the door. Salim walked in, his pistol in his hand ready to shoot. His brown protruding eyes glowed in their sockets rolling from side to side. He looked a murderous lunatic. Hajji feared his heart beats would stop anytime, and he regretted why he wanted to see such an aggressive hideous lunatic, clad in rags not worth even for a rubbish bin. He wore torn shoes and the toes showed out on both feet. The shoe laces were string of sisal tied round the shoes, probably to hold the soles and the body of the shoes together. He carried a basket full of meat in one hand.

"Who is this idiot, mama?"

"He is your uncle I talked to you about last night."

"I have no relatives. I know only you as my mother, you have no husband. Therefore fatherless."

"No son that is not it. You know you have a father who has neglected us ..."

"Shut up mother. What do you want here, you idiot." Salim said dropping the basket of meat down and he took two steps towards the frightened Hajji.

"I -I want to see you son because I have an important matter to discuss with you. I want you to change your way of living. I have been hearing a lot about you and I feel I must try to do something to save you and your mother from trouble.

"We are already in trouble what more trouble are you talking about? She has born troubles for the last twenty years she is not new to troubles. She can stand it with or without me," he said and looked at his mother over the hurricane lamp burning on the table in the hut.

"I know you have but if you do not get out of this kind of life you will one day end up badly and you will leave her in a mess which may even cost her life."

"Up to her, when she feels she's tired she can die any time. I won't worry because I won't be there to see her off." Salim said grinding on his teeth.

"My son, what he is saying is right. I have been bearing many troubles simply because of you. I am not happy about the life we are leading especially you. It's quite risky. One day you will get caught or even kill and ..."

"I am already dead mother, do you think a living man looks like me? See those who are living men." He said and pointed at Hajji. I died long time ago and who is talking to you is my ghost and not me. I can walk out of this room through the walls without you seeing, so don't worry about a dead man. But if my ghost could get the whole of that bastard I will kill him and defecate in his mouth."

"And who is that bastard?" Hajji asked knowing he meant his father Ibrahim.

"Who has killed me? Not your brainless brother? I hate you all. Why have you come to see me?" Salim asked with a shaky voice of someone starting to cry and tightened his grip on the trigger of the gun as if he wanted to fire.

"I want to see you about the man whom you said has killed you....."

"He has something I am in support. He told me about it. I think you will like it son." His mother interjected.

"Okay, go ahead and let me hear." Salim said lowering his pistol and wiped the tears from the coners of his eyes. "If it's stupid you will go out walking on your head. Meanwhile where is my supper mother?" His mother gave him his food. He gormandized it as he listened indifferently to what Hajji had to say. When Hajji finished, Salim rose up after his meal and said, "You go ahead and kill him. You want to kill him for money but I want to kill him because he has killed me morally. Just look at me. Is this how a son of a millionaire should live? And look at my mother she's going naked exposing her ass to the world to see. I swear in front of Allah if he sent you here to find out what I am up to, go and tell him to have his last Juma prayers on Friday and on Saturday he will be sleeping in his golden grave he has built. I am going to kill him. Tell him, and even if you don't, I will get at him. Once I get my mind made up, I always succeed in all my under takings."

"What is your plan after you have killed him next week?" Hajji asked Salim.

"Nothing."

"I was thinking son, I have a powerful lawyer in town here. He is the State Attorney, the government lawyer. I am sure he should be able to protect you. What I mean to say is, I honestly want you to come out of this dangerous life you are living at the moment. I want you to come out in the light and live as a living man. I trust and believe you will be all right. The State Attorney will protect you and our properties against the hand of the law. So now to hit the nail on the head, I would like you, Sadala and me to share the business of Ibrahim between us when he is dead. So before you kill him get him to write his will sharing his business between us. They know your mother is one of his first wives and you should be one of the immediate heirs in the family. Get him to write that you could chose your share and dictate to him to allocate to us our dues. Then you can kill him. But don't take the will with you leave it on him. The police will find it for us. And then we shall only go to receive our dues after he is buried. You know you have a bad name these days that is why you are living in the dungeons. I will clear you of all offences through the lawyer and you will be a free man."

Salim sat astride on the stool and stared at Hajji and imagined himself dressed like Hajji. A clean jacket a bow neck tie a sparkling white shirt and a pair of shoes that reflect light like mirror and probably sleep on a mattress that is a foot thick and eat like a King. It was a temptation, which a frustrated man, like Salim could not resist. He yielded and he accepted defeat. He heard a voice within him telling him all the wonderful things he would get. Servant to wash and iron his clothes. All he need is to walk in them and go out for a show. He could own a car, one of those exotic long springy Zodiac or Citrion for that matter.

"Will you protect me?" He found himself asking Hajji in a voice which seem to come from someone else and not his.

"I promised you I will. There is no doubt about that. All you have to do Salim is to get from him a written will sharing the business between us."

"Let me tell you something which I haven't told anyone even my mother sitting here", Salim said and pointed at his mother with the ribs of a cow he was gnawing. For the last five years I have been monitoring movements of Ibrahim in the evenings. He is always escorted by an armed gun man to pickup his daily collections from various shops, butcheries, and hotels in and around town into his secret room outside Babies' shop. As soon as Ibrahim enters the room the armed guard snaps on the security light in front of the house and sits right at the foot of the door with his gun in his hands. It always takes him hours counting the money and this has been going on for years without any risk. What I am going to do is, make the man at the door sleep, take his gun, and put Ibrahim off completely, take all the money for that day and make away. I am sure the following day when things get to be known, the bodyguard will be in shit. I could use his car to acompolised my plan but I don't know how to drive. What I need is a driver. When all are done we shall drive away with the sleeping guard and leave him in the car near his home after we have removed the money from the vehicle."

"You said the bodyguard sits with the security light on?" Hajji asked.

"Yes he does".

"How do you get at him without being seen?"

"I always sit about six meters only from him. When I told you that I am not a living person but a ghost you didn't quite believe me." Salim repeated and added, "I can get at him as easily as a cat gets at a mouse."

"Another thing is do you know the type of gun the bodyguard carries?" Hajji asked.

"An automatic rifle."

"You know how to handle it?" "Very well."

"I mean if it starts to fire what about the noise."

"That one is fitted with a silencer. I have seen one before when I was working with John."

"Do you know where the bodyguard lives?"

"I told you we were going to abandon the car near where he lives didn't I? And what does that tell you? Salim asks retrogressively and put in some lump of meat in his mouth and began to masticate it."

"Can I pick you up from where you will leave the body guard? I could come with my car and park it near where you think it is safe. Then we could transfer the money into the car and drive away."

"And let the Police track your car up to where you live? Salim asked and smile. You are such a child uncle? I think if you want to play the mad game with me on Saturday begin to put on torn socks like me and to stink human blood like me and die before you come. You understand me. The most important part of it is to die before you come. That is why I said it is a mad game. No, when we abandon the car we shall wear shoes made out of leaves and walk until the tarmac where we shall dance and destroy our shoes in the mud and our ghost will fly home. Who will get us? Allah only will know.

"On Friday evening I am going to bring for you some rubber gloves which you will wear when you go out on Saturday so that you don't leave any finger print anywhere in that room or on the gun."

"That will be great uncle. I am beginning to see you are determined to protect me." Salim said and sneered at him showing his teeth covered with food."

"That takes care of almost everything. Now, I am wondering if I should let Sadala know." Hajji asked.

"Let him get the shock." Salim said. "I see. And who is driving for you?"

"I have all those fixed. All you need is your will on Saturday. The present mad game is for us the bums and freaks."

"Would you know if the bodyguard is able to read and write?" Hajji asked.

Salim chuckle and said, "You'd like to send the imbecile man to school? He is an idiot more than me."

I see, so we could frame up a written will, for Ibrahim to copy on this official headed paper. And you will see that he copies the right words."

"How will it read?" Salim asked.

Supposing we say something like this. I have been assassinated by my own bodyguard. I had trusted him for many years but tonight he has become traitorous he has mauled me and held me at gun point. He is asking me to write a will allocating my business to him as an uncle, but because I know he does not know how to read I have decided to write my will so that my business be shared between my first son Salim Rajabu and My brothers Hajji Rajabu and Hajji Mustafa Sadala Rajabu. The cash money in the bank should be shared between all my wives equally. How do you like that? Hajji said after dictating the words of the will to Salim.

"No objection its sounds fantastic. So will you write it up and let me have it on Friday? I will scare the hell out of that idiot on Saturday evening. I wish you were already dead like me I would have invited you to see how he will vibrate at the sight of the gun. You haven't seen one. I always enjoy them. They shake. It looks as if something enters their bodies and flutters inside them. I smile before I slug them. Stupid people." Salim remarked pleasantly.

Hajji looked at his watch the time was 4 a.m. "We must sleep for a while he said."

"Who? Me?"Salim asked "All of us."

"This is my mothers' house I don't sleep in it. Don't you see her snoring on her dirty mat, a miserable old hug?"

Hajji glanced at the woman sleeping next to him and asked. "Where do you sleep?"

"Ghosts like me sleep anywhere". Salim said and stood up check his gun and walked away towards the door and turned back and said, "remember on Friday the gloves, the drafted will, the headed paper, and a pen in here, at 12 mid night then on Saturday at about the same time come to help me count the money."

"And you, remember to be careful from now until Saturday, don't step in a pit to dislocate your feet before that day."

"I am already lame I can't be any worse. Friday uncle."

"Friday mid night" Hajji repeated and Salim walked out of his mother's hut.

CHAPTER 8

Hajji Rajabu did not have a nice sleep his neck ached him terribly, because he rested his neck on the wooden backrest of the chair as he slept. He was woken up by a cock flapping its wings in the room, before it crowed. He looked at his watch in the hurricane lamp they forgot to put out. It was 5 a.m.

One more hour then I will ride away, before anyone else is up Hajji Rajabu thought and sat up.

It didn't take him long to obtain the headed paper from Ibrahim Rajabu office for the purpose. He got three of the papers and on one he wrote the will, which Ibrahim was to copy in his own handwriting on another blank head paper. There could be a rubber stamp in the room where he counts the money. If there is, it would carry more weight if he got it stamped and signed, and I will let him know that this original draft he must take it away before he leaves the room. He must not be careless with any step. I don't want to be exposed in this.

Salim got one of the sons of Ibrahim who was also left in the cold with his mother and sister. His early life was more stormy than that of Salim. He was arrested and imprisoned twice because of robbery with violence and the latest sentence from which he had just walked out of prison was a motor accident in which he knocked dead a man with a lorry he was driving. He personally surrendered to the police station and when taken to court, he pleaded guilty of the offence and he was sentenced to four years imprisonment.

While there, he behaved well and the sentence was reduced to three years. He completed the three years and walked out in time to find his step brother serial murderer Salim who was badly wanted by the police but has never been caught or imprisoned even once in a plot to murder their father. Salim welcomed his step brother Abudalla Rajabu, in the house of his mother in Islamic way a night after he had met Hajji, and briefed him of his plan to get rid of their father. Abudalla didn't hesitate in siding with him. He willingly threw in his lot.

Abudalla trusted Salim. He knew his plans were always successful. Because of this million of shillings were hanging over his head as a reward to anyone who would reveal the whereabouts of Salim. Salim knew all this and kept low but occasionally shocked the police and even the army when he attacked their barracks and made them run for their lives. Salim would collect whatever they threw behind to be used against them later.

"Your job will be to drive the car to the shrubs near the Awinyo Estate. Three we shall park the car share the cash between us and you can dissolve in the air while I go my way! He never told him the part where Hajji comes in. *The will.*

He thought that if he mentioned that to him he would also press for a cut which he thought would interfere with the agreement of the will. He thought it might bring discrepancies and such discrepancies may bring disagreement which could lead to revelation of the secret. So he told him the parts, which concern him only.

Friday came, the two boys went out together to see their areas of attack. They saw the car, a Zodiac, parked near the house and the driver a tall huge man got out of the car and walked to the door of the room, flicked the security light on and walked back to the car. He opened the door for Ibrahim who tumbled out of the car and began to unpack boxes from the car carrying them one at a time to the room. They counted twelve of them in all. They observed that because of the safety of the place and confidence the two had in themselves the boxes were not locked. He came back and took a black book and walked back into the room while the tall huge man walked out with his gun and sat on the step in front of the door in the bright light. He put his gun next to him and began to stare blankly in front of him.

The two, Salim and Abudalla, lay in an empty barrel only five meters away from him.

"You see how easy it will be tomorrow to put him to a temporary sleep. Bang the top of his bald head and he will fall like a rotten stump or we shall suffocate him by gripping him by the neck and dragging him in the dark here, tie him up and gagged his mouth with a stone larger than his mouth, and he will not know how to talk or shout for many days." Salim whispered to Abudalla who only sneered at his method of mollifying his victims.

"Why don't we do it now". Abudalla asked.

"No, the arrangement is tomorrow Saturday."Salim replied. "You know better."

"I want him to enjoy his Juma day tonight and tomorrow he surrenders his life. Millionairs hate to die. You will see tomorrow he will want to give you anything to make him survive to continue counting his millions as he is doing now. When you corner them with a gun they urinate and diarrhoerate on themselves like children. The thought of living the millions behind is always sickening to them."Salim whispered to Abudalla as they continued to watch the man.

"What does he do with the money?"

"He leaves them in there until tomorrow morning when he banks it."

"You mean no other person beside you know this routine?" "I don't know."

When Salim went back home he found Hajji waiting for him. The meeting was more cordial than the one they had on Monday. The handshake was more friendly warm and affectionate. He gave his mother the usual basket, which he uses for collecting the relief. That night it was containing a dead hen below a cabbage and some onions. A tin of cooking fat was put on top of them all. The hen could have been killed because of asphyxia. His mother received the relief and put them away while she gave him the supper of beans with chapatti. He devoured it with the greed of a man who has been on an empty stomach for days. If there was anything Salim enjoyed beside violence, then it was eating good food. That was why he always comes back home with meat of some kind.

The Director Murdered

"Set for tomorrow?" His uncle asked him as he rolled the chapatti in his hands before biting on it.

"Very much, we are from there now. We went for rehearsal and everything was completed fine."

"With whom are you going to do it?" "Don't worry yourself about that Hajji."

"I should worry myself Salim. If you are going to collect people who are not careful, they may slip off course and mess up everything on the other hand if they are talkative they might blurt everything thereafter. And it won't be nice."

"That is the trouble with you living men. I told you to get in this trade of ours you have to die before. If you join before dying you won't make it, because you will first fear death, secondly you will fear being tortured because it is the livings that have feelings, the dead feel nothing. And thirdly you fear your good name being spoken in the streets that Dr. Hajji got involved in the murder of his brother Ibrahim. How do you like hearing that? I know all your hairs stand on end on hearing such remarks even from me now I see you are cringing away with dry a mouth as dry as that of a convicted man. We who are now the living dead feel proud when you hear your name in the street. You feel you must do more and be talked of everyday and everyhour. So you see the difference between living people and the living dead?" That guy I am taking with me tomorrow has already languished in prison for a total of 16 years. So you see, half of his life has been spent in prison. He is a nice man in our profession. I am sure we will get away with it tomorrow."

"Well I am glad if he is a nice man. I want to remind you on certain points which we didn't discuss last time. These are, one, when Ibrahim copies the will from this original copy, you make sure you take it away with you. Two, if he has rubber stamp in that room make him stamp the letter and sign it. And thirdly make sure you use the gloves throughout. I brought four pairs because I want all of you to use gloves so that there is no way of tracing you with your prints. I am sure as all of you have already been involved in criminal offences you could be having your prints in the police station."

"Perhaps him not me." The Police have my description only not even pictures. They tried to get me when I was staying with my mother in town but now in this cage who can get me. It was once rumoured that I was killed. Well, I know their trick. They might have said that so that I stick out my neck and they get all of me or there was a man whose description matched mine who was killed. Anyway whatever was their intention, I will not be apprehended by these Police here in Kitgum." Salim said and bit on another chapatti. His mother sat with hunched back near the hurricane lamp burning on the table. She watched her son sympathetically and deeply regretted having fallen in love with Ibrahim. *I would not have got this child perhaps*, she thought. *Perhaps if I got him with another man, I would be living happily with the father somewhere. Now he is a robber, a murderer, a criminal, a lunatic.* She felt a lump in her throat suffocating her. She was angry and annoyed with herself especially when she thought of the fact that her daily bread must always be robbed of someone or stolen from someone's farm or gardens.

Saturday came Salim and Abudalla had just entered their barrel when the Zadiac of Ibrahim pulled up at the door of the room. The driver as always got out went to put on the security light and to open the door. Ibrahim remained in the car. When he opened the door the driver came back and took his gun and put it on the boot of the car and began to transfer the boxes into the room and when they were finished. He walked out and sat on the same place he sat the previous night leaving his automatic rifle fitted with a silencer on the boot of the car. Salim saw it and sneered. He heard the door slammed closing Ibrahim inside. He felt his heart slam in his chest as the door closed. He knew unless Allah was guarding Ibrahim he was going to stop breathing any moment. He checked for his own automatic pistol. It was there. He sighed whispered to Abudalla, you remain here and be ready to defend incase of trouble although I don't expect much trouble.

"Yes I will be ready", Abdalla replied and Salim got out making lesser noise than a cat makes when it is stalking a rat. He moved stealthily but swiftly towards the driver seated on the step unaware

The Director Murdered

of any trouble. He sat with his hands flanged backwards holding the back of his head, his legs resting on the bumper of the car.

Salim came and grasped his neck with his fore arm and pressed his throat hard between the forearm and the biceps muscle. The driver felt air going out of him like a punctured balloon. Blood roused to his head and his eyes bulged his tongue shot out. Salim increased the pressure on his throat it was like his neck was being fastened in a vice. Salim murderously bit his teeth together as he increased the pressure still further on the windpipe of the driver. He dragged him away from the door and put him away in the dark. Abdalla ran and got hold of the gun and followed them in the dark. He released the pressure on his neck to see how the fat bulky man was behaving.

"He is going to stay like that for hours. Watch him. If he should stir up before I come back keep him quiet okay?" Salim said and took the automatic rifle of the driver and walked in.

When the driver was being strangled Ibrahim thought he heard something strange outside. He thought he heard someone vomiting. His fatty heart thudded in his chest scattering blood all over his body. He cocked his ears to listen for more of the noise before he closed the door but no more came. He settled down and began to flip the notes like a money machine counting the notes. Salim paying an unauthorized visit walked in the first room, the light was on. He saw a door standing ajar at the far end of the room where Ibrahim was. He stealthily walked to the door and first pushed the nozzle of the gun inside the room, and then walked in. Ibrahim was very busy counting the money smiling at the bundles he had stuck away in a big box, when Salim greeted him, "Good evening Baba I have come to help you count your money to night?"

Ibrahim jumped up with a dry mouth as if he had seen a cobra among the notes he was counting.

"Get out of here you ... "

"Sit down Baba and let us talk. I am your son am I not?" "Please get out I am too busy get out or I call the police." "Do. I will love to talk to you in their presence. You know what you did to me and why I look like this. It is you who is behind my misfortunes and I am not going to let you get away with it. I am not going to allow you to enjoy yourself with your money while my mother and I eat from the bin of the rich ones." Salim said his voice sounding metallic and adamant.

"You will only survive tonight if you copy this will in your own handwriting in this clean sheet of paper. When you finish, stamp it and Sign it then I will go out without pulling a hair from you. You will live your life span and when you die then we shall produce this will to the court for distribution. Let us cooperate and do things quickly. If you don't then you are going to cease to breath now. Go out and see your driver or your bodyguard, he refused to cooperate with me and he might feed the flies tomorrow. Do you recognize this gun?" You should. It is yours and it will kill you. So don't cut your throat with your own knife. You know how sharp it is. You sharpened it yourself. I will cut you with it without mercy. You have heard how merciless your son Salim, the Lion has been operating in and around town. It's me talking to you now. I am the living dead. You once heard that I was killed and it's true I am dead this is my ghost talking to you but watch it my ghost behaves like myself. One question, you are writing the will aren't you?"

"I am not." "You are not?" "No?"

"Salim cock the gun and showed him the nozzle of the gun pulling lightly on the trigger Ibrahims' lips quivered, his teeth rattled, his eyes watered, his nose secreted mucus, sweat poured on his face.

"No don't fire. I - I will write." With trembling hands Ibrahim wrote the will coping from the one Hajji wrote. He signed and stamped it.

"It is here take it now and get out of here," he yelled.

"Read it I mean the one you have written." Salim ordered. "Trembling he read the will."

"That is okay."

"Who gave you these papers?" Ibrahim asked

"You don't know me baba. You will only know me tonight that I am dangerous I have already told you that I am a ghost of a human being. When I become a ghost like this I behave like this", he said and pulled on the trigger the bullet zipped through

The Director Murdered

Ibrahim's arm, blood oozed out. He held it and cried out. Please you are killing me don't do it". He begged.

"I am doing just that tonight. You thought I was going to leave you after writing the will and tomorrow you go to court telling them that you wrote it under duress?"

You are an old clown get this slug and sleep, Salim said and pulled the trigger again and the bullet exploded on his head scattering life out of him. Ibrahim fell behind the table thud and Salim felt the house rocking and creaking as he completed his fall. Salim chuckled showing his yellow teeth which were never brushed since birth. He took the original will drafted by Hajji and put it in his pocket and walked to the door peered behind the door to study any movement outside. He saw nothing except the Zodiac which stood like a mini Aeroplane. He walked out to where he had left Abudalla guarding the unconscious driver.

"How did it go inside?" Abudalla asked. "Fine. How about here? Any trouble?"

"No, not at all I am only enjoying myself. You sent him into a longer sleep he might wake up after one hour from now."

"Come on lets go to work! Salim said and dragged Abudalla by the hand in the room. Abudalla followed him.

Ibrahim with the top of his head blown open, his brain looking like porridge spilt on the wall, laid under the table. When Abudalla saw Ibrahim, he stopped short at the door and held over his mouth.

"What is scaring you idiot, come hold the boxes and we go." "I am shock at the sight of the money." Abudalla retorted.

"You get shock over nothing. I thought you were shocked because of the dead pig lying down there." Salim said and pointed at the dead body of Ibrahim.

"I have seen a number of such bodies fall and I always laughed at them when they threw their hands in the air yapping for sympathy." Abudalla remarked. They took the big iron boxes with bundles of notes and walked out of the house and put it in the back seat of the car.

"Let's go and get him". Salim said. "Who?" Abudalla asked startled.

"The driver! You clotted head. Did we not agree that we would take him with us and make him wake up on the steering wheel with his gun on his back?"

"Yes we did."

"Then why the hell you ask me who?" They went and brought the driver dropped him in the back seat near the box his gun laid on his thigh he looked someone who has been driven around the world and was having a nap in the car as he completes the long boring journey.

"Yes, the key?" Abudalla asked.

It must be on one of them either him, or the pig in the house check the ignition first."Salim advised and Abudalla walked in front of the car behind the steering wheel and got the key stuck in the ignition on the neck of the steering wheel.

"It's here". He yelled.

"Okay let us get going". Salim ordered and climbed in and slammed the door. Abudalla kick the engine it ignited, the fuel gage indicates full. He smile and said I haven't driven in four years we might as well go for a pleasure ride in the cool night. The fuel is enough to take us up to the moon."Abudalla joked.

"With blood on our hands?" "On our faces also."

"Lets go wash it away first before you can go driving if you want salvation." They had just pulled out and joint the tar road turned towards Guru Guru Road where the home of the bodyguard of Ibrahim was when they saw the police patrol car after them. Their bright security lamp fixed on the roof of their car illuminated the road brightly.

"Police' Salim said without looking behind. Don't worry we have enough fuel and the bird seem to be in a sound condition I will beat them. I could even wait for them and show them that I know how to drive." Abudalla said confidently. Abudalla was one of the best drivers in town. He contested in the East Africa Safari Rally three times and always finished third. Although he never got any nearer to the international drivers. There was a lot of potential in him. Only if he kept practicing he would have pulled up tremendously but with so many years of languishing in prison, he never had any better chance to practice. Abudalla was able to drive fast braked hard suddenly and swiveled the car on the rear wheels and begin to drive backwards without stopping. That was the trick he was at. He lured the police in the chase. They chased them, their speedometer flickering between 180-200 kilometers per hour while Abudalla purposely drove slowly at 150-160 kilometers per hour. He glanced into the mirror and saw that the police vehicle was only a few meters away behind them, Abudalla braked hard and swiveled the Zodiac on its rear wheels and began to race backwards heading against the Police Peugeot 504 cruising forwards. He took the police driver by surprise. He knew he was going to panic and drives the car against the nearest electricity pole to avoid the head-on collision. As he predicted the police driver suddenly swung the car away from the Zodiac racing straight against him. With the high speed they were at, the Peugeot 504 hit the electricity pole and carried it off, and smashed head on, on a caterpillar, which was parked at the roadside. It seems Abudalla calculated the spot and brought them to it. The Peugeot 504 was a crumple mass of metal and the occupants, four police men, were smashed beyond recognition there tongue flew from their mouths laid scattered on the road, their skull exploded open and the brain spurted out like white porridge they were disemboweled and their intestine mixed up with the soil gave the place a looked where hyenas have had a good feast. The two, Salim and Abudalla drove away laughing, "beautiful" Salim said and patted the back of Abudalla in the car as they continued laughing exhilaratively. "Never chase Abudalla in a car" Abudala warned and sent the Zodiac racing at 180-190 kilometers per hour. "We shall hear the news tomorrow", he added.

"What will they say?" Salim asked.

"That four drunken police men were minced in their car when they tried to go through a caterpillar park at the road side." I will be there tomorrow morning to witness how they will be pulled out of the car" Abudalla said.

"Come and tell me also I wish I was able to come and witness it too." Salim said.

The Zodiac bounced and swayed as they left the tar road and joined the dust road where they were going to abandon it.

They got to the shrubs and drove the car in the bushes and stopped. Abudalla switch on the inside light and they saw the bodyguard of Ibrahim in the back seat still unconscious. Salim smiled at him and looked at Abudalla.

"He has been asleep all the way. He has missed the fun." He said and patted the driver on the cheek.

"Let him sleep. He will wake up in the wilderness and he might run mad for good." Abudalla commented.

"Let's get started, you share the money". Salim told Abudalla. They got out and went to where they had hidden their baskets to park in the money. Abudalla first pack his baskets followed by Salim. What do we do with these?"Abudalla asked. When he saw some money still left in the box.

"What we do is. We are going to take this punk from the back seat put him on his seat and make him continue to sleep on the steering wheel. We shall put his gun near him here. This money! if you have pocket take more, the rest we shall leave with him here to convinced the police that he killed his boss and stole the money.

"That is wise". Abudalla agreed.

"And make sure you don't drop a leaf of note anywhere until you get to your burrow do you understand?"

"That you don't have to tell me you vulture. I know it better than you do. Put on your leaves' shoes and we go. Leave the punk to sleep he's about to wake up now. And remember our oath, we shall work together for the good of our mothers until death. We shall never betray each other. Allaha will punish whoever will blurt out any secret between us."Salim said and started walking away.

The time was 2 a.m when Salim got home. His mother an obese diabetic woman, who could not stand much stress, laid on her mat in the far end of the hut sleeping. Hajji sat on the chair he had been sitting on since he knew that hut, dozing with sleep, when he heard the knock unique to Salim sounding on the door. He knew he has come and with what news? His heart slammed and scattered all the sleep from his head. He became awake like a starving man in a cold cell. He was almost out of breath as he walked to the door to open for him. The exhilaration he saw on his face enlivened him and he expected good news.

"Where is mother?" Salim asked smiling. "She is sleeping son."
"So early tonight why?"
"It isn't early for an old woman like her. Its 2 a.m now! She said, that is your supper."
"Thanks. I need it very much," Salim said. He took the food and with the greed of a hyena, which has not eaten meat for a day, devoured the chicken he brought home the previous night silently. When he finished he sat up and washed his hand still in silence drank a mug full of water, sighed, sat astride on the stool blowing between his teeth and stared at Hajji.
"How did it go?" Hajji impatiently asked him. Salim walked and took his basket he had stood on the table were the hurricane lamp was burning. He removed the leaves he had packed on top of the notes and emptied the basket on the table. "Go ahead and count." He said as the boundless of notes tumble out of the basket. Hajji caught his breath. He could not believe his eyes.
"Don't be shock this is just a little portion of what we took. My friend took much more than these and what was left behind in the car is even more than what I took. So don't be shock at nothing."
Hajji stared at the money disbelievingly.
Mustafa Sadala Rajabu received the news about the assassination of Ibrahim the following day in the morning with shock and dismay. He was in his office when the usual newspaper boy walked in with the *NATION DAILY* news papers. The main heading read *BLOOD FLOWS IN KITGUM, A PROMINENT BUSINESS MAN IBRAHIM RAJABU ASSASSINATED. The story below read:*
Blood flowed here last night when a prominent businessman Ibrahim was gunned down by an unknown gunman in his apartment. The assassin believed to be his bodyguard made away with large sum of money and the car. A written will was found in the scene of the murder stating that the assassin, the bodyguard wanted him to write the will giving all the businesses to him but because Ibrahim knew that the bodyguard was illiterate and didn't know how to read he wrote the will sharing the business between his two brothers Hajji Rajabu and Mustafa Sadala and his first

son Salim Rajabu who the police identify as the notorious Salim the "Lion" and the money on his account, should be shared equally among his wives. The bodyguard of Ibrahim has been apprehended and he is helping the police with the investigation. But Salim the Lion still remains at large. Anyone with the knowledge to his whereabouts is requested to report to the police station the reward of one million shillings still stand.

Meanwhile a police patrol car with four police men in crushed on a caterpillar last night and all occupants died instantly.

Sadala read the story again and began to analyse it. Is this really true? Of all people how can Ibrahim write his will to Salim Rajabu, a spoilt child, a robber, a murder and a criminal. I don't believe this news. There must be something fishy behind this. It could be Salim himself who did this. But how did he get this paper. Someone must have got it for him. Because I know quite well Ibrahim does not take this headed paper out of the Office. Could it be that Hajji got them for him? But first does he know where he is now staying with his mother. I used to know the mother stays near the rock hotel in those slams area. Police have kept that place under surveillance for three years for him, and they never saw him. I don't understandthis. I will ring Hajji up now and find out if he knows anything about this," Mustafa thought and rang Hajji Rajabu.

"Hello Rajabu here."

"Yes brother it's me Mustafa here. Have you seen today's paper?"Rajabus heart pump fast sending bloods up his head he felt the guilt of killing his brother haunting him. He knew the paper was talking about him. Must he commit suicide or leave the country?

"No." he forced himself to say.

"You'd better get a copy and read it. It was at first verbal news all over town here this morning. We have lost our brother Ibrahim," Mustafa said melancholy.

"What? What are you talking about?" Hajji Lamented pretending ignorance when he heard the voice of Mustafa conveying the message to him sorrowfully. He knew Mustafa and Ibrahim were great friends and brothers. How grateful he was to Salim. If he implicated Mustafa in the plot as he had wanted, Mustafa would have inform Ibrahim and he and Salim would by now be answering murder charges in police, but as it is Salim has saved his neck and there is still room for gambling.

"What killed him?" Hajji asked with a trembling voice. "He was assassinated". Mustafa answered. "Assassinated? Where was he and by whom?"

"He was in his usual apartment where he counts his collection for the day before banking it in the morning just short distance away from Baby's Shop. The assassin is not known but there is a funny will written by Ibrahim saying that Abudu, his bodyguard who has been working with him for the last twenty five years held him at gun point and asked him to write his will to him giving him all his business but he knew that Abudu is an illiterate who does not know how to read therefore he 'Ibrahim' decided to write his will sharing his business between you and me and his notorious child Salim the Lion. He didn't mention in the will who takes what. The specific thing he mentioned was that his money on his account should be shared equally among his wives. Now Hajji, I don't understand why of all Ibrahim's sons Salim the Lion should be included in the will. I am suspicious Salim himself murdered Ibrahim. But what foxes me is how he knew that Ibrahim must write the will on his official letter and what I know of Ibrahim is that he values those papers and he always kept them locked in his office safe. The verbal news also said that Ibrahim stamped the letter, "will" he wrote. Anyway further information is that Abudu has been arrested and he is in the police hospital. I hear he was found with about two hundred thousand shillings and Ibrahims' Zodiac too, was at his place. So you see what is in our hand. I think we have to try to prove who murdered Ibrahim, Hajji'. Hajji felt his skin slugging at the mention of the words that he has to get involved in the investigation of the mur- derer of Ibrahim. He knew then that they could be reached any time, and their names, would soon be in everybody's lips. He would have told him there and then that he was behind the plot, which killed Ibrahim, but he feared death. Life was still sweet and he wanted to live a little longer so he groaned in the mouthpiece like a trapped lion and endeavored to speak.

"Of course Sadala Musatafa we must find who murdered Ibrahim." I will be there with you immediately we are going to the police with you, so wait for me in your office. I still don't believe Salim did it on his own he is a brainless headmuderer. A boy like him, how would he know of a will? But who advice him if it's him?"Hajji said. "I will wait for you Hajji."Sadala said mournfully and cradle the receiver ignoring his plea.

I was going to make the best mistake I have made in my life if I brought this man in. Now what is going to happen is, I will tell my lawyer to implement the will and we will cut this man s' business up. I will explain to him the position of Salim. I will want him to protect him lawfully. No one can prove that he killed any of those people they are talking about. I know Owiny is a smart lawyer and he is going to put up tremendous fight that will shock the nation to hear that Salim the Lion is acquitted. If he is acquitted I will want him to run the Baby's Shop and I will run the hotels and the butcheries while Sadala if he likes will run the farm and the other remaining shops. I know he will relax his idea about Ibrahim. But I won't tell him who did it as long as we live. Rajabu thought as he drove to town to meet Sadala.

It was two years after Salim Rajabu joined the human community and took over the baby shop that trouble between Hajji and Dr, Gunya began. It all started when Hajji's daughter without the permission of Dr. Gunya, went and cut some banquet of flowers from Dr. Gunya's garden. When Dr. Gunya complained to Hajji about the trespassing, Hajji interpreted the complaint as an aggression. Hajji hated anyone talking to him with air of superiority. Although Hajji didn't show it out openly that he hated Dr. Gunya, inwardly he wanted Dr. Gunya dead. However how he was going to do it and go away with it as he did with that of his brother Ibrahim? He knew it was him behind the plot in which his brother Ibrahim was killed and he manoeuvred it out with the help of his lawyer. Would he suc- ceed again if he tries the same on Dr. Gunya? He is sure people won't believe he killed Dr. Gunya because there are no outward signs that he hated Dr.

Gunya. He had heard rumours from other people that he wanted to be the Director of the Institute. Whoever told them? Supposing Dr. Gunya dies will they suspect him for having killed him because of the chair? How was he goingto do it, to accomplish his plan? It looks as if more than Dr. Gunya should die, if he was to kill him and keep the incident secret.

When he thought of Dr. Gunya being the cousin of the head of the state he felt sick at the thought and his stomach loosened as if he has had a sudden attack of salmonellosis. *They will send the best criminal investigator that will track me back to my mother's womb.* The thought made him cringe and flinched from the plot like a snail whose feelers have been touched, but when he thought he would camouflage behind the notorious BDM who were terrorizing the country especially in Kitgum town, he thought it would be worth taking the risk under their umbrella. Hajji nearly jumped up with ululation. Yet he didn't know how to get at it alone. He has to do it so that it looks like an army or some kind of security persons who killed Dr. Gunya. He had to plan where to get him and pinned him down. He thought about this for a long time but he could not find a suitable solution. He found out that he needed an advice of a trusted friend, a friend with a criminal brain, brain which can plan crime and give Allah hard time to investigate, and who could that be? He recalled his experience with Salim the Lion. He advised him to exclude Sadala from the plot to kill his father and it worked well. May be if I trust him with the secret he will advice me and probably set me on the right track or I will let him go at it again.

He has been out of his trade for quite sometime now. He might be itching to see human blood flown. Hajji thought.

Hajji immediately invited Salim to his house and explained to him what he wanted to do with Dr. Gunya and how he intended to camouflage the murder.

"Your idea doesn't sound bad if you intend to murder him and blame it on the BDM, but the obnoxiousness of the idea is, you have to make it look like one and how are you going to go about that? You have to acquire guns, not less than ten and get ten men in uniform of some kind to handle the guns. How are you going to do that? It is not easy Hajji, to commit a silent crime." Salim said and looked at scared Hajji.

"These crimes always shout out behind you that there he is, he is running away get him and you find that you are always a criminal wherever you go with or without anyone around you. You feel burning, jumpy, nervous and suspicious of anyone you see. If I were to become a crime investigator, I would easily pick up a criminal from among a million of people with his hair and put him in the open and tell him that you did it. I know how their eyes blink and how their mouths behave. I can smell them, smell them like a dog smells an animal." Salim said and crossed his lame leg over the good leg.

Sat back in his chair and stared at Hajji sweating cold sweat. He was more scared, than advised by Salim's talk.

Supposing a CID with that talent is set after me after I have committed the crime will I escape?" Hajji sat thinking. He nearly gave up the idea to kill Dr. Gunya. But he hated him, he really did.

I must kill him at all cost if it means me dying afterward I don't care. Hajji thought and pulled out a handkerchief from his pocket and wiped off the sweat collecting around the black callous on his fore head.

"I see you are scared like a girl going in labour suite for the first time. That is what I told you last time that to be a criminal you must die first before you become one. If you are living, you won't commit a crime because its subsequent ugliness keeps nagging in your brain and you feel sick really sick. But if you are dead and your ghost is the one acting you can pull a trigger on anyone including the president. You have that feeling of renunciation, of worthlessness that a piece of glass is more worthy than you. So you see it uncle. If you are serious that you want to go ahead with your plot to assassinate him you must be ready for all eventualities, expect the worst to happen to you thereafter." Hajji scratched the corner of his mouth with his fat black finger and sighed.

"Well I think I am determined to go ahead and get rid of him." Hajji said adamantly.

"Okay, if you are so determined to get rid of him like that, as I said the first step of your plan is correct that is blame it on the

The Director Murdered

BDM. But you must brush off any suspicion later, make it look real, make it look the BDM."

"How?" Hajji asked

"The BDM always attack in a group and they are always armed and in uniform anyway the good thing is that their uniform is very much like the National Army uniform. So how do you go about that to acquire all these?"

"I know of a friend in the army he is a fine man, he could loan us the guns and some uniforms to …"

"Stop your nonsense. You must be a big fool. You think he is going to accept implicating himself in your offence when you are going to get picked up and blurt everything tomorrow and he is thrown in jail without bread and drink. Is he such a thick headed man that he will yield to lead you to their armoury and you make the choice of the best weapons they have there? I don't think so Hajji, you must think of a better way of acquiring the firearms and the ammunition otherwise you could call it a day for the game."

"And let him live?"

"And let him live for one hundred more years, yes." There was a pause between them when Salim sneered at him and said.

"I see you are in a fix. You don't know what to do. By the way, I always see Captain Dramadri drinking alone late in Rock Hotel in full uniform for the National Army. He is a drunkard who does not miss a day. Whenever he is like that, very often he sleeps in the bar and the bar attendants sometimes lift him to his car before he drives home. He is such a louse. I don't know why he was promoted to such a rank and worse still he is the commander of Kitgum battalion. I think that is why the BDM always find it easy to snatch arms and ammunitions from their armoury. Are you getting me Hajji?" Salim asked sneering.

"No."

A clown of a doctor. Salim thought shuckling. You want me to speak in an ABC fashion. Put all criminal jargons into your head, and you listened to them like you hear news on the radio. Now look, Hajji here is Captain Dramadri, he goes to Rock Hotel bar every evening. He is friendly to everyone when drunk. You could hang around him one day and keep eyes on him until he is completely drown in the beer. When he starts to sleep you could escort him home. Then you use his uniform and identity card and his army Land Rover to go and collect the gun and the ammunitions you need from the armoury."

"Then where do I keep the weapons?"

"Why do you embark on a task you are incapable of shouldering?" Salim asked. "You are not ready to risk anything. Keep them at your place who do you think can keep them for you?"

"I can't go with them in the gate without being checked moreover the vehicle will be the army vehicle. We have authorized the gate keepers to search any vehicle entering and leaving the institute compound especially foreign vehicles. So you see why I asked that question."

"Well I could keep them for you here. So, when you have got your guns, and ammunitions stored, there are yet more to be done. You could cable your BBC pressmen and tell them that the BDM have kidnapped Captain Dramadri the Commander of Kitgum 11th Battalion. The news will come out anyway. The search will be mounted for the Captain, they will tear Kitgum into bits but who will get him if you hide him well?"

"You could be kind and return to them their Land Rover. Park it anywhere in the open in this country, they will always get it. Leave no trace of you in it and you won't be traced." Salim sneered and stared at his uncle Hajji, a bulky thickheaded man in criminal plots. "Those are not all for you to do. You will have to get the men who are going to handle the guns and wear the uniform you are going to get from the barracks."Salim added.

"And where am I going to get them?"

"You could leave those to me. I can fix them for you, nice guys, who will not make a mistake. They always shoot to kill. When you send them to do a half job they don't go for it. They go for a complete thorough job."

"Fine, if you are going to take care of that, I have all the confidence and trust that it will be a success."

"Now you tell me Hajji, how you are going to make this plan of yours look like the work of the BDM. Forget the guns and the uniforms we have already discussed.

The Director Murdered

"And the men?" Hajji added.

"And the men, yes". Let's imagine we have already got those facilities how are we going to attack. Go straight on Dr. Gunya any time we are ready to do it or what do we do?" Salim asked.

"I think that's what we are going to do what else can we do? I want Dr. Gunya don't I?"

"Yes, you want him, and you want the assassination to look the work of the BDM. You need to shroud the crime further."Salim said.

"And what do we do?"

"First you boys will go and destroy some government properties in the institute compound like the store for example. Then after the store your boys will go to the gate were the night guards will be. You told me that you are the one responsible for them aren't you? On guard that night, you will put a man of your choice whom you trust will not leak out your plan to anyone. You will tell him everything so that when the men come to them at the gate he will know what to do. The men will ask to be lead to the homes of some listed member of staff , including the names of Dr. Gunya and yours, they will ask the guards to lie flat on the ground on their stomachs and they will be asked where the homes of the staff member on the list are.

The rest of the guards, I expect according to the oath they have taken as you know will not accept to lead them except the one you are going to use who will to lead them to Dr. Gunya's home. The rest of the guards will be properly beaten. Your man will lead the men to your home first and leave two men there and he will continue with one I am going to show you. A real gunman I believe he can shoot a fly fifty yards away. He is an excellent man. This man will go with the guard to the home of Dr. Gunya. When he has taken up position in a good place the guard can run back to you and alert you that everything is ready. You'll then ring Dr. Gunya. He will certainly come to attend the phone and the man will fire at him. He could empty the whole of his magazine on him if he likes but I think that guy will just kill him with a *Twa*." Salim said and smiled.

"What if he is in his room with another person as he often did and that person comes to attend the phone instead of him?"

"You will want to talk to Dr. Gunya won't you?" Salim asked and went on. I haven't finish with my suggestion. When he has finished with Dr. Gunya they will come back to your home and fire a few shots on your door and you wife and the children will scream. But remember when you will be asked, you will say that your home was attacked before Dr. Gunya". Salim said and kept quiet.

"It sounds brilliant only if they could be implemented. One thing which remains unanswered is how are they going to get to the Institute?" Hajji asked.

"They will walk through the gate during the day and keep low at your home. There are plenty of rooms in your place, I think. Then, during the night, before the attack they will change in their combat uniforms. I know their entrance and exit is going to raise some controversy on which you will insist that the men came in over the wall using a rope. It has happened before hasn't it?"

"Yes, twice in fact which I know!"

"Yes these will be good supporting facts." Salim said and went on, "What is still left and which we should not treat lightly is the means of information. What I mean to say is, there must be a way of letting the police and the Western Press know that the BDM have committed a murder in the Institute."

"If I ring them using my phone there is possibility that they may trace it back to my room and these entire elaborated plan will just go up in flame. I have to inform the police anyway because I am his assistant at the moment. I will be held irresponsible for failure to report the case to the police." Hajji said.

All you have to do is talk to the post master of Kitgum post office Hassan Abbas your nephew about all these and on the day of operation, after everything has been accomplished, you will ring and tell him to go and ring the police and any of the Western news correspondence preferably the BBC that the BDM has successfully completed a murder of yet another important man in the country. He is going to brag threatening that more on the death list will be eliminated systematically. Then to justify your innocence he will jam the line to the Institute on which you lie so that if they asked who rang the police reporting Dr. Gunya's murder, they will not think about you.

Chapter 9

Odongkara stretched and yawned as he finished compiling the reports from Lwanga and Opiyo to be cabled to the headquarter. He sat resting his fore arms on the file in front of him and pulled out the walkie-talkie from his pocket, he switched it on and fixed it to his lips.

"Hello Peter." he heard the voice of Mukasa. "How are you Joe?"

"I am not fine, everything is getting messed up. I don't know what to do Peter. I thought I would conceal this case but it seems there are just many witnesses who saw her out last evening in my official car with the two children."

"I thought you would find it difficult Joe to conceal such a case where you already have too many eye witnesses and evidences at hand."

"What do you mean evidence at hand, Peter?"

"The body of the child is lying in the mortuary, isn't it?" Odongkara remarked.

"Yes it is, but that is not evidence that she knocked down the child herself."

"That's right Joe, but when you look at it this way, there are people yelling and yapping there, and they are swearing with their blood that they saw a Peugeot 504, UP 125, rundown that child, and the driver behind the steering wheel, was a lady with two kids, and the lady, was further identified by a mature eye witness as being your wife, I don't see how the body of the child lying in the mortuary cannot be considered an evidence. True, I would have agreed with you if there were no eye witnesses who are testifying that they saw the car and that particular driver run down the child." Joe kept quiet and sighed at the other end of the line. Peter heard the sigh of surrender and knew that he had managed to convince him about the words 'evidence' he had used carelessly. What Odongkara was actually referring to be the evidence was the blood result with John in the Government Laboratory that was obtained from the wheels of the car.

"As I was going to tell you Joe, in that case you are not going to do anything good if you are still holding fast on to your earlier decision that you conceal your wife from the law. I am not encouraging you against your conviction. You are a man who has been guarding the law of this country for the last forty five years. You were a loyal dedicated servant, and now you want your good name and your entire benefit for your service in the police to end up in flames? I personally wouldn't go for total destruction of life at the last moment. I know if your wife report to the police now, and explain that she was actually very shocked to realize what she was doing, I am sure Orwotho would definitely do something more to protect her. It's the attitude you have adopted now that is going to worsen everything for both of you.

I wasn't at home when this accident happened yesterday evening and to pretend to provide you with any protection is just looking for a felony if not a misdemeanour charge. We will be missusing our offices Joe, to protect your wife, and that is not allowed. Your wife must come out in the open and face the fact, then we can use our offices to protect her otherwise at this stage we cannot Joe."

"You know Peter, I am sick with heartache. She never drove my official car before and why yesterday? The first time and she messed her life, my life and the family's as a whole. Why Peter? Can you tell me what I am going to do?"Mukasa asked his voice grating on the line desperately.

Peter kept quiet for a while and said, "Joe, I have already told you that there is always a beginning of a fault how it begins is unknown to us. If we were to know the beginning of all our faults, there would have been no faults in this world because we all would have avoided them. Probably if you went out that way

The Director Murdered

yourself, the accident wouldn't have happened. I think you have to accept the situation as unfortunate. Otherwise beyond this I think I am unable to advise you on this matter." There was a pause between them and Mukasa said, "You know Peter, you are the only person I have so far confessed that, my wife is the one who hit that child yesterday. I have a lawyer in Kampala, Dr. Okumu, he is an excellent lawyer. I want him to defend my wife, should they arrest her. So what I would like you to do now is to keep quiet on what I have told you." Odongkara heard what Mukasa was telling him with astonishment.

Is this not what I want him to do? This man is more confused than his confused wife. Odongkara thought.

"Okey Joe, you do that. I will keep my mouth shut." Odongkara said and was about to hang up when Mukasa came on the line again "And by the way Peter, Dr. Kzza has just arrived what did you find on the car?" Mukasa asked. Odongkara looked at his wrist watch the time was 18.35 hours, he knew his appointment with Betty was in twenty five minutes time. He must speed up with Mukasa if he was not to be late.

"Not much Joe, some streaks of dried black substances on the left front and rear wheels of the car and a dent at the front bumper of the car, otherwise, there was nothing Joe."

Mukasa sighed and continued, "Why did you take the car? I mean you asked to use the Peugeot 504 instead of the Police Land Rover, and your car is just in a perfect condition. The mechanic tested the car. He said he couldn't find anything wrong with it. The stone in the exhaust pipe was removed. I am now thinking you must have had a prior knowledge about this incident and decided to take the car away with you because you believe that if you left the car behind and the news flared up, I would destroy the evidence to justify my wife's innocence. Peter are you such a bad friend? I believe very strongly that you knew about this. I thought I knew and trusted you. Why are you doing this to me Peter?"

You have been the most unfair old man who wanted to wreck my family. I would have divorced my wife because of your adultery. You should have been at your home and not in my house with my wife, your wife would not have killed that child. You caressed and fondled my wife, and you made love to her. I have all the proofs that you did it, you old owl. I should have asked you the silly question you are asking me now. I thought I knew you, and trusted you as a friend, but you went rocking the foundation of my family. I am not going to sympathize with you, you can go to hell, and I am not going to give you the answer to your questions. Odongkara thought irritatively and suddenly said, "I am getting late for my appointment Joe."

Bashfully, Mukasa went on, "I am working in this office for the last time today. I believe things are out of control, with you behind it. I am merely fighting a loser's war. I wish I reckoned earlier that you were fighting me, I wouldn't have told you that my wife admitted she killed the child." Mukasa said gawkily.

"I think you have got everything wrong Joe. You are suspicious I am fighting you for a reason best known to you. I don't know I am fighting you. If you want to retire Joe, to avoid a scandal, I think it is wise to do so and you won't spoil your good record as a policeman. Afterall you have reached the retirement age. I am saying this not because I want your chair. You know it well that if I was after that chair, I would have taken it from you many years back, but I am still young. I don't want to get locked up in administrative office work. I love fieldwork. That much you know well."

"I will consider the advice you have given me just now", Mukasa said ruefully.

When he heard Odongkara advising him to resign, Mukasa thought,

This is something I didn't think of before, I could tender in my resignation now and immediately pack up with my family. We will drive out of town and the country. After all, I have my brother living in Kisumu. We will go and live with him for three to four years. After everything is quiet, we shall sneak back home settle in any quiet place. I don't mind living without my pension, but my wife should never go to suffer in prison.

"Hey Joe, do not overwork your brain. This matter is very simple. Let's forget it at the moment. I have something for the Kampala guy." Odongkara interrupted his thought when he notice a pause between them.

"You do!"

The Director Murdered

"Yes Joe. It has been very hectic since morning and we have come out with some findings. We have been putting them together and we are ruling out the claim you heard over the foreign radios, that the BDM was behind the murder."

"You are?" If that is true then Kampala might lose interest in following up your investigation?"

"Why Joe?"

"They were interested in the case because you heard that the BDM claimed they have a list of names of some dignitaries in this country plus some foreign diplomats who are on the death list.

Kampala wanted to know about this claim and if true, sent some troops to tear Kitgum to pieces until everyone of the BDM in Kitgum is picked up. Their activities is scaring foreign diplomats here. They want to close up their embassies and go out of the country. It is very embarrassing to the government Peter. There must be proofs, which the government can exhibit to the foreign diplomats that their lives are not in danger and that is to prove to them that Dr. Gunya was not murdered by the BDM but by other hoodlums. I believe you will do that for them and report to them directly." Mukasa said.

"What is your job Joe? I have to pass through your office." "I am starting my leave tomorrow Peter."

"What the hell are you talking about? You – you don't mean it." "Of course I do."

"Umm." Odongkara groaned and sighed, "Well Joe, get someone else to sit in that office to do your work will you?"

"D/SP Ebokorite is here from Kampala he takes over from me." "Why such a sudden leave and where are you going to spend it Joe?"

"I am not quite sure. I might take it here or go home to Mukono." "And your wife?"

"She goes with me of course."

"Good luck Joe. It's a pity you have to leave before I am through with this tricky investigation."

"You were giving me your result for today when this topic of my leave popped in. What did you stir up Peter, which made you confident, that the BDM is not reponsible?"

"There are many things that are happening here Joe which are erroneously blamed on the BDM and they accept it!"

"I think it is because nearly all the people in Kitgum are BDM sympathizers. So, whatever is done there is done to promote BDM notoriety. This BDM seems to be for all those who are bent on criminal activities and anti government elements residing there so you see they are part and parcel of each other. Mukasa agreed."

"That is right Joe. From what we have found in our investigations today, Dr. Gunya's case is far from BDM. There are two schools of thoughts, in the Institute, about the case. The first, there are some people I interviewed this afternoon, including the Deputy Director, Dr. Hajji and the night guards, believe that the invasion of the Institute, and the assassination of Dr. Gunya, were the works of the BDM. And that they came into the Institute over the wall, using a rope or ropes. We are yet to establish that. This group can swear that the BDM invaded the Institute and killed Dr. Gunya on the eve of the revolution day.

However, the second group of people I also interviewed this morning consisted of the storekeeper of the Institute and the servant of Dr. Gunya, are very skeptical about the radio claim of the BDM. They think that the assassin of Dr. Gunya is within the Institute. So you see Joe, we still have a tremendous task ahead of us. They don't accept the over the wall route as the entrance for the invaders even if it had happened before. The numbers of the invaders were too many for the over the wall route before they could have been recognized. They suspect that those people might have come in during the day and hid themselves within the Institute walls. I have to talk to more people who live within and outside the Institute to ascertain these two schools of thoughts. Lwanga found some very interesting clues, in Dr. Gunya bedroom which we have so far sent for identification. They found a 0.38 automatic pistol in his bedside locker but the funny thing with it was that, there were a lady's finger prints on it and nothing for Dr. Gunya. It means a lady took it there."

"A careless lady." Mukasa said.

"Well, I won't jump on to that. She might have thought if she did it that way, she would not be found. The same prints were found on the hilt of a knife buried under the pillow."

"Of Dr. Gunya?" Mukasa asked.

"Yes. A very lethal, sharp knife you could use it for shaving hair on any part of your body. The inscription on the blade is, *'made in Britain by Smith and Smith Company Limited*. These were all in his bedroom. In the dining room, Opiyo found two empty cartridges of bullets, which I think killed him.

They have all been taken for identification by the ballistician in Kampala. We should get the results from them any time from now. Finally Opiyo also found a photo album packed from the first page to the last with girls' photographs below which he wrote their names, and addresses and locations. I am going to use it to trace the girls and chat with them a little. Their last finding was a fake identity card for Food and Beverages belonging to a Salim Rajabu. And you know what, one of the shops which caught fire last night in town belong to a Salim Rajabu. We still have to verify the connection between these two Salim Rajab.

"Why do you call the identity card fake Peter?"

"Because it has no number on it."

"I see!" Mukasa murmured absent mindedly.

"Salim, the owner of the burnt shop is on the run. I think if we lay our hands on him, we shall be very near to our target of the assassin of Dr. Gunya.

"The case sound one of the most interesting one Peter." Mukasa said. "I wish you would be in the office to witness the end, but unfortunately you want to go away."

"I think I must go Peter, I need a rest, a tranquil place to rest my head and that of my family."

Odongkara looked at his wrist watch he had only five minutes to be out. He must stop talking to Mukasa if he was to get to Rock Hotel Avenue 26B by 19.00 hours as he had promised Betty.

"Joe, I must be going. I will get in touch with you again any time from now. Will you be in the office?"

"I don't know, I will try!"

Baby shop was serving both as a wholesale and retail shop. Customers were able to purchase the children wears and toys from Baby shop at wholesale and retail price. On the eve of the New Year Day, which happened to be the revolution day, many people came to buy toys and wears for their children. One of the people who came was a close family friend of Salim Rajabu, Isaac Ibrahim. Salim welcomed Isaac at the back of the baby's shop. Isaac was a heavy smoker. When all Isaac wanted to buy was loaded in his car, Salim and Isaac went to his office at the back of the shop for a chat. Isaac continued to smoke as they talked. After their chat, Isaac drew in a last lung full of smoke on the cigarette and crushed the smoldering butt in the ash tray and they both walked out of the office. Isaac did not quench the fire on the cigarette completely. The wind blowing in the room through the ventilation activated the fire like a black smith at his furnace. The cigarette glowed and caught up with a crumpled piece of paper Salim had thrown in the ash tray. The paper with the aid of the same wind blowing in through the ventilation transferred its home on the heap of receipts on the table. The receipts welcomed the smoldering paper. They also cracked, popped and issued smoke. The table said why not? It's a fun I must not miss. It started showing dark spots and snap and hauled many small fire as the wind told them, I am just a catalyst but enjoy your fun. The heat generated by the smoldering table was hot enough to worry an inflammable fluid. There was shortage of fuel in the country especially petrol and kerosene. Because of that the little that there was had to be rationed among motor vehicle owners.

Salim the Lion thought he was a different man. He defied the government warning which stipulated that anyone caught hoarding fuel would be prosecuted and if found guilty of the offence would be sentenced to three years imprisonment or a fine of five hundred thousand shillings or both. Well, the drum of petrol stood not very far away from the smoldering table. The heat tickled the petrol in a huge laughter which exploded into a deafening sound that shook the whole of Baby Shop and set very flammable object in motion. The whole shop was engulfed by the fierce fire which ate away everything like hyenas. The hand grenades and the ammunition, which were hidden in the shop all begun to laugh, cough and sneeze explosively in the heat driving everyone nut. "Has the third revolution started?" they asked. The BDM with their supporters clapped their hands and smiled beatific, while others in the government systems heard it with headache. The hand grenades coughing expectorantly, hauled spittle of lumps of fire right across the road. The Town Council was bogged down into complete redundancy. Their trucks for carrying away rubbish from the town were all grounded because of mechanical conditions so that the parking ground in the council premises because a dumping ground for dangerous mechanical conditions DMC vehicles.

Because of that the rubbish bins infornt of the shops were pack with rubbish up to the street. Pop in shop had its wall still newly renovated with oil paint. It looked a new building and a step towards rehabilitation. But the hand grenades which coughed and hauled spittle of fire from Salim's shop dumped the fire on the rubbish overrunning the premises of the Pop in shop. It was not long before the current of wind blowing excited the fire in the rubbish. The rubbish snapped popped, glowed and vomited tongues of little fire which sprang up onto bigger papers and the Town Council work was done transferring the fires onto the oil paint on the walls. The fire rattled up the walls like hideous dragons, cremating the paint. The fire found the ceiling board soft wood palatable and they soon charred, and hissed and flinched from the attack of the fire but were fixed. They yelled and wailed as the fire gormandized them. They remitted the fire onto the entire roof and supporting timber shook, and gidded as the fire licked them. They sagged, swayed and colasped bum. The Pop in shop was dehabilitated by the fire. It left the place smelling all sorts of smell, acid smell of burning wood, sweet smell of burning perfumes, pungent smell of chemicals, irritating and offensive smell of garbage, mention all were there.

Salim, returning from the Institute to take the guns to the boys who had already taken cover at Hajji house, waved to Saban at the gate and drove off. Saban was put on both day and night duty by Hajji Rajabu to make sure that nothing went wrong at the gate. During the day Saban was alone to allow the movement of the guns and the gunmen to the institute but at night he was accompanied by three other night guards. The explanation for making Saban to work both day and night duties was that he had requested to be off duty for two days to attend to one of the sick wives in the hospital.

Saban memorized the instruction given to him as much as he could. When they heard the bums and the pumps originating from Town, they were exhilarated at first, thinking it was going to be an easy camouflage to Dr. Gunya's death. Who has not heard the gun shots and heavy sounds of the blasting hand grenades which cracked the window glasses and shook every house within vicinity sending everybody gripping over the heart?

Salim heard the blasts. He loved the sound of guns. He used to say when you hear a gun blast you know at least blood was leaking out of some veins and he loved to do it himself. He loved to see bright red blood oozed out from a human body and see their body fall like fallen trees and sprawled in front of him.

Salim slowly drove to town and wanted to go in his shop to see the money Isaac had paid him but to his surprise when he got near the Town center, the smell of burning plastic toys and, children shoes and clothing hit his nose and nauseated him. He felt like driving back but he persisted. He finished the round about at the town center and turned on the OAU Street where the Baby Shop had stood at the extreme end. He saw what to him looked like a nightmare. The bright glowing fire still cracking and creaking and hauling fire across the roads. He was flabbergasted. He accelerated the car and got to the burning shop. He got out of the car, stood akimbo and stared at the burning shop with fierce vicious look. He felt bile spilling uncontrollably in to his mouth and spat it out. Salim's main concern was not the weapon burning in the shop, but the money, the wealth which he was beginning to enjoy had turned into ashes and miseries, the miseries he used to know when his mother was still alive, had come back to shake hands with him. He went back in the car and sat, not able to think. He was hallucinated.

What next? Drive into the fire and end there? No, he thought and ignited the engine, reversed, turned and drove through to Aguru Avenue to his home. When he got home he explained to his wife what had happened to their shop. The wife was frightened. Her fear and worry to the contrary of Salim was not the money but the weapons which were kept in the shop.

"What are we going …

"To what?" Salim interrupted her staring at her viciously. "Let's get out of here quickly. Get the children into the car. The police will soon be after me." Salim said as he put his 0.38 pistol and the knife in his pocket. In silence Salim drove the family along Kitgum Gulu Road until he got near River Aswa and turn into a dust road into the forest. When he got to the most remote area of the forest he suddenly stopped and ordered the wife out of the car and to lie face down. She was trying to ask why when Salim bung the side of her head with the butt of the pistol and she fell down crying. Salim turned and shot to death the children and man handled their mother to unconsciousness and left her for dead. Salim abandoned his car at the site of the murder and went to his hide out flat where he laid down on his back thinking what next. He remained there until the following day.

Mrs. Salim, Hajati Atek slowly came round from the unconsciousness she got from the kicks Salim gave her in the forest. She sneezed twice yawn and opened her eyes. She felt a nagging pain in her head the pain which was excruciating enough to cause abortion. She held her head in her palm and with the dim light of the setting sun she saw her three sons lying on the grass with their limits sprawled away from their bodies. *Were they sleeping?*

She thought and dropped on her back on the grass unable to Stand. The splitting migraine like pain could not allow her to concentrate her thought. She felt a lump at the side of her head and a similar protuberance was at the back of her head. *What happened to me? Have we had an accident and my children are dead?* At the thought that her children were dead, she stirred and sat up holding her head, she crawled to where the three bodies of her sons were. She stared at them with horrified shock, they were dead, and blood which flowed from their gun wounds dried on them matting their shirts on their bodies, flies flew from the wounds to their eyes and back. She was too shocked to scream or cry. "Who shot them?" She asked and she vaguely recalled that Salim drove them out saying they were leaving town and going in a safe hiding place. She recall that they drove following bush path and when they got into the bush Salim ordered her to lie face down and he shot the children. She heard the gun blasts with heartache then he turned to her and kicked her on the side of the head and at the back of her head and she blacked out. Their car was still standing there. *Was he still around?* She thought and shuddered at the thought and fell down on her back again. She waited, listened but nothing stirred. She had virtually forgotten the nagging pain in her head she must go and inform the police, he must be arrested and answer for the death of her children. Hajati Salim Atek crept on her knees and hands furtively avoiding snapping twigs and grass as much as she could. She slithered among the grass like a snake and came out of the scene and began to run hysterically following the bush path towards the road. Did she know where she was going? Did she know which road to follow? It was her instincts which guided her from the bush towards the main road. She crossed the main road and stood right in the middle of the road it was 19.00 hours. She didn't know which way to follow, she felt vertigo, and she nearly fainted. She stood panting and slowly lower herself in the middle of the road knelt on her knees and with her hands on the road her head dropped she remained like a grazing goat for a good five minutes and staggered up on her feet. Then something happened to her she found herself getting strength and she broke in to a run. She ran not towards Kitgum but towards Gulu. She ran with tears streaming down her cheeks and down her chest. She didn't know what she was doing. She was mad. She ran and walked and looked behind and imagined she was seeing Salim chasing her with the gun in his hand. Because of that she ran faster and faster unable to tire out.

What was going to stop her if not a lake, a sea or mountain? She made the seven miles to Gulu in two hours and she arrived at the gate of the police station in Gulu as Mukasa left his office and drove out to his house. He picked her up with his head lump and nervous as she was, when Hajati Salim saw the car she imagined he was Salim driving after her to kill her. So, she walked and hid behind the fence. When Mukasa drove passed ignoring her she jumped back on the road and began to run after him. Mukasa saw her running after him and wondered what she was up to. He hid his car and came back by the line of the shop to intercept her.

The Director Murdered

Salim was to participate in the invasion of the Institute personally and Juma Rajabu, one of the many bastards of Ibrahim Rajabu, was the gun man who was to shoot to kill Dr. Gunya. He was among the group who entered the institute during the day. Therefore with or without Salim Rajabu the Lion the operation was to go as planed. When Salim didn't show up for the operation, Dr. Hajji wondered what happened to him. Using his office telephone, he phoned to Salim Rajabu the Lion house to tell him that the operation was successful and that the boys were already back to their respective places. About there times he called without a reply. This worried Dr Hajji. He became anxious to know. *Was he shot dead last night during the gun shot in town? But Salim is always very careful with such incidence.* Hajji thought

It was until the following day when the news of the assassination of Dr. Gunya was in the lips of everyone and the investinvestigation team from Gulu police Criminal Investigation Department lead by Odongkara arrived in Kitgum Medical Research Institute that Hajji again tried Salim house number because he wanted to let him know that the investigation into Dr, Gunya death has started in the afternoon by Odongkara. Still there was no reply. So he tried his private flat know to him only late in the evening.

"Hello, Hajji here", Dr. Rajabu said as soon as he heard Salim pick up his receiver.

"Good evening." "How are you there?"

"Salim, I am ringing you to tell you that the situation is getting off our hands and ...

"Which situation?"

"Well what we did last night."

"It's what you did last night. How do I come in? Count me out of that Hajji." Salim retorted with a note of embarrassment in his voice.

"The problem is yours. You know why you kill Dr. Gunny. You stand by it and solve the problems. Remember my warning when we leagued up to kill Ibrahim, I told you that to be a true criminal, you must die before you commit the crime."

"But Salim, you are not going to desert us and walk away." "Yes, I am going to do it and I am now out of the game. I have nothing in this world now worth living for."

"I know Salim, but my lawyer could still protect you." "Against what?"

"The guns found in your shop. They are going to be identified as the guns from the armoury of the army barracks. And you know the guns were reported as having been taken out of the barracks by captain Dramadri. People believed that Captain Dramadri had defected and joined the BDM. You heard the news yourself. We were quite covered up by that news, but now with the guns in your hands and one in Dr. Gunya's house we are going to be traced and asked where Captain Dramadri is. It's going to be known that we killed Captain Dramadri and used his uniform and identity card to obtain the weapons...."

"I am not bothered about the weapons. Salim interjected interrupting Hajji, I knew they were going to be found out anyway. But all I wanted was to accomplish your need and leave you to shoulder the consequences. I now need one thing and that is to tell the police that you killed Captain Dramadri and took his uniform, Identity Card, the Land Rover and used them to obtain the weapons for killing Dr. Gunya. And because of security at the gate of the Institute, you left the weapons with me. I might be charged lightly for storing stolen goods, but you, I don't think even your smart lawyer there will save you."

"Don't talk like that Salim." Hajji begged Salim in grating voice with anger and annoyance. He felt hollow in the depth of his heart, the hollowness you feel when you hear you have lost a love one and yet refuse to accept the reality. He felt numb on his arms, the knees ached as if he was chilled. "Salim, is it because of your shop that burnt down, I will help you to put it up but don't turn me to the Police."

"How am I going to avoid that?" The weapons which burnt in my shop belonged to the army and I am sure, unless the ballistician is out dated, he will identify them as the weapons which disappeared from the army barracks. Now Hajji, am I going to say I did it or what?"

"I appreciate the offer of assistance you have just mentioned, but tell me how I am going to avoid the Police digging for me everywhere. Already, I am sure they know I am on the run and the roads leading out of this town is thronged with nothing but plain and uniformed policemen looking for Salim Rajabu the Lion. You are there seated in the open worrying about what is going to happen to you, once the police lay their hands on me. So tell me, it might save me too, what do we do to avoid them getting at me? I am not going to do the thinking this time Hajji, you think and I act. If you think badly, I will act just that and when I mess things up don't blame me because that will be you acting. If you kill someone with a gun, the gun is not charged but it is you who handled the gun. So it is. You will be the assassin I am the gun."

"Salim, I am sorry, let's not fall out with each other but I think we need to discuss this more seriously. We could come out with something new and useful for both of us. I overheard the interview between the CID and some people here. I think they have given us out."

"What do you mean given us out? They have given you out. That is what you want to say perhaps." Hajji paused and went on, "anyway Salim, it is clear that the storekeeper, and the house servant of Dr. Gunya, were not bluffed by the announcement on the radio that the BDM killed Dr. Gunya. They remonstrated that the death of Dr. Gunya was the work of the BDM. They pointed out that Dr. Gunya was assassinated by someone within the Institute. I didn't know that Shaban would forget all we told him about the plan before we acted. He was badly shaken up during his interview and his talk was very incoherent. He did not follow what we told him to say."

"I am not surprised that he didn't. He is an old snake without brain now. He must have strained himself very hard to recall even one phrase of what you told him. Now Hajji, what do you want us to discuss seriously?"

"Odongkara is meeting Betty, our telephone operator Salim."
"So what?"
"I think we must stop the meeting Salim."

"Why? And how? Why do you want to interfere with their appointment? If you want to poke your nose in other people's affairs you go ahead. I am not going to involve myself in unnecessary trouble now."

"I think you need to Salim, because you remember last year about this time I talked to you about the plan to obtain the weapons for our job. My direct line, I am using now, was out of order and I used the line through the switchboard and am suspicious she bugged in the line and guessed what we were talking about. I am worried if she meets this man tonight, she might mention to him the beginning of the plot and he is definitely going to work his way up until he gets on us."

"So what do you want to do?"

"Stop them from meeting. I tried to delay her today after duty to stay on. I pretended that I had an important call to make at seven and wanted her around, but she refused saying she would not stay behind because she had an appointment at 19.30hours. This emphasizes the importance she attached to the appointment Salim. She told me that if I wanted to make a call at seven p.m. she would leave me the line open."

"What do you think you have done Doctor?" Salim asked. I think you have blundered. Your request to stay her behind has aroused suspicion. She is now wondering why you were trying to interfere with her appointment. Iam sure that is going to be the first thing she is going to discuss with him and you can see what a mess you have done. So, if you intend to follow him now, don't risk it because he is going to get you with your hand and lead you to the place you fear to go. The court, and then to jail, or have a gallows. Anyway where are they meeting Doctor?"

"No place was mentioned except that I know he must be going to Betty's residence, 26B rock Hotel Avenue. She shares a flat there with her sister."

"And you want to go there?" "Hang around the place, yes." "And?"

"Try to stop their meeting. I am telling you one thing Salim, if this girl meets Odongkara tonight then we should all go on running because I believe she knows quite a lot about this case.

The Director Murdered

She is going to be the third person to testify that the source of the death of Dr. Gunya is intrinsically occulted in the Institute and that is going to make him intensify his search in the Institute."

"And find you." "Yes, and find me?"

"You see Doctor, I have seen that you are very scared of death, you love to live and yet you risk your neck in some of the events which throws hand grenades of scare on your face that makes your lips dry and your eyes water and stop your heart beats. You have nocourage to do it yourself but you want to sit in your office, do your work, go home, drink tea with your family, romance and relax in the arms of your wife, while your children dance and sing and watch television and eat sweet and delicious cakes, when we, I mean your stooges, are out in the cold night fighting all the evils of the darkness ranging from the mosquitoes bites to the bites of bullets and all you tell us in the end is thank you, you are heroes."

"What have you done for the boys who risked their lives, came to the Institute and did all you wanted them to do especially Isaac Juma, who shot Dr. Gunya for you? What have you done for them besides may be, lunch at your place and cups of coffee in the evening? I mean, you throw idiots into danger while you keep low. When anything blows up you cover your head you and flinch. You have no courage, no heart of a man who wants to do something against the law. As far as this Odongkara meeting Betty case is concerned, I tell you, count me out. I won't be able to help you in it. I have a shock, I am nursing like a baby. My shop, my wealth, my family and my life have all gone up in smoke. My future is smudged by this loss. I am not coming, and for the next one week I want to rest and think my destiny. I am now thirty five years old a good age to die, although a little too early, but a frustrated man could call it a good age to switch off with one exciting event. Rob the bank and get killed in the robbery or feed some big fish with bullets just for the sake of it and get caught and hung." Salim said resentfully.

Hajji listened patiently. He sighed, and stared in front.

"Is there nothing you can do to stop them meeting tonight Salim?" Hajji insisted.

"Personally I will not participate perhaps the best I can do for you is to ask Abudalla and Juma Isaac to help you. That is, if you intend to use a motorcar to accomplish your aim, then Abdalla will be your man. He is an excellent driver. He knows how to maneuver vehicles of all sorts and if you need a man who can shoot to kill, then I think you know the man who has engendered you the present problem you are trying to escape from. He shot doctor Gunya and scattered live out of him with few bullets. If you want him to stop Odongkara's heart beat tonight, contact him. He ...."

"Salim!Salim!Salim!" No voice came back on the open line. Salim! Salim what is wrong?" Hajji earnestly called him. But all he could hear was the open line, snaping, buzzing and whizzing sounds. "Salim are you there? What is wrong? Finish what you are saying. Where do I get Abdallah and Isaac? Where?" But no voice came only the wind buzzing on the mouthpiece greeted his ear. He was infuriated and exasperated. He felt humiliated and deserted. He cradled the receiver and cried.

Chapter 10

When Salim brusquely stopped to talk, to Hajji Rajau, his black cat, Magic, had crawled into his bedroom where he had laid on his back talking. Magic was believed to monitor movements outside the house and warn Salim accordingly. He had a way of warning him when the visitor coming in was friendly or unfriendly. Magic sat on the pillar of the gate most of the time and when a stranger came in through the gate, Magic always went to him or her and browsed around the visitor to detect the attitude before it ran fast in the house to warn Salim about the incoming visitor. When the visitor was friendly, Magic always came, browsed around Salim, and said Mew-mew mew, and led him out to meet the visitor, but if the visitor was an enemy, Magic always ran in and stood on the table without touching him and stared at him snarling with its fangs jutting out of its mouth the way they always do when about to fight.

That evening, Magic crawled in and sat on the table and glared at Salim snarling. Salim knew he was the number one wanted man by both the police and the army so the warning by Magic told him that something was wrong. He quickly threw the receiver of the phone on the bed and heard a powerful knock on the door. Salim didn't know what to do he stared at the door to his bedroom and at Magic as if to ask him for an advice. Magic said 'mew' and jumped down from the table and walked towards the door leading to the bathroom. Salim saw him and followed him, with the pistol he stolen from John, in his hand. He limped after Magic into the bathroom and out into a corridor which led out through the back door. Along that corridor, Salim had packed empty wooden cartoons box from which he once unpacked his refrigerator. Magic went and sat on it and again said "mew" Salim understood the message and the invitation Magic was conveying to him. He wanted him to go into the box and hide there. He smiled back at Magic and entered the box and closed the lids. The tiny little horizontal cracks on the box seeped in some air to rescue him from asphyxia. He had just closed the lid of the box when he heard the door squeaked, and swung on its hinges and banged on the wall. The Putty holding the glass gave way and the glass shatter tingling on the floor.

Salim smelled the acrid reeky smell of death in the box he laid in.

I am going to be caught in this box like a eunuch without firing even a shot at any of these people. May be Magic knows why he led me into this box, let me be ready. Should anyone come to open this box, I will send his hideous face up in the air with bullets, Salim thought and heard Magic jumping on the box. He heard him purring followed by the crunching of bones. He knew then that Magic was protecting him further by eating whatever he had just caught on top of the box to show the belligerent intruder that the box was empty. He heard the heavy footfall of military boots, typical of army men, pounding on the floor of his house that shook his heart in the chest. How he wished he was out to try his gun at one, but when he heard the many footfalls, he knew he wasn't going to patch with them. He flinched, quailed in the box, and pretended he was a corpse. He heard one man walked along the corridor where he laid in the box and Magic crunching his bones on top of the box. The man came and stopped near them. Magic groaned and he heard the man said, "I am not after you and your mouse. I want your master, the notorious Salim. Where is he?" He said and tried to smoothen the fur of Magic. But Magic snarled at him showing him his fangs and the little tongue dance in the mouth furiously.

"Okay take it easy", the man said and pounded away in his boot. "There is no one in. Are the people down stairs checking the garage?" He heard the commanding voice, asked.

The Director Murdered

"Yes Sir. Every place is sealed up at the moment. We should find him if he is within this place. We shall pull this house in bit until we get him. He won't escape." Salim heard the voice said determined to get at him.

"But sir, one funny thing is, his telephone is open. It seems to me that he left the place hurriedly when he was talking to someone on the phone. He could have seen us coming in, and then he sneaked out through the back door."

"That is what I think. Searching the place now looks to me a waste of time we could leave one or two people only here to guard the flat while we go and try his home near Rock hotel."

"Yes I think that is an idea. At least we now know that he is still within Town."

"Who are going to remain here Sir?" "Would you like to remain?"

"I don't mind."

"Okay, you and Ebonyo will remain behind. But be careful, Salim is very dangerous. You have heard people say all sorts of scaring remarks about him. They say he's able to transform into grass, razorblade and anything that is useless, even into an animal. I almost thought that cat in there was him." The commanding voice said and added "But I don't believe such fairy tales. I think they just want to emphasize how tricky and cunning a man like Salim is." The commanding voice said and walked out through the back door along the corridor where Salim was lying in the box with Magic winding up his meal. He came and stopped near the box and looked suspiciously and smiled. "Are you Salim?" The man asked. As if he had heard it, Magic shook its head and eyed him with the corner of his eyes.

"Menya" "Yes Sir"

"Come here will you?" Menya came running to the commander. "Will you keep watch on this cat? See that it does not leave the house."

"Why Sir?"

"I don't know why I am growing superstitious. You know what happened, I came and asked the cat whether he was Salim, and know what it did? It shook its head. It could have been a coincident, but sit here and watch him." The commander said and walked out. Menya looked at the cat and pulled one of the empty cartons and sat on it. Salim felt sick in the box. Sweat oozed from his skin and evaporated in the tiny space making it humid, warmer and stale. He knew if he remained there for the next one hour, he was going to suffocate to death. He must get out, and the sooner he did, the better. He leered through the cracks in the box through which he was getting air, and saw Menya seated with his eyes fixed on the box. He guessed he was scrutinizing Magic who had already finished his meal and was sitting on the box licking his lips, its tail wriggling on top of the box like a dying snake.

How do I get hold of this man? Salim thought. He saw him holding an automatic machine gun with three magazines of cartridges looking death themselves. Any miscalculated move will make him minced meat. He fidgeted in the box and fell a chill, which climbed his vertebrate up to his brains. There was no way of escaping from the box because of Menya, rooted, in front of the box obeying orders. His army uniform torn on the breast pocket, his boyish face looked feminine, he sat with his gun laid across his bosom and, he kept fixed eyes on Magic. *He is so much taken up by Magic. Supposing I jump up suddenly from the box and surprise him. He will first get scared and may be flee for his dear life leaving the gun behind. If that happens, I will grab the gun and challenge the man outside. What if they are many? I think first, this young man must die a quiet death, then I will sneak furtively outside and see who are out and with his automatic machine gun, I should patch up with three people and not more.* Salim thought and found himself sweating furiously.

Magic said "mew" in acknowledgement of his thought and scratched his nose with his paw and stared at Menya. Salim screwed his eyes on the soldier and mused. *Should he make any mistake and look away I will spring on him like Magic and scare life out of him.* The message was transmitted to Magic. He jumped down from the box and walked across the room and climbed a window behind the soldier. Menya saw the cat move and dexterously snatched his gun from his bosom, cocked it to cover the cat. Salim saw the dexterity of Menya and it frightened him. He marveled it.

The Director Murdered

Menya, a twenty five year old corporal, was a tough soldier who had all the potentialities of becoming a commander in a foreseeable future. He was brave and had a metallic physique his facial and body built were deceptive enough to categories him among the weakling and undernourished. Menya moved following and covering Magic with his gun, his back against Salim lying in the box. He fixed his eyes on the cat sitting at the window licking its fur with its small tongue.

Salim with his gun in his hand got up from the box inch by inch. He lifted the lid of the box slowly and poked his head out of the box and looked at Menya. A slim, wretched looking boy whom Salim thought he would put off with one little blow only. He did not want to waste his bullet on him. He was running low in ammunitions so he wanted to use the few left in dire trouble only. Should he scare the boy with the gun and asked him to try to hold the ceiling boards? or just grasped his neck the way he did once with the driver of his father. He did not know if the boy would fire a shot at him if he did scare him by surprising him.

I'll try. He thought and moved forwards furtively like cat stalking a rat. Salim did not realize that when he was edging his way out of the box, Menya saw his image being reflected on the window glass in front. Menya saw him poked his head out of the box, got scared at first, but when he realized it was the man he was waiting for, he relaxed and pushed up his strength in all his limbs, his gun ready to fire, he shifted his gaze from Magic and focused them on the image of Salim resurrecting from box. He saw him come out of the box and stealthily lowered the lid of the box down and began to walk limping towards him. He was ready for him. He saw him put the gun back in its hostler and crept behind him. Menya suddenly relaxed. He knew Salim had chosen wrestling and if he preferred that, then the gymnastic, wrestling and the boxing club he was doing every evening was going to be useful. Salim came to a distant of a yard only and saw his reflection in the glass. He knew he sold himself, Menya was only acting. He had seen him from the very moment he started edging his way out of the box. There is no way now he must do it and do it fast. Before he moved any nearer, Menya swayed his gun covering him.

"Hands up." he ordered him.

Salim stood as if he just missed treading on a cobra in front of him and his hand flew in the air wildly. He knew he won't be shot if he obeyed his command because there were plenty of questions for him to answer, therefore, killing him was going to be a loss of valuable information they were searching for.

"Okay man, you've got me tonight." Salim said smiling. Menya didn't reply his deceptive smile. He remained stern and hard.

"Walked to the wall." he ordered.

Salim wobbled to the wall and plastered himself onto the wall with his hands up in the air.

"You want me to touch the ceiling don't you?"

"Shut up your idiot." Menya rebuked him as he wrenched the gun away from him and search his pockets. From his breast pocket, he took a sheathed knife and asked him to turn to him.

"Go sit down on your coffin." Menya ordered Salim. Salim wobbled and sat on the box astride. Menya darted in front and slapped him hard on the face. It sounded like wood breaking. Salim wipe his slapped check. It felt hot and scalding as if it was flashed with boiling oil. He looked at the soldier graphically and sneered contemptuously at him.

"If I get you one day boy, I will make you eat your own faeces." Salim said with sneer.

"You shit." You think you are going to escape again? Try and you will never give any evidence anywhere. My fingers are itching for the trigger. Even if I kill you now who is going to prove I killed you in cold blood? The world knows you for your crimes and you are described as dangerous as Sulphuric acid but I am going to neutralize you permanently."

"Will you?" "Yes"

"Let's wait and see if I talk to anyone giving the so call evidence. Magic was still sitting behind them saying "mew-mew-mew" desperately looking at Salim sitting in front of Menya, helpless. Salim knew Menya was a tough man by the feel of the slap he gave him a few minutes ago. He seems to have a strength that could fracture many jaws in the rings. Salim looked at Magic sitting at the window facing him.

The Director Murdered

Next to Magic on the window was a big kettle of water which Salim used for going to toilet. It was full of water. Salim saw Magic moved towards the water kettle. He knew he was up at something.

The water kettle was the most likely target. He watched. As he predicted, Magic went and jumped on the water kettle, it left the window and came down 'bum.' The sound was like a twenty kilogram rock dropped on a cemented floor. Menya startled and turned to look at the fallen kettle. Salim took the opportunity and sprang on him. As he did, Menyas finger started the automatic machine gun and it rattled as the two men struggled to gain control of the gun. Ebonyo who was guarding the house from outside rushed in alarmed at the sound of the gun in the house. He thought his colleague Menya was being killed. As he burst into the house, he stopped two straying bullets with his forehead and chest. It was bad heading. The bullet entered his brain and minced the grey matter into bloody porridge and went through. The other went through his sternum bone and scattered it into pieces creating a window in his chest.

Whoever told you, you could head a bullet, it is not a tennis ball. Salim thought when he saw Ebonyo sprawled down throwing his gun disorderly in the room. Salim had sprung on Menya and brought him down like a lion killing it's prey. He sat on his back smashing his forehead on the ground as he watched Ebonyo received the bullet on his head and chest. Wet blood poured from the cut on Menya's forehead down to his mouth and eyes. He knew if he didn't use his gymnastic skill, the murderous Salim was going to make sure his head was a soft as butter. With his free legs and the heavy boots he had on, he swung his left leg forward and hit the back of the head of Salim 'thud', it stroke him hard enough to scare him. He was warned that Menya was not completely overpowered. He repeated the kick on the ribs. It hurt. He felt his intestine clutching and twisting inside him. The stomach jarred and churned at the bang. The heart oscillated in his chest he wasn't sure if there wasn't a crack on the lungs, if not the liver.

His mouth tested blood. The saltiness and raw smell of blood seeped into his mouth. He split blood mixed with saliva. It worried and angered him. He became furious, and viciously murderous. He increased the grip on the neck of Menya. He wanted to squeeze life out of him before he thought of another trick to bother his ribs. Menya was worked up. He fought desperately to get the man off his back. He lurched forward with both legs and locked his feet just below the chin of Salim and kicked upwards. Salim felt his jaws screwing into each other, his neck parting from his chest, his head boiled at the kick. He dazed and lost grip of Menya's head as he fell on his back. Menya, with his head dripping blood, gidded and swang forward to attack Salim who was already on his feet standing limply on his strong leg, looking ferocious and aggressive enough to scare courage away from a coward. Menya charged forward with his hands stretched out, his fingers hooked and spaced out from each other, his left feet forwards and the right behind, leered at Salim indignantly. Salim bit his lower lip and wobbled forward challenging Menya. With a quick ostentatious dart, Salim dived down grasped Menya's legs and Manya tacticfully fell on his back. Salim got on Menya grooving for his throat. Salim was beginning to tell Menya that he was an idiot, when Menya coiled his feet and stood them on Salim's chest and kicked hard. Salim flew away as if he was fired from a missile. He hovered over the table and landed down at the back of the table in a big saucepan, 'thud'. Menya knew even if he was to get up, he was not going to put much resistance.

As they fought oblivious of the pistol and the knife Menya put on the table, Magic went and tried to carry them away but they were too heavy for it to carry. So it sat near them mourning and warning his master, Salim, buried in the saucepan. Salim pulled himself out and ambled forward to meet Menya who had got up and was on him, his black face plastered thickly with bright red blood pouring from his forehead into his eyes blurring his view. He needed help but this bastard in front of him must be fixed before he bled to death. Magic on the table near the gun and the knife, said "mew" and Salim look its way and saw the gun and the knife on the table but they were behind Menya. How he wished he could by-pass him and get at any of them. He would make him say his last prayer first and slit his throat right down to his scrotum. Menya saw the excitement in his eyes and knew he wanted either the gun or the knife to use against him. He would have used them but they wanted him alive at the Military barracks for the guns found in his shop. They wanted him to talk and tell them who killed Captain Dramadri. Therefore, he must get him alive.

Magic heard heavy footfalls outside the house and jumped down from the table, ran, and sat at the window and looked outside. He saw five armed men walked out of an army Land Rover and took cover around the house. He ran back and sprang on the table and said 'mew' before it snarled, warning Salim that there were more trouble on his hand. Salim didn't know what to do. He knew he would soon be arrested. He retreated from Menya towards the main front door seeking for emergency exit. Magic saw him retreat and shook its head approvingly. Salim retreated and Menya charged him towards the emergency entrance. Salim rested his back on the door, with his hand behind turned the door knob and pushed on the emergency entrance, it swang out and Salim disappeared behind the door and Magic jumped out after him leading the way for him. Menya with blood pouring from his head fainted and collapsed on the floor. He fell face down in front of the emergency entrance where Salim disappeared with Magic.

The automatic machine gun, which rang in the house and fell Ebonyo, sang loud and clear funeral songs. Everyone with good ears heard it and knew something was amissed. They took cover. The gunmen knew that their game was on. They took theirs and laid low and watch the development with interest. The security men knew work was at hand they must go to see what has happened.

For Captain Ben he knew where the sounds of gun were coming from and who was causing it. *Salim is killing Menya and Ebonyo*. Ben thought and quickly collected his men guarding the home of Salim near Rock View Hotel. They got into their Land Rover and drove off towards Aguru flats, the secret residents of the hoodlum, Salim. They got there, jumped out of the Land Rover, ran crouching towards Salim's flat and bust in the apartment. The place was quiet. Only the smell of the gun, mixed with that of blood filled the house. "Two of you cover the house from outside while we go upstairs to see what is up there." Captain Ben ordered and started crouching towards the steps followed by another Corporal avoiding the light from the house. It was when they were at the foot of the step when Magic saw them coming up and seriously warned Salim that he was inhell of trouble. Captain Ben tumbles into the house and took cover behind the door and watched the house carefully. He was outrageous when he saw the two Constables Menya and Ebonyo sprawling on the floor in their own pool of blood. The ceiling board blown by the machine gun, the hunks of the walls chopped off by the bullet, the pulverized glass windows scattered by the bullet, laid in heaps near them. Ben jumped forward hysterically and reached Menya. He turned him over. There was no gun wound on him except for a crack on his forehead, which was draining, him dry of any blood. He felt for pulses. They were weak and feeble. He jumped on to Ebonyo, the minced brain and the open window on his sternum bone told him that he was a corpse. No human being could get shot as he was and still breathe. He didn't bother to practice his doctorate on him, all he did was to order the constable to assist him carry the unconscious Menya to the Land Rover.

The emergency entrance in Salim flat was connected to a tunnel dug underground by a ladder that aided to ascend and descend to and from the flat respectively. The secret tunnel led from the base of the flat, at a safety height of about four feet and joined the outside world covered with a metallic plate which looked like a manhole for a toilet. Salim descended the ladder, grooved his way along the tunnel up to the outside door where there was yet another short ladder four feet high serving the same purpose like the one in the flat.

Salim climbed the ladder and with the top of his head, lifted the rectangular cast iron plate and walked out. He crouched near the fence surveying what was going on, in his bushy compound. He saw them talk and the captain gave an order which was answered with a salute before Menya was driven away to the hospital leaving this time Captain Ben and the Constable who helped him to carry Menya to the Land Rover behind. Salim saw them walked back to the flat with their guns in their hands.

"You wait here and watch around the house. Fire at anything that moves, do you hear me?"

The Director Murdered

"Yes Sir."The constable said and saluted. Captain Ben disappeared in the flat while the constable paced up and down in the bushy compound walking as far as the fence where Salim laid crouched. How he wished he got his gun with him, he would have licked him with a shot. He wondered what the Captain was doing in the flat, what if he sneaked his way back and collected the gun. He didn't know how strong Captain Ben was.

How about trying him? But the thought of meeting a tough officer, after a duel which has left him more crippled than he was before, made him flinched as Magic growled warningly. The constable pacing the yard near them heard the growl, reeled and turned towards their direction to catch the sound again. Magic this time said 'mew'. The Constable saw him and cocked his gun and fired but the bullet jammed in the barrel. Magic said 'mew' and Salim giggled at the soldier as he struggled to remove the second bullet from the gun.

"What is wrong with the bloody gun?" the soldier said furiously. He snarled shaking the gun, nearly throwing it down. He removed the bullet and tried again, when he failed for the third time, he was frightened and scared.

I must let Captain Ben know my gun is faulty. He thought and walked up to Captain Ben. He got him searching every nook of the house his face tensed and provoked.

"What do you want up here? I told you to watch outside and shoot anything that moves."

"That is what I was doing Sir. There is a cat outside the fence. I tried to shoot at it thrice, but at each attempt, the bullet jammed in the nozzle of the gun. I don't know what is wrong with the gun?" The constable said. Captain Ben stared at him disbelievingly and snatched the gun way from his hand. He examined it and when he found no fault with it, he tossed the gun to him. It slammed on his chest and it trigged off the automatic machine gun, which began to sing. It released a few bullets off before it was stopped. The Constable was amazed and so was Captain Ben. They both looked at each other without words and walked out off the flat into the bushy compound. "Where is the cat?" Captain Ben asked embarrassed at the incident.

"It was under the fence just opposite that tree." he said pointing at a tree which stood beyond the fence under which Salim and Magic were crouching.

"Let's go and see." Captain Ben said leading the way walking powerfully cross the compound.

Is it true that this man is a conjuror? How has he walked out of this place without a trace? Is it him who has transformed into that cat? Why did his gun jam thrice each time he tried to fire at the cat? Captain Ben thought.

Magic was on the fence when they got at the site. Captain Ben tried thrice to shoot at it but all the time he tried the gun jammed. He was furious.

"We must kill the cat." He yelled. Magic heard him swear, but it growled and said "mew." That provoked Captain Ben as if he never was a lover of pet. He felt like chasing the cat until he got it, but with the night in, he wasn't going to do much. Magic, to pull him down further, jumped down from the fence and began to walk in the bushy compound keeping space between them. Captain Ben took a stone and hauled it at Magic. It nearly got him on the head but it jumped away and continued to say mew-mew-mew as it walked near the fence where Salim laid with only his nose showing.

With the disappointment and annoyance, Captain Ben and the constable walked back to the flat and began to search the flat carefully. They found the .38 automatic pistol of Salim and the knife on the table along the corridor to the store where Menya and Salim started their fight. Captain Ben took the gun and examined it. He found on the butt of the gun an inscription written, *British Embassy Property*. Ben smacked between his lips and said, "How did he get this gun". *British Embassy Property*! Umm! We shall find out more about this. The police will do that for us, this is their work now." He took the knife with a razor sharp blade with a black hilt. On the blade it was an inscription, made in *Britain by Smith and Smith Company Limited*. He examined it and put it back in its sheath.

"We shall let the police have this too. They could be useful evidence for them." He said as he shoved the gun into his hip pocket and the knife in the thigh pocket of his military trousers and closed the flap with the button.

Chapter 11

Peter Odongkara had just finished bathing and was toweling himself in the bathroom in front of the mirror fixed on the wall. The water draining in the bath swirled wizzily making a hollow cone as it drained. He heard a faint buzzing of the telephone. He hurriedly cleansed the bath and walked out putting on his bathing gown. It was when he opened the door to his bedroom, that the sound of the telephone ring, saturating the atmosphere in the room, poured, into his ears like cathedral chimes on a Pentecost day. He tumbled forward thinking the persistence caller could be someone important to his investigation. He snatched the receiver from the cradle of the phone and talked in it.

"Hello, this is Peter Odongkara."

"Hold on the line for Mrs. Odongkara Sir." He heard the voice of the receptionist at the counter. Odongkara sighed and wiped off the droplets of water at the back of his head.

Why is she ringing soon? I thought I told her I would ring her up when I am not busy and here she is impatiently calling. What's on her sleeves? Odongkara thought

"Hello honey"

"Hello darling. How are you and the kids?" "We are fine, thank you?"

"And you are you alright?"

"Very hectic down here darling."

"You must rest darling. I have been waiting for your call since morning I could not wait any later than this. I have been trying and trying to get through to you, but I don't know what was wrong with the line."

"You're lucky you didn't get through because you wouldn't have got me."

"How is the New Year Day being celebrated there?"

"With gun blast everywhere, not for the virtue but for the vice." "I want to talk to you about something very important."

"But dear, I must go." "You must go?"

"I am going to ring you when I come back. I am already late for an appointment. A very, very important one which I shouldn't miss. I believe I am going to get a lot from the person I am going to talk to and that will ease my task here. It will make me sort out things here pretty fast and be back home to you soon." Odongkara said and look at his wrist watch the time was one minute to his appointment with Betty.

What is the important message she wants to tell me, I am already late. Odongkara thought and nearly cradle the receiver but when he thought that it could be associated with Mukasa case , he decided that she should summaries for him the message but she could detailed it later.

"Can you tell me roughly what the important message is?" Odongkara said with an edge to his voice and rubbed the water trickling down his neck from below his hair.

"Mukasa came home this afternoon and I didn't like what happened?" Jane said running out of breath.

"I see. At what time was that?" "14.25 hours."

"Let's do it this way darling, I told you that I am going out to meet someone important in our investigation here. I thought I would stay out, but now, I must come back with the person here in my hotel suite to enable me to talk to you before eight p.m. I think that will be okay darling. I will ring you up."

"I'll wait."

"Thanks very much darling and bye from now." "Bye darling and good luck." she said and hung up.

Odongkara put on his black suit, one of the many suits he bought when he was studying criminology in Britain, a milk white shirt with blue neck tie and walked out of his suite, locked the door and walked out along the corridor and descended the steps into the lobby and dropped the key to his suite on the counter near the receptionist, a slender round faced girl, with a small nose. She looked at him with her attractive white large eye with long curly eye lashed and smiled at him invitingly. Odongkara stopped, looked at her, and returned the smile with yet another paralyzing one, which caressed her over her spine.

"I am out for about one or two hours. Keep any messages for me will you?"

"I'll do that Sir." The receptionist said as she hooked the headphone on her head and began to talk to someone ringing the hotel. The taxi drivers were all seated in their taxis waiting anxiously for anyone who wanted a ride in the night. At that early part of the evening they were still many and competition for passengers were high, but as the evening wore into night and gun blasts begin to greet the people, all taxis disappear and so would the travellers. So, in that early part of the night, every taxi man tried his best to get customers. When Od"ongkara walked out of the hotel, all the taxi men rushed to him each one asking him to go in his car. If it were not because of his dignified smartness, they would have scrambled for him grabbing him on by hands. Odongkara walked to a new model Peugeot 504 Salon as the driver triumphantly bounced up and down went and open the back door for him. Odongkara climbed in and the driver slammed the door closed, ran in front to the driver's seat, sorted out the key, ignited the engine, and eased the car out of the parking ground, happy with his victory over his friends.

"Where Sir?"

"26 B Rock Hotel Avenue', know where it is?"

"Yes Sir. The secretary to the Mayor and her sister, a receptionist at the Medcal Research Institute, live there."

"You've been going there often?"

"Not quite, but I took some people there in the past."

"I see. None of the girls is married? I am a visitor to this town, and have been given a message to deliver there to one of them, called Betty."

"That is the younger of the sisters of the Mayor's secretary. She works for Medical Research Institute. They are both unmarried."

"You are born citizen of this town?"

"Yes I was born here, reared here, my little education I got here, and now, I am working here and will die here."

"What are you?"

"What you see now, I am doing my job."

"Your name may be I will need your car again." "Sarafino Okoth and you?"

"Peter Odongkara."

"I shall remember your names well. You're here for business or something? Sarafino asked.

"Visiting." Odongkara replied

"You are staying long? Many people don't like this town these days because of fear of stopping bullets. The guns are about to begin singing, they sing throughout the night and the bullets fly like fire flies and if you move carelessly, you could stop one or two and that is not a good fun." Sarafino said

Odongkara smile behind Sarafino and asked, "Who are these firing the guns like that, and where do they get the ammunition they waste every night?"

"We really don't quite know who they are. Some people say they are the people's National Army, some say they are armed thugs, and some say they are the BDM."

"What is BDM?"

"You are from outside the country?"

"Yes, I returned from New York only yesterday."

"Yes, you look a black American."The driver said and they both laughed.

"BDM is equal to Black Devil Movement. There are some guys who are not happy with the people's revolution and have decided to go to the bush. They want to topple the Government elected by force of arms."

"How popular are they?"

"They are very popular in this town because they have the sympathy of the people here."

"Including you?"

"I am a peace lover. I don't like seeing dead bodies. Therefore, although I was born, reared, and grew up here, I don't support the method the BDM have taken to achieve their aim. I am not a politician but I think peaceful means of solving problems is more civilized than the savage force of arm, which cost lots of lives. Look, a week ago, we lost a boy from our village. The father was furious when the group of BDM brought the boy at night and threw it near our home to be buried. When he was alive, he was useful, but when the bullet passed through him, he became garbage."

Odongkara was impressed by his talk. He made up his mind to talk to the driver.

"Okoth as you know I am a visitor to this town, I need to know more about this place, the safe and the dangerous corners of the town, so that I don't run into problems. I think I need your help."

"You are most welcome Sir. All I can tell you is this, there is no safe place in this town. I do not know if you are going to stay long here or are you going to sleep here?"

"No I am coming away soon, may be with you."

"You see Sir, we are living in what is known to be a civilized generation, but you find that the people, who claim that they are civilized, actually are more savage than the people they think of as savages. Civilization says you must respect all human beings, their lives and properties. But here in this town, the civilized people who should be showing the rest of the people their civilization instead are showing their savagery by importing in all kinds of weaponry as if to kill elephants but they use them against helpless people like you and me." Okoth said and swung his car into the path to apartment 26B Rock Hotel Avenue. He got out and opened the door for Odongkara. Odongkara pulled out three hundred shillings note from his pocket and gave them to him. Its only one hundred and fifty Sir, are you paying for return also."

"No. I don't know what is up. You could hold on for a while let me find out. Odongkara said and walked to the door with the elegant steps of a theater professional and knocked on the door.

A tall slender built girl with, kiss-me-quick rosy lips opened the door. She had done her hair backwards and tied it with a ribbon of orange and green. The smooth forget me not, baby like face, shone behind an expensive skin lotion, which saturated the atmosphere with its fragrant scent. She was dressed in a long sleeves white frock with white laces on the waist and the open V shape collar ending were the base of her powerful breasts jutted out from her chest. The white high heel shoes, which exaggerated her height, made her silver coloured earrings, dangle well above Odongkara.

"Hello, come in." she said with a pregnant smile exposing the hidden beautiful teeth. "You are welcome." She said and led the way to the sitting room furnished by a lady who had the money and bought what she wanted to buy and put them where they should be in a living room. She waved Odongkara to a sofa seat.

"I am sorry I am late. Have I kept you waiting?" Odongkara said knowing well that this could be no other girl but Betty.

"No, you haven't."

"Can I help you with your coat?" She asked when she saw him hesitating to sit down.

"Ha' come on Betty, you are too Europeanized." He said and laughed.

"No I am not. I don't want a wrinkle on that smart coat."

"Just a while, there is a car waiting for us down stairs, are we ready to go?"

"Not yet, my sister hasn't come back, she has gone to collect some breakfast for us in town, and should be home any moment. She promised she won't be long."

"Well that means we could release the taxi man and ring him up later."

"That is alright". Betty said and added. "He can go, we could ring for another one. That's not a problem."

"Okay, let me release him. I'll be back in soon." Odongkara said. "Where is your wheelchair Betty? I want to push you in the street to night." Odongkara said when he came back in. She laughed and said. "You will push me next time, it's late for tonight. Did you believe I was a cripple?" she added.

"No, I didn't but I wanted to see you all the same even if you were crawling on your stomach."

"But why?"

"Just because the voice was special and unique." Odongkara said cajolery.

"Don't paint me Sir." Betty said.

"Now you are back to your "Sir" with my permission you can call me Peter always.

"My kind of job has made me too used to the word. Even now, I almost said it."

"I know when you live with the people who always want to be respected and honored, you always get your tongue twisted to say the words of adorations they love. Your Lordship, your Excellencies, your Honors and what not, because you say such words hundred times in a day. I guess Dr. Gunya used to make you say a lot of "Sirs" to him in a day."

"No, not him. In fact he was a very simple man who never demanded for respect from people."

"Who does?" "It's this Hajji." "Rajabu?"

"Yes, he is too much of a nuisance especially to the junior staff. He wants them to say 'Sir' to him all the time. And when he drives, and meets you, you must stop and wait until he has passed you, you cannot move. He wants the junior staff to treat him like a little god around here."

"What about the rest of the senior staff of the Institute. Do they demand such respect from you too?"

"Well I think they are alright, there is no problem with them." "What did Dr. Gunya used to say about Hajji attitude?"

"I think they onetime clashed over that issue when the junior staff complained to Dr. Gunya over Hajji's harassment. This made Dr. Gunya to call for a general meeting in which he expressed his disappointment at the way some senior officers were handling the junior officers."

"Did he mention him by name?"

"No. Dr. Gunya wouldn't have done that."

"What were the reactions of the people after his address?"

"I think the people were impressed and they liked the idea, especially the junior officers."

"Did that not spoil the relationship between them? I mean Dr. Gunya and Hajji?"

"Well of course, it did, they never privately met, but in public, they pretended to be friendly."

"What about this rumours I hear that Hajji Rajabu was preferred by the people in the Institute to Dr. Gunya. Is there any truth to that?"

"To the best of my knowledge no one in the Institute want that man there, leave alone being a Deputy Director or what?"

"Even you, you don't want him there?"

"Not even his foot marks. Do you know, I don't know what Hajji was up to this afternoon?"

"What did he do?"

"He wanted me to stay on until 19.00 hours." "Why?"

"Because he had an important call to make." "Where?"

"I don't know."

"Did you sometime stay behind for such duty?" "No."

"Why do you think he asked you to stay on tonight?"

"I quite don't know, but I suspect he wanted to disrupt my appointment with you this evening."

"Why should he do that Betty?"

"I don't understand him", Betty said with shrug of her shoulders. "Has he ever disrupted any of your appointment?"

"No."

"How did he know you have an appointment with me anyway?" "Did you not talk to me?"

"Yes, I did."

"And he was in his office next door, wasn't he?" "I don't know, I can't swear to that."

"Yes He was", Betty said assuringly because she first checked for Odongkara in Haji's office before she got him in the boardroom. "So, he followed your conversation with me from the beginning up to the end. He always does that to his fellow members of staff. He spies on them from his office to hear if they back-bite him or talk about him."

"That's strange Betty, for a well learned man like him to behave childishly like that."

"It is not only childish but primitive."

"What baffles me still is why he wanted to disrupt your appointment with me tonight."

"May be something is worrying him?" Betty put in curtly. "Has he ever made a pass at you?"

"Nonsense, not him at least, a louse, a clawn, a pig headed man." "Sorry if I hurt you Betty, but you just think, you are only an employee of the Institute just like him, except that you are both employed in different fields and status. Strictly speaking he has no right over your private affairs. "That's' right", Betty snapped in.

"Nor of any other person in the Institute", Odongkara took the floor and went on. "If he is doing that, then he is very wrong. Not even our parent can do that, and he certainly has no right whatsoever, to approve or disapprove your appointment with any man if he has no link with you."

"I would rather have links with some city bums than go with Haji" Betty said and suddenly said. "That's Anne coming."

"Your sister?" "Yes."

"She has a car?

No not now, she had a Fiat 127, which was robbed off her at gunpoint about a month ago."

"I am sorry to hear that." "Never been traced?"

Where? Here once you lose a thing no one bothers to trace it. You report to the police just for records purposes otherwise, there is nothing that can be done. The police are so scared of the gunmen of this town that they look as helpless as we civilians who need their protection and help. Some people lost their car and even got wind as to where their cars were, but what could the poor helpless police, do? They also want to live a day or two longer. They cannot walk in the bullet 'dung-dung' and sprawl just because they want to wrench a car off a murderous robber armed up to his teeth with the entire modern lethal weapons. That ..."

"Hello, hold on?" Betty said and got up to open the door for her sister when she heard a knocked on the door. Odongkara sat with his finger clasped, his thumbs drumming against each other, he wondered how he was going to bring Betty to continue with the trend of the interview he was already beginning to enjoy. Would she get back to it? He must cajole her tactfully back to the topic.

Anne with two bottles of milk and a loaf of bread, walked in being followed by the driver of the Taxi giving her a hand carrying a netted shopping hand bag containing two tins of butter and jam, a dressed chicken, some sausages, lumbered up the step and when he got in, gave the bag to Betty who was at the door way. She received it and took it to the kitchen. Then Anne and Betty came back to the living room, where Odongkara was sitting.

"Meet my sister Anne, Peter. Odongkara got up and shook hands with her. He felt the softness of her hand, which fondled him deep in his remote sex bag. He looked at the tall slender, subtle beauty standing infront of him. He quivered at the desire of having her. Bring any tall, slender woman to Odongkara, you buoy up his sex appetite like boiling water. He surveyed her from head to foot. The roundish shining face, with the small nose put at the right spot of a beautiful nose, the slightly enlarged eyes, the ears, which stood away from the head with the smooth curve of the pinnas, gave her indubitable beauty. Odongkara looked at the flat belly which looked a good bed, and a narrow waist which look hot and suspended on smooth shappy legs. He swallowed a mouthful of saliva and looked away to Betty.

"Nice to meet you Anne." He said and slowly withdrew his hand from Anne.

"Same to you sir."

"Peter is here in town to help us to find out what happened in the Medical Research Institute last night, and Anne is my elder sister and a Personal Secretary to the Mayor of Kitgum Town." Betty introduced them.

"That is a big job and responsibility you have at hand, Anne."
"Thank you, that's right." Anne acknowledged Peter's remark and added why are you sitting like this without drinking anything?"

Anne, who never enjoys talking about herself to others, said switching them to a different topic.

"I offered him coffee." he said no, beer no, every fluid no, so we sat talking."

"As a matter of fact we were waiting for you ..."

"Before you drink?"Anne put in interrupting Odongkara.

As they talked, the machine gun of Menya fighting with Salim in Aguru 26 shattered the stillness of the night. They looked at their wrist watches the time was 20.35 hours.

"There you are, you can go out and hit the head line in the News papers tomorrow, because you will have become dead ends of those straying bullets.

"Tonight they have started firing a little earlier', Betty said.

"If that's how it is, then we must leave Anne before we get into trouble." Odongkara demanded.

"How are you going?"Anne asked. Odongkara felt a little embarrassed at the question but put in curtly, "Taxi."

"I hope you get them. Our men here are not very brave. A gun blasts like that send them seeking for caves to hide in. I am sure most of them are on their way home and to wait for their deaths in their houses which they erronously think are the safest places.

"Betty, will you ring Booze Bay Hotel and let Okot come for us as soon as possible! Odongkara ordered

"Yes, please." Betty said and walked to the telephone to put the call through to Booze Bay Hotel. In less than five minutes Okot arrived in his Salon 504. He parked and hooted once.

"We must be going Anne. Sorry to leave you alone."Odongkara said.

"It's alright. I am already an old woman. I stay behind to look after the home, let the young ones have fun" Anne joked and smiled showing her powerful evenly chiseled, immaculate teeth. Odongkara looked at here, swallowed thickly and eyed her romantically.

The time was quarter to 21 hours when Anne closed her door and went to the kitchen to organize her supper.

Chapter 12

Salim, sthealtly crouched out from where he was lying, with Magic purring under his armpit, mingled among the bushes and walked out to the road. He continued to walk at the side of the road avoiding being spoted under the street light. He wobbled on the lame leg, not sure of where he was going, or what he wanted to do. Although he several times used, and knew the road very well, all seemed strange so that he did not even know where he was going. But he knew that something was happening which he didn't know how to overcome it. His head had stopped thinking. As he walked confused, a lorry sprang out in the corner in front and came crusing towards him. He saw it coming. He thought he knew the lorry. Yes, he knew it. It was a Bedford lorry UVY 980 of the Anyma ginnery. Abudalla his step brother drives the lorry. He knew the man behind the steering wheel must be Abudalla and no other man. He stepped in the street and waved towards the lorry to stop.

Abudalla had been out off town for about a week he had driven the bails of ginned cotton right down to Kampala. So whatever happened in Kitgum in the week, he was green about them. All he knew was about the activity of the BDM and arm thugs within Kitgum Town. Abudalla saw what he thought was a ghost at first. *Salim! What could he be doing out on foot at night like this. What about his car what has happened to it.* Abudalla thought as he drove and slow down to a stop near Salim who had stepped a little off the road to give him room to park his lorry.

"Hey Salim what are you doing here?" Abudalla asked. "As a matter of fact I don't know my brother."

"What has happened?" "Everything."
"What do you mean everything?"
"Just that brother."
"It's getting late to be loitering on the street, where are you going Salim?"
"I told you I don't know."Salim said as tears run down his cheeks.
"Come on don't be an idiot."
"Worse than an idiot in fact. That's what I am now." Abudalla's hut, where he slept, was no better than pigsty. He,
since they splited the money they robbed from Ibrahim Rajabu, their father, never had any ambition of putting up anything for himself. He never thought of a descent home. He knew acquiring such a fortune with no base, everythinking man would raise eyes at him. So why waste money putting up a descent building instead of eating up every cent. He had no wife no family, in any case, the idea of having a family never crossed his mind. He was contentended with his driving and eating. So Abudalla fed himself and drank coffee like water with the money he got from the split between him and Salim. He bought new dress for himself when the old ones were real rags. Shoes he used the motor tyre sandals, which always lasted for years. He slept on cotton mattress with only one blanket. There was no chair no table no furniture in the hut. He had a clay pot for cooking, a metallic bowl and plate, a clay water pot and a tin mug to complete his assets.

When he met Salim that night he didn't know where to take him. He looked to be in trouble. But he must go and park the lorry in the depot before they walked to his hut which was enough for him only. Additional man would bust the hut. As he thought Salim with the instinct of animal recalled that Hajji Rajabu rang him wanting him to do a job for him. He remembered how he was brought on his feet when Magic warned him when Captian Ben bust into his flat. He remembered that at that time he was talking to Hajji Rajabu suggesting to him that if he had any work to be done he could try Abudalla and Juma Isaac who were able to handle any violence. He recalled vaguely that he stopped talking to Hajji Rajabu before he told him where the two men could be reached.

"Oh brother, Hajji wanted you to do a job for him tonight."
"What job?" Abudalla asked.

"I am not quite sure but he was talking of a guy meeting their telephone operator tonight. He wanted me to stop them from meeting."

"Why?"

"I think he is worried the lady might talk too much and blurt out everything what she knows between him and Dr. Gunya and that will give a lead to him."

"What if the guy is going to release his sex burden in her only and not interested in his Gunya-Hajji affairs doesn't he think interfering into such meeting would even make him suspect number one. In any case when he was getting his neck in the yoke did he think he would pull out easily? He must think now, fast and in the right direction otherwise he is going to regret it. You, and I are used to problems but him, with his kingly attitude, will not afford to sleep in the grass and chew raw cassava. He is in for a gallow."

"Why don't we see him now?" Salim suggested.

"For what? I am too tired I want to go and have a rest. I am from Kampala just now. I don't want any nonsense. Climbe in and we go."Abudalla said and open the front door for him. He helped him up and he sat down. He looked at him and ignited the engine and they drove off. They had just joined the 'Rock Hotel Avenue when the taxi of Okot taking out Odongkara and Betty to Booze Baby Hotel nosed to cross the road they stopped to let the lorry pass first. They fell after it and overtook it as it was going to reach the Town center.

"Now tell me Salim what happened to you?" "Many things."

"What are these many things? I don't know why you are answering me like that. Don't you trust me with the story? I don't know whatever we didn't do together."

"Well let your desire be satisfied. My shop got burnt down last night and what does that mean to you? The guns the hand grenade, the ammunition you stock pilled in my shop blew off last night as if it was the November incident when the BDM tried to topple the government was back. The fire hauled from my shop by the blasting hand grenade started fire in the Pop-In shop and it's also down to ashes. I was gripped by the loss of my properties. I became insane. I decided to lose all I own. I took my family to Abera forest and I blew every living cell in their bodies they are sleeping in the forest. My Benz, I deserted it in the forest anyone could go for it. I took a taxi back to the flat. And Hajji rang, when I was talking to him, when Magic warned me that I was in trouble. I jumped out of my wrecked bed, and walk to a carton box where I hid. The army broke in, they search every inch of the room they could not get me because Magic protected me. He caught a rat and sat with it on top of the carton. He continues to eat his meal while I lay in the box. It was when they were gone except two, that I tried to break loss. I walked out of the box stealthily but the glass at the window accused me. The punk I wanted to strangle had stood with his back against me he had fixed his eyes on Magic who had sat at the window. I think he saw me get out of the box and crouch behind him. He didn't show any knowledge about me. It was when I straightened that I saw my image in the glass then it occurred to me that I sold myself out. He turned to me and asked me to touch the ceilling boards with both hands. I tried and he emptied me completely. I became as useless as a broken pot. He ordered me to sit down on the carton what he called my coffin. I sat, and we chatted. Magic didn't move from his place at the window. As we chatted Magic startled us? He jumped on kettle I used for my toilet. The kettle fell down with a solid noise. He wheeled round to see the falling kettle. I was on him. I wanted to crack his head. As we fought the bastard had already release the safety catch on the gun and set it ready to go. His finger triggered it off as we fell and the bullets began to rain. One of his friends who was down stairs didn't know what was happening in the house he came upstairs running as if he wasn't trained. The raining bullets licked him on the head and the chest. He fell down creating a stream of blood. I think the gun, which fired off scattered the bees on me, more of them heard it and they came to the rescue of their friends. Magic again warn me as we fought that I had more problem in my hand. I escaped outside through my emergency exit. I hid under the fence with Magic making all sort of noises. I regretted the absence of my gun. If I had it I would have licked all of them. They were walking near me, nearly troading on my head. Six times they tried to shoot at Magic but their gun jammed. I nearly laughed at them. To frustrate them further Magic walked in the compound and they tried to stone him but he dodged the stones walked back to me. I picked him up and here we are.

"Who set the fire to your shop? Abdallah asked.

"I don't know but I guess it must be Isaac who came to buy some goods on Sunday the eve of the New Year Day. He was smoking like a chimney."

"Could be him, do you think he intended it?" "How should I know that? It could be."

"That is sad Salim. I am sorry to hear about the loss?" "Have you any money in the bank?"

"Just a little which is not enough to feed me for a week with the present inflation. That is one of the reasons why I blew off my entire family. I want to be left to suffer and eat from the rubbish bins of the rich without a wife or children bothering me. Even that little money in the bank is useless to me because I can't get anywhere near the bank before I am picked up."

Salim saw Abdalla sighed as they pulled up at the Medical Research Institute. Abdalla introduce himself to the gate keeper as the son of Hajji and with the mention of the name of Hajji the gate flanged open and the lorry rolled in and the gate closed behind it.

Hajji finished his SA1A at 18.00 hours, went to toilet and came back to the sitting room where his nephew Abudu Abas and his daughter Sarah sat. Hajji took a chair opposite his niece and rubbed his callous forehead and stared at them.

"Things are no good now. What I planned in two years blew off last night. It all went well until last night when things started going wrong. The shop of Salim which served us for a long time burned down exposing all of us in the open. All the bullets and the cartridges used here last night are going to be identified as having come from the barracks. That wouldn't have mattered much if what we stocked in the shop of Salim remain occulted. We don't have much room to argue on. Salim is around although the newspaper reports say he has vanished with all his family. My main concern is,

The Director Murdered

there are already people within the Institute who are ready to bet their lives that what happened yesterday is an internal issue and not external. They ...

"Who are these?"Abudu Abas interupted. Abudu Abas was the son of the sister of Hajji Rajabu he worked with the National Post and Telecommunication as telephone operator as early as the Colonial days. He, because of his aptitude in electronic, he was sent to U.K. to be train in telephone electronic engineering. When he came back, he was made the chief of the engineers. Abudu an obesed Muslim was diabetic patient who was a little more handsome than a hippo. He had a big mouth with thick lips, which cracked and bled blood in hot weather. The big red eyes stood out on the fat big baldhead like tennis balls. Abudu adjusted in the chair and stared at Hajji expectantly. "It's our storekeeper and Dr. Gunya's servant is another and worst still is our telephone operator with whom the CID is meeting tonight. I don't know what we can do about that? I think I must prevent the meeting because if he meets that girl, she is going to give him all information that will lead onto me."

"How are you going to prevent them from meeting?" Abudu asked.

"I don't know. Salim could be having an idea." "You said you know where Salim is?"

"Yes"

"Any telephone there."

"Yes."

"Ring him up and seek for his help." "I did that an hour ago."

"And what did he say?"

"He is not willing to help. He suggested I tried Abdalla or Isaac."

"Where do you get them?"

"That is the problem. I wanted him to tell me where to find them but he hurredly left his receiver as if the walls were collapsing on him."

"Funny, wasn't it?" "Indeed it was."

"Well Hajji while that remains unsolved its true as you have said at the beginning that all that have been planed in two years started falling apart yesterday. You told me that the gun we gave to this girl and the knife were found in the bedroom of Dr. Gunya is that right?"

"Yes that is the problem of involving women in a tricky game like this. They make it stink sooner. So what do we do about that?"
"I think there is very little we can do now. Because the weapons are already in the hands of the police. I over heard that finger print of a lady was on them, which I don't doubt they belong to her.

The similar prints were found on the door. So you see. How do you go about such a thing?"

"But no one knows she was his girlfriend?"

"What about his servant, the old man knows all the ladies who passed under that roof. Ask her if am lying."

"Is it true Sarah?" Abudu Abas asked. "Yes, he is very correct."

"Does he know you were his girlfriend?" "Yes he does."

"Beside there was a photo album of all his girl friends dead and alive, found in his house. Every photo contains the name of the girl, her age and address. This was also found in the house. Am I lying Sarah?

"No."

"Is your photograph one of those in the album?" Abudu asked. "Yes." Sarah replied.

"Well that tells us where we are with the case. Only Halla will save us from it. They are going to contact all the girls, that can be reached, and their fingerprints will be taken, and obviously hers will match to those on the knife and the gun, then the questions come, where did she get the gun and the knife and why did she take them in Dr. Gunyas' bedroom? Anyone can answer that. In my opinion, now, before the worse comes to the worst, Shara must go away. She must disappear from here." Hajji commented.

"To where? That will expose you too." Abudu remarked. "So what do we do?"

"I don't know". But …

As they talked Abdalla swang the lorry at the round about in front of Hajjis' house parked, and cut off the engine. He got out and Salim slipped down with his cat under his armpit. They walked towards the door and knocked. Hajji got up and opened the door for them.

"Oh! How nice it is to meet you this evening. Salim you don't look well". Hajji commented. Salim walked passed him in without talking to him. His Magic glued under his armpit.

Abudu and Sarah, were frightened at the sight of Salim when they saw them.

"You have a bruised face what happened? Sarah asked. Salim kept quiet and stared at Hajji.

"You know you have caused me all these loss. If I am going to die today tomorrow or when, you are responsible Hajji. I have lost all what belonged to me because of you. Your ill intention plunged me into irreversible mess. What can you do about it now you big headed pig". Salim interjected.

Every body was shocked at the fury of Salim. They know him as one of the most dangerous descendant in their clan and he could stick a knife at anyone, be his father or mother. They didn't know his weapons were already in the police.

"Still you idiot rang me up asking me to come to your aid because you want to stop the meeting between these two people tonight. You can go ahead and stop them. But I assure you there is nothing you can do about it or about this case now. If I were you, I would have started thinking of the nearest country to flee. I have often told you that you must die before you act against the law otherwise you will lead the most miserable life through out your life. You will sit with your head stooped like bats, which have never seen the sun. Because, you know the law and the police are looking for you. For your information, my wife and my children, are now six hours dead and you Hajji is responsible for their death. Their ghosts will haunt you. Salim said and walked out of the house. Abdalla got up and followed him outside.

"Salim!" Abdalla called. "Yes."

"What do you intend to do now?"

"I don't know." Salim said with a waved of a hand and continued. "You return your lorry to the depot it's getting late. I am going to the street, my home. Don't be worried about me." As they talk Abudu joined them outside.

"Salim, please, listen to me." "Tell me what you have to say."

"Not here. Shall we go to my house where we will talk?"

Salim pause smoothened the hair on Magic and Magic said 'Mew'. He looked at Abudu and at Abdalla and said Okay I'll come with you." Abdalla climbed his lorry and slammed the door of his lorry shut and drove away leaving Salim and Abudu behind.

Okot drove at 80 k.m.p, got to Booz Baby Hotel and found that the parking ground was deserted by all the other taxi.

"They have all vanished?" Odongkara asked as he opened the door of the car and got out.

"Because of the gun shots which went off a few minutes ago. Did you not see how they were streaming back?" Betty said and got out after Okot had opened for her.

"We are always scared of these gun men when they start firing like that they fire at anything that moves even at the mosquitoes. The fireflies have stopped flying at night because of the guns. The bats used to be here in thousands they have all migrated because of the gun blasts. It is a new trend of life, no creature is used too". Okot said and received the two hundred shilling notes for his fees, thanked Odongkara, entered his car ignited the engine and drove off.

Odongkara and Betty walked to the reception and Odonkara asked for his keys. A new man was on night shift duty. The girl, whom he met before he went out at 20.00 hours, was gone. The new man, a short plumb, one eyed man, the other bad eye could have been destroyed in an accident, leered at them.

"Our keys." Odongkara said. "What number Sir?"

"Suite 12"

The man cocked his head and took the key to Suit 12 and gave it to Odongkara.

"Any message for me?"

"Yes Sir." he said and gave him a chit and stared at Odongkara with the one eye as Betty looked at him piteously. The Note Read Chief a *fat short man with pig like head was looking for you in our hotel here. The staff of this hotel was kind enough to make us aware of the insecurity in the town. They warned us not to be outside our rooms after 21 hours so please note that. Signed Opiyo and Lwanga.*

"Yes these are my colleagues they are putting up at Rock Hotel." Odongkara said after he had read the note folded, it slipped it in his pocket.

"You would better go for your supper. It is nearly time for the dinning hall to be closed." The receptionist advised. Odongkara glance at his watch it was 10 minutes to 21.00 hours.

"Thank you for reminding us. After their dinner the two went to the bar. The bar was strictly for the residences of the hotel.

"Mr and Mrs Odongkara suite 12." Odongkara said to the man at the gate as he walked in with Betty. The man leered at her and smiled. He knew Betty well and he knew Betty was as unmarried as a Catholic nun. Odongkara looked at him and asked anything funny. No sir the gatekeeper said and turned on to the residence that was walking after them. Odongkara and Betty walked and sat in a two seater table planted at the corner of the bar where there was not much light. From where they sat they were able to see everywhere in the bar with ease.

"What do you drink whisky, beer and what beer?" Odongkara asked

"We are staying long aren't we?" Betty asked "Of course yes."

"Then keep whisky out. I'll take Bell Beer."

"Oh great that is my choice too." Odongkara said and walked to the bar and bought four cold Bell Beer and brought them to the table where they were sitting. I am sorry I have to do this because I have a very important call to make. I will keep you lonely for about thirty minutes. I am sure you will excuse me you won't be offended if I call you darling? Will you? He asked and dimmed his eyes and looked at her from below. She also dimmed her and smiled, and said it's no offence to me if you say it yourself."

Odongkara put his hand on her and gripped ecstatically and walked to the telephone boot in the balcony. He lifted the receiver and heard dialing tone and slip two fifty cents coins in the box and dial his house in Gulu. In a few moments he heard the telephone rang and his wife picked it up.

"Hello darling." Mrs Odongkara answered as she recognized the voice of her husband.

"Hello honey nice to hear your voice late at night in the New Year night. How are you again? You sound very lonely."

"You know that yourself darling I am really lonely. The children are now in bed."

"What did you cook for them?"

"We ate half of the turkey and drank some wine." "No whisky?"

"I always drink whisky when you are here to fondle me!" she said romantically

"Well keep fit I am almost through this end. I am sure tomorrow I will crack the nut, and I will be back to follow up the Mukasa story."

"That's what I want to talk to you about darling. I am worried." "What are you worried about?"

"Because Mr and Mrs Mukasa came to me this morning and they were pleading that I should provide alibi for Mrs Mukas for that case. I was scared darling you know I am not meant for public speech. How am I going to speak in a court? How am I going to defend her? I can't surely I cannot. Let her find another person. I … I …"

"Well darling what did you tell them?" "I told them that I couldn't do that." "And what did they say?"

"They said I should do so on tribal ground because no one in our tribe has ever ignored a fellow tribesman in trouble and if I do then I am going to be the first."

"So do you want to be the first or go with the tribal legendary if I may call it?"

"I am going to be the first. Darling why did you send them to me?"

"What? Did you say I sent them to you?"

"Yes. Mukasa said you agreed that I should accept that the wife and the family were with me yesterday evening between 20-21 hours the time when she ran the child down."

"Nonsense. Absolutely nonsense. Mukasa talked to me about that but I said it's up to you. If you think you can withstand the eventualities then you could provide them with alibi they need. I didn't tell him to come to you. How on earth can I do that Darling?"

"I am sure many people saw Mary on Onekalit's farm and they will say that out. Then how odd can I insist she and the family were in our house. I don't want it darling I am not going to enmesh myself in this case."

"Well darling I had given you the choice. I talked to Mukasa about that. I warned him that he's messing up everything by covering up his wife. I thought she would get a lighter sentence if Mukasa acted intelligibly but he's treating this case with a lot of misgivings so I have left it in his hand. He wants to capitalize on the lots of lawlessness going on in the country at the moment from the men in authority shoot someone with a gun no investigation even if the investigation is done and the culprit is found nothing is done about it. Tomorrow he shoots another nothing is done and he gets the lust to kill. Well some are born lucky. I thought it would really be wise for Mukasa to follow the straight road of the law. He thinks I am misadvising him. I am glad darling you have seen the danger and you have acted wisely. Do not get mixed up in the matter you could draw four years in jail for defendinga criminal."

"And you know what Mary said to me, she said I am to blame for what she did last night. And that I am going to be responsible to what will happen to her family."

Odongkara sigh and said, "Is it a blackmailing now? That you know better."

"But why?" Jane asked pretending innocence of what she did with Mukasa on that fatefull evening.

"Umm. Why should she say you are responsible for what she did that evening?"

"I don't know darling."

"To me it sound you did something which could make her uses it to blackmail you if you don't provide her with the protection she wants."

"I … I … can't recall it." Jane lied

"I don't know either." Odongkara said. "Finaly what I would like to advise you about is, whether it's a tribal, traditional legendary, or myths, that you people have never let down anyone of your tribemate, I would if I were you think twice before I get entangle in this case. The complainants have hundreds of powerful genuine witnesses who are ready to vindicate that Mrs. Mukasa was the driver of the car which hit and killed that child last evening. No lawyer will be good enough to disapprove them. This is why I don't understand Mukasa at the moment. He knows about all these and yet he insists on concealing his wife from the law."

"May be he is going to use his position."

"Not when the complainants have already got all the evidence against the person who will be identified as the driver of the car which hit and killed the child and the accuse has not yet until now reported to any police station!

"I think he is disappearing."

"Disappearing? What is that?" Mrs Odongkara asked "He talked of starting leave tomorrow."

"Don't tell me."

"Worried?" Odongkara asked teasing his wife.

"Why? None of my business why should I be worried?" "Don't blow your top darling keep your veins in peace don't wreck them. Anyway that is between you and me yet." "Of course darling."

"Keep up your decision to have nothing to do with the Mukasa affair only our sympathy should be extended to them but to enmesh us in the drama! No. I am going to be an observer. Do you get me clear? Make no mistake at it. From now have sweet dreams and kisses."He said and smacked his lips on the mouthpiece and hung up. Odongkara walked out of the telephone boot to enable a lady waiting outside the boot the chance to talk. He had wanted to ring John in the Government Laboratory to find out about the sample of blood he left with him in the morning but he thought he had kept the lady outside the boot too long. He greeted her and waved her to the boot.

"I am sorry if I kept you long madam."

"No sir it's all right." The short fat flat head woman said and slipped in the telephone boot and closed the door behind her. Odongkara never in his life glanced twice at short ladies. He naturally dislikes them especially the short fat belly type. When he waved her in, he continued to walk away towards the bar ignoring what the lady said. Odongkara walked to the table where he had left Betty sitting in the corner her chest well above the table, her breasts jutted out like growing horns of a young bull. She smiled at him erotically and Odongkara felt the warmth of it stirring his sex virility to boiling. He walked and pulled his chair back sat, on it and rested his forearms on the table.

"You're welcome back." Betty said.

"Thank you. I am sorry I kept you very lonely." "I was all right here."

"Were you? When you haven't sipped even a bit of the beer, don't you like it?

"I love it but I didn't have the appetite without you around." "Oh lovely, okay let's have a drink." Odongkara said and shot the beer from the bottle in his glass and toss to their health and they began to drink.

"That is better to drink when you are two." Betty said and continued "You have that feeling of togetherness and when you talk you drink without realizing you are drinking but when you are alone you know you have it in front of you and all the time you are conscious and you find that you gulp it at a fast rate and you either get bored with it or give up soon." She added and they laughed. Odongkara gently nipped the back of her hand and they eyeballed each other erotically.

"Well Betty dear, the cripple. It's nice to be with you this New Year Day. It was quite a busy day but now I have some room to swallow a few drops of beer with an incredulously beautiful girl I've ever seen near me." He said and sipped his beer.

"Don't coat me with all those lovely commend you handsome peacock. I don't deserve all those hunks of praise." Betty said sternly without any seriousness.

"Oh come on! You know who you are, who can dispute that?" Odongkara insisted resting his palm on the back of hers. Betty said nothing thereafter but took her glass and swallowed in two mouthful of beer.

"When do you go back to Gulu?" She asked. "Are you bored with me already?"

"Oh no! That's not it. I just want to know how long I am going to have you with me!" She said and drew in more beer. Odongkara had wanted to start his interview and he had already planned how to corner her and put her back to where they ended in the flat. But he was lucky she started it herself and therefore although the trend of thought was changed he knew the theme remains the same.

"I will go back to Gulu anytime from now when I find who killed Dr. Gunya." He said lowering his voice.

"So you still have some days to stay here?"

"I don't know if it will take me some days, weeks, months or even the whole year I will be with you here."

"I wish it could take you a year so that I see more of you!" She said and giggled romantically. Odongkara knew the beer she had emptied was beginning to work and loosen her tongue. A little bit more will make her spilt out the beans when he starts a serious interview.

"I too wish the same?" Odongkara said and flick the nipple of her left breast nearer to him. She shuddered and looked at him with a dreaming eye.

"Not yet time for it." She warned. Odongkara folded his arm and said.

"Okay. I am sorry, I'll wait."

"Be a nice peacock it will be alright." Betty assured him.

"You are putting out burning fire with petrol? Supposing we put off the fire with water?" Odongkara commented feeling sexually aroused by her comment

"Go ahead and bring the water." She said

"The water is this, when I was with you in your flat I asked you a question, which still remained unanswered."

"And what is the question?"

"Wait a minute let me fetch more beer the bottles and glasses are empty."

"Go ahead I am here to drain the bottles dry." Betty said and they both laughed

"My wallet is well loaded. You can't empty it." Odongkara returned the joke.

"I will make a permanent big hole in your Wallet that you will never mend it peacock."

"Try and see if you will." "A bet?"

"A bet."

The Director Murdered

"I am joking", she said and laughed as Odongkara walked to the bar to bring more beer taking the empties along with him. The bar was a self-services bar. As a matter of fact, Betty was a little better than a teatoddler. The two bottle she had, had atomized every sexual feeling in her. She was talking loudly so that Odongkara thought of going to the suite but because he wanted to squeeze all she knew about Hajji and Dr. Gunya relationships, he decided to sit on. He knew it wasn't going to be to long. *She must talk sense and not drunk talks.* He thought as he came back with four opened bottles of beer.

"Who is going to drink all those bottles you've collected?"
"You are a joker. Did you think I was serious about what I said?"
"I knew you were joking of course. We are just passing time." "I normally don't take more than four bottles of beer to be honest with you."She said stooping on the table.

"Well that leaves you with two bottles more Odongkara said as he serves a beer in her glass.

"Yes Betty what about my question. Why do you hate Hajji so much?"

"I feel like not talking about the ape, Betty answered nauseously." "Not even for …"

"For your sake of course I will tolerate mentioning his name. I wish Dr. Gunya was as villain and evilish as him and he acted fast and it was Haji who was dead, I would by now, be running mad in the street."

"Now! At this time of the night? With all the gun shots? And why the Jamboree?"

"He is an old hypocrite, who, at first sight anyone would say Haji is the nicest man and the best man that has ever lived on this planet. His smiles are deceptive to everyone. When he hears of other misfortunes he shed crocodile tears. He is a real snake in the grass and he is dangerous. He is antisocial and he knows only his home and his working place. This is not because he is a better researcher than any of the researchers, but simply because of his personality, exaggerated by his belief, which prohibit alcohol. As I told you he is an introvert self-seeker he is rapacious and finally a tribal. But his strongest temperament is introvert self-seeker and rapacious. He could do anything in this world to defend them. Hajji has always wanted to be the boss of the Institute because of his long service there. But because of Dr. Gunya qualification and manigegerial ability and cooperation with the workers he was appointed to head the institute. I think Haji has not taken the appointment of Dr. Gunya benevolently. He has looked at it as a despise and humiliation. This is what I hear people say don't quote me anywhere because I have no proof." She said and squeezed Odongkara's knee under the table reassuringly. He smiled and nodded his head.

"Umm." Odongkara said. "So what do you think about the death of Dr. Gunya do you belief the story, I mean the news in the foreign mass news media which associate the BDM with the murder?"

"It is difficult to answer that question – I get the temptation of calling you darling I don't know why?"

"Because I am your darling and you are mine that is it."
"Stubborn peacock", she said.

"Why is it difficult to answer the question?"

"Because here in this town you get three groups of armed men, one our security men by these I mean the police and the army. Secondly the so called BDM and thirdly the armed thugs who actually acquired their arms during the revolution and now because they do not know the use of the weapon they are pumping anyone who walk their way with the bullets. If I am to say my observation about these three groups of armed men, you will find that even among our security men, I mean our army and police you find some of them who go out doing all sorts of bad things around beating people robbing and looting houses which sometimes end in deaths. And when such things happened, the BDM is blamed for it. And silly as they are they always accept and claim they did it. I don't know why."

"Because they want to be known outside, and that gives fear to the foreign government to give us any assistance because of an insecured country." Odongkara said.

"Oh I see I hadn't known of that." Well this is the problem with us Africans. Whenever we are notoriously being heard of like

The Director Murdered

that we feel proud, we feel we are king of kings because we are killing our own black brothers. They can't sit together and talk and accept one as superior we cannot all be Head of State."

"It may not happen in Africa in the near future." Odongkara said carelessly

"Why?" Betty asked.

"That seems to be our way of life in Africa." "Sad, extremely sad."

"I agree with you, but we've gone away a bit from our discussion." "I know, I was only elaborating my regret about importation of arms to the country to kill our own black brothers and sisters! You want my opinion about the news on the radio which claims that Dr.

Gunya was killed by the BDM isn't it?" "Yes quite right."

"Well, it is a pity Odongkara, you men must begin to value human lives it is the greatest gift God has given human beings and no one has the right to remove it from anyone forcibly.

"I understand but …"

"I know you want me to talk about Dr. Gunya." Betty said and looked at Odongkara hallucinately. Odongkara knew the beer was breaking her fast.

He wondered if she will be sober enough to talk sense. Odongkara took her palm in his and squeezed gently when she had slightly raised her voice.

"How nice you do it!" She remarked and smiled erotically. "I will do it better after here."

"I know you will, peacock." Let's talk about Hajji now I know you are impatiently waiting to hear from me. The incidence, which happened in the Institute, is very suspicious. As I said you will appreciate the fact that these three groups of armed men I mentioned are terrorizing people in town here like cholera. Eh! They are all doing a lot of havocs to innocent men and women. Everyday, every night someone must bleed blood to death. How far are we going on with this? You see, there are people who are getting blown up by their friends who either have grudges with them because they collided over a woman, jobs or business or some of those petty quarrels and those trivial problems. They always plan death for them. I am telling you peacock keep your ears open and hear how we live in our Town but please I know you won't qoute me anywhere."

"I won't Betty."

"Yes they always plan deaths for such fellows and they always make a smart game out of it. Looking at the robbery and the assassination of Dr. Gunya, our Institute is supposed to be the safest place in Town with its fortress. There has never been any incidence of such nature in that place since the BDM started their existence. The place is naturally feared because of the name. People think deaths is line up along the path to the Institute like bees in the hive. So if one wants death go near Medical Research Institute and you fall dead, like a fly fumigated with insecticide. So who dares to go near the place? Only the people who work there and those who are made aware of the safety of the place, by those who work there. So you see peacock, last night incidence leaves many questions unanswered.

But … she paused and slopped more beer in her glass and drained a mouthful and gulped it, the throat grunting. But … that is where I ended. You know peacock it is not possible for people of the number mentioned to pass over the walls without being notice. The security lights are scattered everywhere after an incidence where two men stole a small cartons of drug over the walls and even that they were arrested. What if twelve men dared that, would they go unnoticed? Really? I don't think so. The rest of the jokes about the Institute drummer you already know. They have told you but answering your question, I differ from the news we heard on foreign news media that the BDM are behind Dr. Gunya assassination. I think you need to think and ask few question and you might stir up the assassin of Dr. Gunya. She sighed and blew out air which smelt of traces of alcohol but she looked sodden drunk.

"You said Hajji and Dr. Gunya never got along well together."

"Hajji doesn't get along well with most people in the Institute, not even with his wife at home perhaps." She said and they both laugh.

"Does he make calls outside very often?" "He does."

The Director Murdered

"Does he call the same numbers or different numbers?"

"Well he used to talk quite often to a man whose shop got burnt last night."

"Yes!" Odongkara exclaimed

"Salim – He has a very funny story according to what people tell me and I wonder why if Hajji is a descent man as he seemed to look, should associate himself with such avillain?"

"Salim is the name?" "So I hear."

"What did he converse with Salim whenever he rings him up?" "Salim is as illiterate as a wild ape, he doesn't know a word in English so they always communicated in Arabic or Nubian. But one day, not near, along time back I heard them talked of course in Arabic but they mentioned about *Bunduki* which of course is gun and *Kaptain Dramadri* and *Uniform* I didn't know what was the matter and by the way I never told this to anyone except you because I have loved you at the mere voice I heard on the phone this morning."

"This afternoon." Odongkara corrected. "Time not important", Betty snapped. "Yes Okay tell me." Odongkara coaxed her.

"A month after I heard them talked, it was alleged that Captain Dramadri of Kitgum 15 Battalion disappeared with hundreds of sophisticated guns, ammunition, hand grenade, and uniforms. The Land Rover in which he removed the guns and ammunitions, hand grenades and uniforms was recovered near Abera forest. It was widely rumoured that he defected and joined the BDM. I am sure you heard about it. So, that claim made it difficult for me to talk about what I over heard Hajji talked about to Salim. I thought perhaps they had pre-knewledge about the defection of Captain Dramadri. And if really Captain Dramadri defected why abandon the Land rover. Don't the BDM need vehicles? I think they badly need them." Betty said and looked at Odongkara while licking the rim of the glass of beer in her hand which she had lifted face high with both elbows pivoted on top of the table.

"You are damn right Betty."

"Don't ask me more question now I have closed my station. I – I need to sleep Iam fed up of drinking this bitter liquid."

"You want to drink another sweeter liquid?" Odongkara said and drained the beer from his glass and got up.

"Yes that is what I am set for now. She whisperd in a voice which made Odongkara fidgait with a tickling sensation which crept over his spine. His mouth watered, he felt his heart beating faster as Betty rose from her chair towering up to his face. He moved the chair for her and she slipped between the table and the chair her arms folded over her powerful breasts, she walked in front of Odongkara. The people of the bar turned to look at them as they walked out.

They got to the suite and Odongkara opened the door and put on the light and Betty walked in. He helped her with her coat put it on the hook at the door and removed his coat and put it on the next hook on the door.

Betty slammed on the chair in the lounge and closed her eyes as if someone in dire need for sleep after a terrible long journey.

"Are you sleeping?" Odongkara came bent over her he felt the warm breath which shot out from her nose, titled upward. It heated him real hot and triggered off his sex virility he could not help it he fixed his lips on hers she felt it like an iron brought near a magnet, she open her lips and they kissed. She groaned and moved and wriggled on him. Odongkara squeezed and sucked her tongue and they became breathless and they gasped for breath.

"The sweetest kiss I have had in years!" Betty groaned with her lips between Odongkara's lips.

"I thought you were sleeping." "And you woke me with a kiss?" "That's right."

"I won't sleep before I make you sweat your last drop of water in this handsome body." She said patting his chest, and threw her arms round his neck and raised her lips to his again.

Odongkara lowered his head and their lips met again. When he was conscious enough Odongkara lifted Betty from her chair walk with her to the bedroom and put her on bed and began to undress her.

"Wait my bladder is over flowing with the damn beer I have drunk let me go and pour it out." She said and staggered up on her feet Odongkara escorted her to the toilet.

Odongkara could not sleep before he fitted all he had collected during the day together to see if they made sense and where to start from the following day. The conversation he had with Betty the girl who laid dead asleep under the same blanket with him that night her head resting on his arm was very informative. He thought he must verify the talk with that of a neutral staff of the Institute preferably one of those white girls. If I find out that the same will be said, there will be nothing wrong with arresting and charging Hajji with the murder of Dr. Gunya. It looks everyone is suspecting him to be the man who engendered the assassination of Dr. Gunya. The burglary in the Research Medical store is just a silly cover up which exposed him other than concealed him.

Odongkara looked at his watch lying on the bedside table next to the bed and wondered if John the Laboratory Technician was still awake. He always left the club at 22 hours and went to the laboratory before he went to his home. A routine he never missed even for one day. Odongkara felt the warm breath of Betty pumping on his face he looked at her and smiled. He removed her head from his arm slowly and rested it on the pillow. She squirmed a little in her sleep and turned her back against him moaning and she fell into a deep sleep. Odongkara saw the smooth linning of her naked, back which curved down to two round smooth salacious buttocks.

I will wake her for more at dawn not now let her sleep I have other things to do before mid-night. He stealthily slipped off bed and walked out to the telephone boot and lifted the receiver and slipped two fifty cents in the box and dialed John's Laboratory. He heard the phone ring and John's voice came on the line.

'Hello John here"

"Hello John this is Odongkara." "Oh chief that's you? How is it there?"

"We are fine with gun blast everywhere now." "But why are they doing that?"

"I wish I knew the answer John." "Do they shoot at human being?"

"At times but mostly they are firing for the lust of it."

"What a joke. They have all those ammunition to waste? I think they have too many and there is no space for them anywhere and that is the best way of storing them."

"I don't think so!" "Then what?"

"They might be covering something we don't know."

"May be." There was a pause between them and John knew Odongkara rang for his result he left with him in the morning before he left for Kitgum.

"I did your work and the result is ready." "How is it?"

"You want it on the line?"

"I don't think it matters really."

"Well, then wait a minutes let me get it over to you." John said and Odongkara heard him flapping through papers.

"The blood is of course a human blood according to the radial immunodifusion test." John stated after he had reached the right paper. And the person is belonging to group B of the ABO blood group system and is Rhesus D positive so in summary the person is group B Rh D +ve. That is what I did for you."

"Beautiful work. Dr. Kizza got back this evening didn't he?" Odongkara asked.

"Yes he did."

'Did he deliver the car?"

Ah yes. You-you mean – Ah – there you are. I am surprised. No wonder the result ties up."

"What are you talking about John? I asked you if Dr. Kizza delivered the car to Chief Orwotho. And now you are telling me something else.

"Oh well as for the car, Dr. Kizza delivered it and I sampled the blood stain on the front wheel of the car and the rear wheel of the car. I found they were human blood and the same blood group with that you brought to me."

"I think they should be the same John." Odongkara remarked and went through the story for him. How he detected the bloodstain on the wheels of Mukasas' car and how he grew suspicious, and took the sample for analysis.

"What do I do with your result?"

"Keep it I will receive it when I get back. I sampled the blood for fear that the evidence could get spoiled."

"Genius!" John said.

"I want to have very little to do with the case now that it has sprung out in the open without me."

"Yeah I think you have no dealing with this case. Only if there was some concealment of destruction of evidence then you will have to probably come in with your result that you gave me this morning as witness of the complaints."

"That is right John."

"Don't you think he will suspect you for taking the car along with you this morning?"

"So is there any case about that?" "No not at all".

'It doesn't matter John. I am sure he's now thinking on that line but he cannot revert the case on me."

"No, he cannot of course." "How is he John?"

"I had a glimes of him this afternoon he's broken down. He looked very worried."

"He goes on leave tomorrow." "Does he?"

"I think so."

"You think we should alert the police about the rumour so that they keep watch on him?"

"No need John the law has got long hands like branches of trees. Let him go if he wants to but I assure you he is worsening the situation for himself. This might be the headline in the Nation Daily tomorrow, *THE FUGITIVE CHIEF OF POLICE CID GULU HAS VANISHED WITH ENTIRE MEMBER'S OF HIS FAMILY.* "And there is, when the law will begin to trace him. Once brought out, he will draw death sentence instead of twenty years in jail."

"That will be sad."

"Okay John I must go back to sleep I thought I should talk to you a little before I sleep. Greetings to your family John have a good night enjoy the best of the New Year Day left, and keep yourself safe."

"And you too. Do not over work your brain and have a good sleep for tomorrow's task." John advised him.

"I will John." Odongkara said and hung up.

Odongkara came back to the suite and stealthily opened the door to the bedroom. Because of the warm weather Betty had thrown away the blanket from her body and she lay on her back one leg thrown down at the side of the bed. She looked someone dead. He came and switch on the bedside lamp and saw her breathing her flat smooth stomach muscle extending and relaxing at the rhythm of the respiration. He fixed his gaze on her. He stared at the sleeping eyes. They looked magnificent even when closed into a deep sleep like that. He shifted his gaze down following the smooth long neck and the sensational breasts gave a *roadblock* to movement of his eyes. He fixed his eyes on them he could not help bending down to look at them critically. He felt her feminine warmth piercing him through those breasts, which seem to explain her womanhood.

Should I wake her up with a kiss and we bump? Odongkara thought erotically and sifted his gaze slightly down her pubic region and saw the jet black tuff of hair which stung his sexual deport excruciatingly. He was dazed and his heart began to pump faster. He looked at his wristwatch the time was 23.30 hours.

Can thirty minutes do? Why not? He thought and without a second thought he found his lips on Betty's. She stirred groaned, moaned and clang on his neck pressing him on her. She opened her lips and they kissed, Odongkara fell on her and adjusted her legs.

"You must sleep now you peacock it's enough for tonight be a nice chap okay?" She said and kissed him lightly on the lips and rested her head on his arm and closed her eyes. Odongkara snapped out the beside lamp and began to think of all he heard during the day. He first thought of the warning note of Opiyo and Lwanga.

Who is this man with a pig like head that wanted to see me? What did he want from me? Did he have any information about Dr. Gunya assassin or did he want to cause me trouble?

He shrugged in the dark and brushed off the thought. *Well I will wait and see tomorrow if he comes again.*

Then he turned his thought on the interview he had with the staff of the Institute. He meditated over them one by one starting from Hajji, store kepper, night guard and Dr, Gunya servant. He found that there were conflicting reports from Hajji who claimed he had an excellent relationship with Dr. Gunya but he found out that the reverse is true. *Why is he lying? It looks I might have to concentrate around him tomorrow. I only need to confirm the statements of Betty here, that of Dr. Gunya's servant, and the storekeeper by a neutral source. I know tomorrow I will get the results of the ballistician concerning the identities of the bullets, which killed Dr. Gunya and there is where the search will begin. What about the gun and the knife found in his house what of the fingerprints? We haven't attached them to any girl. May be that is what Lwanga and Opiyo should work on tomorrow. They should see if they can with the aid of the album, fix their fingerprints on any of them especially the one who took the gun and the knife into the bedroom of Dr. Gunya. Mzee, the house servant of Dr. Gunay, should be able to help them to locate these girls. I am sure he knows where they live.* Odongkara thought and lifted his arm slowly from under the head of Betty. The arm had become numb because of the continuous pressure of her head on it. He turned and pressed her on his chest and felt the warmth of her body on his chest. She moaned, and coiled her slender body on him chewed her mouth and continued to snore lightly. He looked at his watch the phosphorylated hour and minute hands distinctly fluorishing in the dark, showed the time as five minutes past one a.m.

CHAPTER 13

The Chief Magistrate Grade 3 entered the High Court Hall at 8.30 hours and the audience stood up as a sign of respect to him. He walked and sat in his throne and the audience sat down on their seats. The Chief Magistrate adjusted his wig on his head and push his spectacle up his head and looked at the Court Registrar who immediately pulled out a file, cleared his throat, adjusted himself on his chair and read the indicament of Hajji Rajabu.

"Criminal case number 217 Hajji Rajabu of Medical Research Institute has been indicted of a murder charge of Dr. Gunya the Director of the Medical Research Institute." He paused, and ordered Hajji to take his stand in the witness box. Hajji Rajabu unfettered walked to the witness box. On top of the high form next to the witness box were two books. The Holy Bible for the Christian and the Koran for the Muslim.

What are your names? The Court Registrar asked.

"Hajji Rajabu Sir."He replied.

"What denomination are you?" The Court Registrar knew Rajabu was a Muslim but he didn't want to take him for granted because of his names. In court case there is no assumption. One must speak everything from his or her own mouth.

"I am a Muslim sir."

"Okay, take the Koran in your right hand, and repeat these sentences after me." The Court Registrar said. Rajabu took the Koran in his right hand held it up in the air and prepared himself to repeat whatever the Court Registrar was going to say.

"I Hajji Rajabu." Rajabu repeated.

"Promised that in the name of Allah."

"Promised that in the name of Allah."
"Shall say the truth in this court."
"Shall say the truth in this court."
"Nothing but the truth." "Nothing but the truth."
"You can put the book down." The Court Registrar said. Rajabu put book where he got it.

"Rajabu what language do you speak best?" the Court Registrar continued to ask.

"I speak English best sir."

"Well Rajabu you have been charged with the murder of Dr. Gunya."

"Do you plead guilty or not?" "Yes sir."

"What do you mean yes sir?" "I mean I plead guilty."

When Hajji was speaking the Magistrate Grade 3 Wankoli was very busy taking notes on a lose sheet of paper. The Court Registrar set up and looks at Wankoli. In return Wankoli looked at the defendant. The defendant a tall smart swarthy handsome man with jet blackhair brushed at the side of his head got up and adjusted his neck tie and walked majestically towards the witness box.

He bowed to the Magistrate and look at Rajabu. "Your name sir?" he asked again, straightening his neck tie.

"Hajji Rajabu."

"How old are you?" "45 years old."

"What is your occupation?"

"I am a Principal Research Officer in the Medical Research Institute, beside, I am the Deputy Director of the Institute."

"How long ..."

Betty, who never slept beyond six a.m. woke up from her sleep, stretched and yawned. The birds were singing melodiously in the trees outside the hotel. The morning sun squeezing its cool rays through the gauzed ventilation into the room illuminated it brightly. She flicked of the blanket from her breasts and looked at the handsome face of Odongkara smiling in his dream. She mused at his lips quivering in the dream and decided that she should kiss it. Why not, last night he disturbed my sleep I must also wake him up, after all it's daybreak now. She thought and threw one of her legs over him and coiled on him squeezed him.

"Umm. Oh, it's you honey." He said waking up. He stirred and found he was between her legs. He knew what it meant he didn't need any excuse or apology in less than a second he was in the mood and they rolled round in the double bed.

"Do you know?" Odongkara asked Betty.

"No."

"You woke me up when I was in the High Court with Hajji charged with the murder of Dr. Gunya."

"He might as well be. There is no any other person suitable for the indicment for the murder."

"I am very suspicious about him now. If I didn't talk to you I wouldn't have been very suspicious. All the same I will make some effort today to track the quarry to his hideout. I am grateful for the information you gave me." Odongkara said and hugged her holding her by the slender waist and kissed her on the lips passionately.

Odongkara glanced at his watch. The time was seven thirty. "We must begin to prepare for breakfast and duty. It's getting late."

"I wish we were living in the world of Adam and Eve where there was no work." Betty commented.

"I wish we could", Odongkara said and jumped out of bed.

Betty followed him and she walked away to the bathroom first.

It was when Odongkara was in the bathroom and Betty was dressing up when a knock sounded at the door. Odongkara heard it but because he was in the bath he could not attend to the person knocking. Betty knew Odongkara was unable to attend to the person so she walked and opened the door. The newspaper boy was at the door with heap of the newspapers *Nation Daily* in his hand.

"Want a copy Madam?" Betty did not answer him at once she looked at head line first. It was in big black capital letters. It read CHIEF OF POLICE CID GULU MURDERED. She took one paper and stared at it.

"I will take one copy." Betty said and went back in the room and got one shilling coin and gave it to the news paper boy.

"Thank you very much Madam." The boy said and walked away to the next-door selling his newspaper. The story read.

The Director Murdered

The *CHIEF OF POLICE CID GULU D/SP* Joseph Mukasa has been found murdered in his house in Gulu suburb and all members of his family vanished without a clue. Mr. Mukasa was last seen driving with his wife from the home of his Deputy Assistant Superintedant Police Mr. Peter Odongkara yesterday at 12.00 hours. Mr. Mukasa was shot by an unknown person on the head and chest in bed and he died instantly. Mr. Mukasa born in 1920 joined the Police in 1937 as a constable he served as a uniform police officer in the ranks of constable, corporal, sergent and shifted to the CID police service and gradually work his way up the ladder.

1962 after the Independence, Mukasa, because of his talent and ability was promoted to the rank of Detective Superintendant of Police. He is survived by a widow, three sons and three daughters. Meanwhile the police is looking for Mrs. Mukasa the wife of Joseph Mukasa for questioning about the hit and run car accident which killed a boy yesterday 31 December 1970 evening on Keyo road. Anyone who knows the whereabouts of Mrs. Mukasa is requested to report her to the nearest Police Station.

Betty put the news paper face up on the coffee table in the lounge and walked to the bedroom and continued with dressing her hair starring at her picturesque beauty in the dressing mirror.

Why was he murdered? This is yet another case for him to solve. I guess he is going to get muddled up with these cases. He hasn't quite finished with this and now he might be required to go back to Gulu today to solve yet another mystery of a murder case. I pity him. Betty thought and heard Odongkara drained the water in the bath. Odongkara cleaned the bath put on his bathing gaon, opened the door, and walked out of the bathroom humming a song. When he got to the lounge towelling droplets of water from his head, while thinking and admiring Betty's indubitable beauty and her intelligence, he stopped as if he was held at knife point when he saw the newspaper. He snatches the paper from the table as if he was competing for it with someone. He rolled his eyes over the headline disbelievingly.

"It's incredible. It can't just be. No! Not at all. Betty heard him shout hysterically. He jerked the door to the bedroom opened and found Betty sitting in front of the mirror applying the lipstick she had brought with her in her beauty kit.

"Hey darling have you seen this paper?"

"Yes. I bought it. I thought you might need to have a look at it."

"Thank you very much. You are an intelligent girl Betty. I just cannot bring my mind to believe the news. Mukasa dead? Sure! And his wife and children vanished! Was it a suicide? Or his wife murdered him and fled away with the children, and why should she kill a man who wanted to protect her. I don't understand." Odongkara lamented aloud.

Odongkara sat on the bed and stared at the paper in his quivering hands as if he expected to get the answer to the why to murder of Mukasa. Betty got up from the dressing stool and came and sat on the bed, beside him, and threw her arm around his neck.

"Take it easy darling. I am sorry for the news." Betty said consoling Odongkara.

"He was a good colleague. A good work mate and a good family friend.

Who has killed Joe? I must go and bring the culprit to book. I know I will do it." Odongkara swore.

In their hotel Lwanga and Opiyo also got the shocking news of the murder of Mukasa. Opiyo took up the telephone and began to dial Odongkara and it was at the same time that Odongkara stablised himself and took his phone and began to dail the two boys to give them the information. Opiyo found the line engaged and Odongkara also found their room engaged.

"What the hell are they doing with their phone early in morning?"

Odongkara said resentfully. While Opiyo at his end cursed him for talking too long to girls. "He must be talking to a girl. He can't miss them Opiyo also said indignatly and cradled his receiver, at the same time when Betty advised Odongkara to cradle his receiver and wait.

"They might be trying to get through to you and you are trying to get through to them and you get the mid air jam."

"May be." Odongkara reluctantly agreed and cradled his receiver.

After a while Opiyo got through to Odongkara. "Hello Sir this is …"

"Yes Opiyo I know you are the one speaking have you seen the paper?"

"That's why I am phoning you. I have been trying to get through to you.

For the last five minutes but I found your line engaged." "So was I."

"I thought you were talking to some places." "No I was trying to get through to you." "What do you make out of the news?"

"Not much at the moment. It sounds a suicide and it also sounds murder."

"Why a suicide?"

I am not sure, but I think he might have realized the wrong he did to try to conceal his wife against the law and he was unable to withstand the scandal and shame and he decided to end that way. You know to go to jail at the last moment when you are about to retire and earn your pension is not a very entertainable matter. I guess he saw his uselessness and worthlessness to his family if he should go in jail for some years and lose his pension."

"And why has his wife run away with all the children." "Perhaps she knew he was trying to protect her against the law,

about her hit a run car drama. Now, she sees no protection and she is now in the open, so what else could she better do than to hide.

"It still does not make much sense to me sir how an old house wife like her could desert the corpse of her husband and flee into hiding without caring for anything in the house?" Opiyo said

"How do you know she didn't empty the house dry with nothing else left behind except the carcass of Mukasa on the floor? I know those types of ladies. Most of the time, when their husbands die they look at them as someone who has never lived and cared for them. A dead husband is a step towards prosperity because all his wealth, if any, will be in her hand."

"So you think that is what Mrs. Mukasa is up to?"

"No I think in her case, she could be running away from the law. What if she killed Mukasa herself and fled? Because Mukasa was reconsidering turning her to the law? All these are possibilities but let us tackle this one in our hands here first, which we should solve, I guess, today." Odongkara said and added "I think we are going to divide ourselves into two groups again. But first we must all report to the police headquarter. Then, you and Lwanga with the help of Mzee should, locate as many of those girls in the Album as you can. See if you will attach the finger prints you got on the knife and the gun yesterday to any of them.

It seems to me that lady was the last visitor in Dr. Gunya's house before he was assassinated. So if we get the owner of the finger prints we will not be very far from the end of our investigation. The lady could have been leagued up in the plot to kill Dr. Gunya because of her finger prints on the gun and the knife. She seems a good clue if found. Meanwhile, I would like to verify the statements I collected from all my clients yesterday with one or two more interviews from neutral sources in the Institute."

"What do you mean neutral sources?"

"I do not think those whites would be bias. I doubt. I trust they will tell me what they know and I guess we should stir up the quarry before midday."

"Okay sir. By the waySir,"Opiyo said quickly coming back on line. "Did you get our note last night?"

"Yes I did. But never saw any man. You didn't ask him why he was looking for me?"

"We did but he would not tell us."

"Well don't worry about him Opiyo. I'll catch up with him in the day today if he seriously wants me."

"He looked suspicious to us."

"Everyone in this town looks suspicious of various offences.

Let's forget him but I will be on the look out for any fat pig headlike man. I never had the chance of seeing one."

"Meet you at the Police station then." "How are we going? taxi?"

"No. Don't waste your dough the police car is coming here. I will pick you up on our way to the station meanwhile cheer." Odongkara said and hung up.

He got up from the bed stretched and started to dress. When he was talking to Opiyo, Betty had finished touching her face, lips, eye brows and put in her white lacy pink frock she came in the previous evening. She took the newspaper lying on the bed and walked out to the lounge and sat reading. Odongkara change in a gray suit with blue necktie over a white shirt and walked out in the lounge. She heard him open the door and folded the paper she was reading and tossed it on the table in front of her.

"You look splendid. She said and got up and threw her arms round his neck and lifted up her head. Odongkara lowered his and their lips met. They remained like that for a good five minutes.

"And you look florid naturally florid all the time." Odongkara remarked.

"Thank you, let's go for breakfast I am hungry." Betty complained.

"So am I. Let' go." Odongkara said and whisked her off her feet lifting her in the air holding her by her slender waist and put her at the door.

He took her coat and put it on her back. She wrinkled in and walked out of the suite after Odongkara had opened the door for her. He carried his briefcase outside, locked the door, and took the key to the reception desk, before they went for their breakfast.

Immediately after their breakfast Odongkara hired a taxi to take Betty back to her sister and then to the Institute for work. He felt lonely as he paced up and down along the lobby waiting for transport. It was not until 8.20 hours when the police car pulled up in the parking ground in the hotel ground. Odongkara had been waiting impatiently at the hotel lobby for the transport for the last twenty minutes. He didn't know what was happening. He was assured by Paul that the vehicle was going to be sent to pick him up at 8.00 hours. He glanced at his watch time and time again and he was on the verge of hiring a taxi when he saw the police car with its red roof light rotating entering the hotel gate. The driver shoved the Peugeot 504 in to the parking ground and stopped. He opened the door of the car and jumped out of the car and opened the rear door of the car for Odongkara. He walked down to the parking ground and climb in the car and the driver slammed the door closed and walked to his seat and ignited the engine and they were soon out of the gate.

"I am sorry I am late." The driver apologied as he sped away to the police station.

"Please drive through Rock Hotel we have to pick two of my staff there." Odongkara said brushing aside his apology.

"They are already at the station Sir." "Are they?"

"Yes Sir."

"Do you know them well?"

"Yes if you mean the Detective Inspector Police, Opiyo the photographer and the finger print, Detective Assistant Inspector Police, Lwanga, and then they are at the Police station waiting."

"They went in a taxi?"

"I think so. Because when I came back from refuling the car I found them already chatting with the O/C at the reception desk."

"You had some problem in refueling the car?"

"Yes the petrol wasn't delivered in time we had to wait." "Oh well ..."

"I am sorry for the delay?" The driver said apologetically again.

Five minutes drive brought them to the police station. Before the car stopped dead, Odongkara was already out walking towards the police office with his brief case in his hand.

"Hello gentlemen good morning." He greeted the O/C Police Kitgum, Opiyo and Lwanga.

"I am very sorry I am late?"

"It is not your fault Odongkara that you are late. It's our fault we should apologise to you for having kept you waiting for your transport at the hotel." Opiyo and Lwanga couldn't wait. They came away in a hired taxi." Paul replied.

"I nearly did the same."

"We thought you had come away without us." Lwanga retorted. "I couldn't have done that. I told you to wait in your hotel for the vehicle he was sending for us. Anyway that is a trivial issue let it not take a second more of our time. Good we are all hear. Let's get to serious work now. If we could get near to our quarry today I will be happy. I don't want to dwell on the same case for a long time. Today the second day should bring us very near to the man we want. So as I was telling Opiyo, this morning I have set up the programme of the day like this.

First we are going to hear the ballistic results from Kampala. I am sure they have all been received. Then, we shall divide ourselves into two groups as we did yesterday in the afternoon. You and I, Odongkara said addressing himself Paul, will go to the Institute to interview one or two more people. I mean other people who wouldn't be bias. I had thought of one or two of those white researchers whose homes were on the list to be visited. I want to do these to compare their version of the story of what happened in the institute with what we have collected so far and the conclusion of our enquiries today. And tomorrow we should be doing something else perhaps on the track of the person who put Mukasa to sleep. And Opiyo and Lwanga should go on the hunt for that lady who left her fingerprints on the knife and the gun found in Dr. Gunya's house. I guess they should sort that out with the aid of the photo album and the Mzee, the servant of Dr. Gunya, should be able to tell them which of the girls visited him lately. I suspect the girl who left the gun and the knife must be one of the last visitors to Dr. Gunya's house. This is my set up. Then in the afternoon we should meet and see what we can make of our morning researches. Anyone with an additional opinion?" Odongkara asked and looked around at them. They were quiet. "Well if that is accepted as the base on which we can work today, then can we get started with the ballistic report, where do we stand with all the guns found in his house where do they come from?"

Odongkara said and sat up and looked at Paul.

Paul cleared his throat adjusted his buttocks in the chair and began "Yes gentlemen before I begin to give you the result from Kampala about the specimens of guns and ammunitions we sent to Kampala, I have a surprise for you. I tried to let you know about this last night but I didn't get you in your hotels. The whole story is like this," Paul said and went through the whole story for them how he became suspicious of some of the abandon building in town to be the possible hide out of the armed wrong doers and the people involved in criminal activities around Town. He told them how he dispatched a surveillance team from the police to go and spy and check physically on such houses. He told them how they stirred up the Aguru flat 26 to be a hide out of one of the hoodlum Salim Rajabu the Lion. He told them how he contacted Captain Ben the Commander of Kitgum 10th Battalion and how Ben with his men had a duel with the thug and how they captured the gun and a knife from the thug who got away. He regretfully informed them that in the event, one of the soldiers was shot dead accidentally when he ran into strayed bullets. He concluded and produced the gun and the knife captured from Salim by Menya.

"Here are the weapons he said and gave the automatic pistol 0.38 with the engraved letters on the butt reading. *The property of the British Embassy.* "Property of theBritish Embassy!" Odongkara said shaking his head. "This is interesting. I don't know if it will league up with our case. If it does then we have a wider chase to make. We have to contact the British Embassy to find out who owns this gun and how it got out of their embassy. He said and passed the gun to Opiyo and Lwanga to have a look at it. He took the knife, which was lying on the table of Paul. It was sheathed like the one found in Dr. Gunya. Odongkara stared at the knife with astonishment. "What! He yelled, pulled off the studded strap of the sheath and pulled the knife out. Its razor sharp blade had the trademark stainless steel. *Smith and Smith Company Limited and Made in England* engraved on it. He studied the knife and pushed it back in the sheath and gave it to Opiyo.

"These are very interesting clues" How do we tie it on that found in Dr. Gunyas' house? The finger Prints on the one found in Dr. Gunya's house is belonging to a girl. Did you say this terrorist found in Aguru 26 is a man?"

"Yes he is a man. Ben thinks he is a man call Salim the owner of the Baby shop which got burnt the night before last night. People rumour all jokes about Salim. They believe he is able to change himself into grass, snake, pen or anything if you are closing on him and that is why he can't be caught."

"So, how will we tie this man on that girl? Well, we shall see", Odongkara said.

"I think I can now go ahead with the ballistic report from Kampala. First, let me start with the guns discovered in the shops. I mean the Baby shop belonging to the furgitive Salim, all the sample of guns and hand grenades were identified by Ben as the batch of weapons which disappeared from the armoury of the 15th Batalion in Kitgum last year. These guns were alleged to have been taken out by Captain Dramadri the former commander of the Battalion who has disappeared without a traced up to now. It was highly rumoured that Captain Dramadri defected and joined the adversary force of the BDM. The bullets which blasted in the fire, the few collected and sent to Kampala, were identified as those for the guns found in the shop according to the ballistic report from Kampala. The bullets and the catridges collected from the scene of the assassination were all fired from automatic rifle Uzi gun stolen from the barrack's armoury and so were the bullets and catridges, collected from the front of the house of the Deputy Director Hajji Rajabu. All we now can swear to is, the automatic Uzi guns, found in the shops, and the hand grenades, plus the bullets, were all from the barracks armoury, the bullets and catridges which killed Dr. Gunya and those found at the door of Hajji's house were identified as having been fired from the same type of gun. We belief that their origin are from the same source. Further more this type of gun, the Uzi gun is not for any other person except for the army. Unless brought in by the so called BDM there is no way of getting this type of gun in the hand of any person. Finally the knife you found in the house of Dr. Gunya, Paul went on.

"It was found under the pillow of Dr. Gunya. It makes a difference when you say the knife was found in the house and under the pillow. I always prefer specificity no generalization is good enough in law." Odongkara interrupted Paul. Paul apologises and went on.

"Yes, the knife found in the house under the pillow of Dr. Gunya, was also identified by Captain Ben that, it's their weapon. They have just started ordering some of these knives from Britain to help them with their field work. They are all stock up in the armoury.

"Did he tell you that they noticed the loss of these knives when the guns and other ammunitions were taken from the armoury?" "A carton of about 144 knives walked out with the guns on the same day."

"Well, then that is beautiful. I see now two things, we have to get this Salim, if we do, we shall solve the mysterious disappearance of Captain Dramadri. I have already got wind not only from you but from one of my clients I interviewed yesterday that he should have some knowledge about the disappearance of Captain Dramadri. If we get him we should be able to locate the person or persons who stole these weapons from the barracks. On the other hand let's get this girl, who took the knife and the gun under the pillow and in the bedside locker of Dr. Gunya respectively. If we get her I am sure she will talk and when she talks we shall have broken the code. We have to hunt the foxes and catch them. So thank you very much Paul for all these very useful informations. It's now up to us to get to work. As I said you and I go to the Institute. Opiyo and Lwanga go to Mzee. Take your guns with you. Girls of that type are as dangerous as a lunatic elephant. They can fight like tigers. So be careful don't think you're going to deal with your shy girl friends that submit to any of your demand. Take some handcuffs with you too they might be necessary." Odongkara said and got up, packed his papers he was writing on, and stuck them in his brief case and walked out.

When Salim accepted the invitation of Abudu Abas to go to his house, Abudu Abas, with his daughter Shara, the girl friend of Dr. Gunya, drove away to his home situated at the junction of Patric Lumumba road and Nkuruma Avenue. They got home, Salim and Sarah, walked in the house

"You are welcome Salim." Abudu said and extended his hand for a handshake.

"Thank you." Salim said and graped his adisposed hand shook it and sat back in the chair.

"I am sorry for what happened to your shop!" Abudu said remorsefully.

"Thank you." Salim said and kept quiet staring at the roof.

There was a pause among them and Abudu said suddenly. "Now what is your plan for the future?"

"What future and plan do I have? I have no future therefore, no plan. Plan for who anyway, with all my family sleeping in the forest now with flies all over their bodies. They are fat big sausages for maggot and flies now. Myself I have no worry for what happens to me I am just a dead man, a walking ghost or walking corpse. All I regret very much now is the lack of my gun. If I had it with me I would have been optimistic to live for a day longer but without a gun now without a knife without anything protective I am a little worst than the dead." Salim said, his eyes glittered with tears. Abudu looked at him and looked away.

If Salim is now so desperate and in need of escape from Town, the adamant terrorist has now become helpless like a piece of rotten potatoe what is going to become of them who naturally were porridge in the game of crimes. Abudu thought and sweat oozed from his pig like nose. He wiped off some of the sweat on his callous forehead and sat back.

"Well Salim if you think you have no future here why don't you leave this country and go to my brother in Mombasa? There you might start a different life and do something new."

"How do I go to Mombasa? Walk from here to Mombasa with my one leg on which I am not able to walk as far as ten miles?" Salim asked.

"You know Salim, Hajji and I have decided to get Shara out of this game.

She goes to Mombasa tomorrow in the morning and I think you should go away with her. I am going to provide transport for both of you."

"And you are going to remove all the road blocks on the way where the security is looking for me?"

"How did you get as far as Abera forest last night?"

"I went through the bush road I am sure they have now discovered my car and the dead body of my wife and the children minus me and the hunt for me dead or alive is intensified."

"So what do we do?"

"Sarah saves her neck and I remain here. I know it's not long before I die."

"You are not going to remain here Salim. If you know whether you go or remain here the end is the same why don't you risk going?" "I'm not going to risk going to Prison Abudu, I would rather die now than go in jail. I will never go in prison. We are suffering all this because Hajji lured us into a dangerous game. I don't know why we backed him up. He said all would be alright." Abudu said regretfully. "I think it would have been, if my shop didn't expose us in the open. The burning of the shop is my main regret. Although Hajji himself sometime does very foolish things which make him suspect. For example yesterday he foolishly tried to stop the girl at their switchboard from meeting the guy working on the case now. Don't you think that arouse suspicions?"

"And I got myself mixed up in it." Abudu said regretfully. "How?"

"He asked me to go and get that man. I think he is called Odongkara."

"To get him where?" "To his house." "Why?"

"Well he claimed for dinner which I think it was designed to interrupt their meeting."

"And you went?"

"Yes I did, but I didn't get him in the hotel. I was told he wasn't staying in that Rock hotel. I was even shown the list of names of the residence who have booked in yesterday, his name wasn't in the book.

There were two of his colleague Opiyo and Lwanga booked there.

When I asked them where he was staying they said he was staying outside with a friend. I asked for the address of the friend but they told me that they didn't know. I thought it was odd. How could a senior officer like that go to live with a friend other than in the hotel? Well he could have done that but he certainly could not have gone away without leaving his address of location to his colleague. I didn't insist on finding out the address because I didn't want to arouse their suspicion.

"And you think you didn't?" Salim wondered. And added "I think you have blundered. How on earth could you have dared go on such an errand? He should have gone to invite his guest himself. Why send you? These men are here to investigate what happened in his home, I mean the Institute. He is at the moment the boss. The thing he wanted. But I don't know if he will live to be the boss anyway. I now warn you, you are in problems. You might get these men on your back very soon. They are not going to take your visit in the hotel for granted. So watch it."Salim warned.

Abudu shigh and said, "I didn't know in any case I drove away home and told him the story. He became scared and knew if he met Betty all was going to be ruined."

"But how was he going to stop them meeting? The best way of doing it was to silence one of them for good. In which case, you brew more trouble for you and more killing in your hand. And something which Hajji will never do. He wants to sit in his house and command from there. When you get wounded up like I am now, he dives below the trouble and remain safe. If I had my gun tonight I would have shot him first thing in his house. He is lucky he will live many years." Salim said, his murderous brown eyes shone with rage.

The time was 9.30 when Opiyo and Lwanga got to Mzee's home.

He was at home clearing his compound. When he saw the police Land Rover entering his home. He dropped the slasher he was using for cutting the grass in the compound and walked to meet them.

"Hello, Mzee how are you?"Opiyo said and got out of the Land Rover his camera hanging at his side by the strap. He slammed the door of the Land Rover shut and walked in front to shake hands with Mzee. After they had exchanged greetings of courtesy, Mzee lead them to his house, which was scantly furnished with the basic furniture expected of a man of Mzee's status and earning. He sat them on some kind of wooden chair made from local material. After some petty conversation about themselves, the weather and rocking prices of consumables, Opiyo went on the point of their visit to Mzee.

"Yes Mzee". Opiyo said introducing the topic.

"We are seeking your help. I know and trust you are going to be of tremendous help to us." Opiyo said.

"Where I will be useful, I will not hesitate to help."

"Fine." Opiyo said and pulled out the knife and the gun they had brought from the police station. Do you know these weapons? Opiyo asked Mzee.

"I know this is a pistol and this is a knife, if that is what you mean."

"Have you ever seen them in the house of Dr. Gunya or in his possession?"

"No."

"You are sure about that."

"I am an old man who believes in telling the truth."

"I see, I am asking you this because yesterday we found this knife under the pillow of Dr. Gunya and this gun in the side locker of his bed.

On these two weapons we found fingerprints of a girl, we suspect that the girl must have been a close associate of Dr. Gunya. Because to get as far as the bedroom, the person must have been his good acquaintance. Now what we want to do is, to trace the owner of the fingerprints on the knife and the gun. There were also the same prints at the door, which belonged to the same girl who left these two weapons behind in the house. And another girl fingerprints appear only at the door. We feel you could have seen the last girls who visited Dr. Gunya before his assassination. We also have here the photographs of, I think, his girl friends, names and their address, may be if you don't know them by names you could point out from the picture who came last." Opiyo said and handed the old man the Album. Mzee received it, but didn't open it and after holding it for about five minutes, he returned it quietly to Opiyo. Opiyo received it and began to open the Album while listening to Mzee talking.

"I know all his girls by names and where they live without the aid of this book. I can count all of them from cover to cover. I know Dr. Gunya kept this album for security reasons but all his girls never suspected that. I don't know why he had to do that. May be natural instinct or an inspiration. I thought all his girls were alright except this Sarah. I was always worried about her each time she came into the house. I nearly warned him against the girl, but I was quite sure, that he himself wasn't very happy with her. He always gave her a luke-warm reception each time she came. I wondered why he didn't get rid of her completely. He ..."

"Mzee." Opiyo poped in. "Yes Sir."

"Supposing we start like this. Who is this Sarah you are talking about?" I see here she is dressed like an Indian lady. She is about twenty-five years old now lives on Patrick Lumumba Avenue. Is this the same Sarah you are talking about?" Opiyo said as he stared at the photo of Shara in the Album Mzee had returned to him. From her photograph Sarah didn't look a hot girl. She looked smug and frigid. The smile she gave in the photo was repulsive it gave her the look of a weeping Chinese girl. The fat thick nose carried a ring with a bead, made the nose look like that of a pig. The earrings were two large bangles, which dangled from lobes of the large pinnas. She looked offensive. Dr. Gunya could have got involved with her because of sympathy! He wanted to have feeling of ugly woman. If not, then was it because he wanted to have some experience with circumcised Muslim girls? But then why pick on this hug?" Opiyo thought as he stared at the picture of Sarah.

"Yes that is the Sarah. She is the daughter of Abudu Abas the chief telephone engineer in the Post Office. The address is correct they live just at the junction where Patrick Lumumba Road and the Nkuruma Avenue meet.

"What do you know about her?"

"She is a Muslim girl full name is Hajati Sarah Abudu Abas. She owns a small grocery in town near the post office. I hear her father found for her the apartment for the business. It was part of the post office building but you know, these days, when you have anyone big in your line, you could almost get the impossible – possible."

So that is how she got that premises where she is doing some kind of business. What surprises me is how Dr. Gunya got himself mixed up with her. You can see for yourself if you compare her with all other girls in the pictures. You find that she deserve the cool reception he always gave her. She seems to have no other boy friend other than Dr. Gunya. I don't know if he fell for her because of this fact."

"Did they ever quarrel in the house?"

"Not an open one which I know but I always suspected they never went on well because of that I did not care the attitude Dr. Gunya put on whenever she was around."

"You think she might have planned to kill Dr. Gunya when she sensed she was going to loose him, her only friend?"

"I think that is a wise guess which needs further investigation."

"What about the others who were his girls how was he behaving towards them?"

"They always got VIP welcome and treatment. Especially this manageress of the Rock Hotel. Whenever she came in, he asked me to keep away because you know, he feels my present there, a man he treated like his father, was a hindrance to their social meeting. I always gave them way and kept in my corner without any interference. But whenever Sarah came, the gloom in the house always bore on me so much that I feel embarrassed. She would flirt round him but he would sit like his portrait."

"It sounds then that this girl was trying to force love out of Dr. Gunya for one mistake he made one day."

"Could be, he might have made a pass at the frustrated girl jokingly once and she thought she would never get another chance."

"One last question for you Muzee and that is, how often have the girls collided here during their visits to Dr. Gunya.

"Dr. Gunya was very wise in setting their visiting days and hours. At time he got two girls visiting him in a day, but never at the same time. No! Not that I know off. Okay Muzee thank you very much for talking to us very frankly. We are going to check on Sarah immediately before we check on the other girls."

"I would personally advise that you check on her first. She was in the house on Saturday the 29th December last year. And the Manageress was in, on Friday 28th December and Dr. Gunya was murdered on the night of the 31st December."

"Thank you very much Mzee. When we need you again we shall call on you for assistance."

"Do not hesitate to do that. I am always at your disposal. Where you will need my help in this matter, I am willing to cooperate with you until you bring the man who assassinated Dr. Gunya to book."

Chapter 14

Abdu Abas gave Salim a room next to the master bedroom. Salim spent a sleepless night. He was haunted by the ghosts of his children he had just slain. He had a troubled sleep. He shouted and screamed and hysterically busts out of bed and sat down on the floor holding his head lamenting. He whispered funeral songs and asked for his gun. "Hey, where is my gun? Give me my gun I am being killed please give me my gun. Look they are killing me." Salim shouted and screamed and bang the door. Abudu Abbas didn't expect those actions out of Salim. He regretted why he brought the lunatic in his house. No one in his house slept properly everyone was scared of Salim. The children all ran into the room of Shara and crouch near the bed expecting Salim in their room any moment. Abudu Abbas sat on his bed his wife laid a heap of meat near him trembling with fear.

"Why did you bring this lunatic in here the man with the blood of many human beings on his hand? Don't you see what you silly idiot have done? Get ready to fight back." she complaied to the husband.

"I did not know he would be like this. It could be it has just started. You know he has killed all his family today."

"He did?" His wife asked surprised. "Yes."

"And you didn't tell me this before. That is very serious. What is going to stop him from getting at us now? Beside this, he is going to attract the attention of all the neighbours and tomorrow we are going to be the subject of discussion. All what you are trying to hide here is now exposed to the world. You're going to be accused of hiding a wanted man. The police are going to be here first thing in the morning so you have to prepare for the worst tomorrow. You ... " "I know I have messed up things now, but don't be despondent we shall sort it out."

"How, you clown, you know Salim is being hunted for by the police and you shamelessly bring him in the house to cause us more problems! Already you have plunged Sarah into a big problem. You foolishly were convinced she could be turned in to an assassin, something she never dreamt of, nor ever thought of doing. You forced her into fictitious love making with Dr. Gunya and now she is in problem. Her fingerprints are in every coner of the house of Dr. Gunya. A girl who never knew how to avoid police tracking. Well let me see how you are going to use your fat pig like head to clear our names from this mess. Let me tell you one thing, should the police show up. I am going to disassociate myself from you and I will tell the police all I know. I don't want it and will not have anything to hide. It's your greed for money which is making us to suffer. You sold your daughter because you wanted money from your silly uncle Hajji the murderer. Will you get that money now? Will you? May be after you have served some years in prison I hate you a – a ..."

"Please shut up or I kill you now before you do anything treacherous."

Abudu Abbas warned his wife his big fat eyes glowing in his head viciously. She saw the rage and knew he wasn't joking with the pistol lying on the bed side locker. She knew the mad gene in their clan could trigger up any moment and she would get the *bang* in the head that might shut her mouth for good. She flinished and cringed from him cowardly coiling away from him.

Salim continued to shout and bang the walls and door so that, one of the quiet recidential area became the noisest slum area for the first time in years. Aba was embarrassed, he had to go out and stop him. *If it meant killing him he was going to do it.* He thought and took the pistol 0.38 Salim gave him from among the loots they got from the army armoury and walked out to the room of Salim. He found him shouting with closed eyes. Magic, his cat sat at the window watching him pathetically. "Hey Salim, Abudu said and griped him hard by the shoulder, and shook him violently. "Umm,

umm who are you?" Salim startled and opened his eyes and found himself standing with Abudu in front of him with a gun in his hand.

"What is the matter Salim?"He asked as Salim was cringing away from him at the sight of the gun. Another weave of fear took all of him.

"Why Abudu? Why do you want to kill me? You call me in your home yourself and you want to kill me?" Why did you not let me go my way if that …?"

"Shut up I don't want to kill you but you were shouting banging the doors the walls and everything in your room here. Just take a look at all these things you have scattered all over the place."

"Shouting? Did I shout? My goodness I am sorry Abudu I never did anything like that. I thought I was having a terrible dream. I am really sorry Abudu. I must get out of here as fast as I can.

"Not now but as soon as it is day break you must disappear."
"I will do that. I don't want to bring you problems."

"I am already in problem."Abudu said.

It was not until 2.00 a.m. that Sarah and the rest of the family fell asleep again. As a result the waking hours scheduled for her depature to Mombasa which was to be at five, passed with a quiet sweet dreams so that she woke up at 8.00 hours.

"Oh my dear I am late, the bus might leave me" She thought and jumped up from the bed went into the bathroom and spash some water on herself came back into her room packed her luggage and dressed up. She was amazed at the quietness of the house. She walked to her parents' bedroom door and knocked.

"Umm" she heard her father answer, groaned and smirked his lips. "Oh dear the sun is already up in the sky? She heard her father tell her mother. She merely turned her bulky meat in bed and yawned. She also smirked her lips and rolled out of bed. The bed gave sqeak of gatitude as she got up from it. They put on and walked out of the room. The time was 8.30.

"Oh Sarah I am sorry for all these. Let me hurry up. You will now catch the 10.00 o'clock bus."

"Have you made any breakfast yet?" "No daddy."

"Make something we still have time for the second bus to Kamplala."

He said and went to the bathroom to wash up.

At 9.30 hours they had just finished their breadfast and had transferred all her suit cases and all she wanted to carry in the sitting room, when Opiyo and Lwanga in the Police Land Rover swang in the compound of Abudu Abas their pistol ready for any action in their coat pockets. They stopped at the round about. Magic was sitting on a stone at the door way. When it saw the police vehicle it ran in groaning and snarling at Salim. Salim knew there was trouble. He snatched Magic and wobbled to the bedroom of Abudu where Abudu himself was.

"There is trouble out there give me the gun you go out in the living room."

Abudu's heart banged scattering blood through him like water flowing through a shower. He fell hot and sweat oozed out from every pore on his body. His hand trembled. He stares at Salim disbelievingly.

"Has his madness erupted again?"

"Get out to the living room and give me the gun," Salim ordered. But Abudu thought Salim was tricking him to get the gun from him and wipped the entire family. He was still shifting the thought in his head when he heard a hard knock on the door then he got convinced that Salim was talking sense.

"You go, I will cover you. Nervously Abudu got out to the living room. He went out and stood at the door. He was startled to find he was looking at Opiyo and Lwanga the chaps he met in the Rock Hotel the previous night. Opiyo and Lwanga were equally shocked to find themselves looking at the man they described as a man with a pig like head.

Abudu stood barring the door as if he didn't want them in.

Opiyo took out his identity card and showed it to him.

He read it and Lwanga did likewise. "So?" Abudu retorted.

'We would like to talk to a girl called Hajati Sarah Abudu Abas we guess she lives here?"

The Director Murdered

"Abudu hesitated and stared at them with a mouth which wasn't sure of what to say. He tried to speak but no words came through.

"Is she in trouble?"

"No we just want to talk to her. We got her address to be this home is she in?" Opiyo asked again losing patient and began to walk in pushing the bulky man backwards into the house.

"Come in". He at last stepped aside and let Opiyo and Lwanga in. With his camera at the side and the album in his hand Opiyo walked in first followed by Lwanga with his fingerprint kits. Abudu closed the door behind them and walked in after them. Opiyo notice the suitcases and baskets standing on the floor.

"You are on a journey?" he asked Abudu.

"No, my daughter is going to see her Auntie in Mombasa."

"Mombasa!"

"Yes."

"A long way off."

"Yes she is already late for the bus."

"Who is your daughter we hope she is not the girl we would like to talk to?"

"Yes she is."

"Where is she? We could finish with her quickly and let her go her way.

Abudu went in the room of her daughter and called her out. Sarah dressed in Islamic style, walked out of her bedroom in slippers. A short bulky dark girl with no trace of beauty came and sat on a chair opposite Opiyo. She timidly stared at them with the brown eyes, her ringed nose quivered fearfully as if she was sniffing at a bad smell. The collous face was rough with pimple. She at list looked a fair lady in the picture but as Sarah, if she was not born of a woman she would have rightly been called a female gorilla.

"Good morning Madam" Opiyo greeted her and looked away.

"Good morning sirs" she greeted them.

"You are on a very long journey." We are sorry to hold you up for a while.

"It's alright sir." she replied with her hoarse manlike voice.

"If you could cooperate with us on this matter we should let you go as soon as possible."

The thing is we are trying to get assistance from those who knew Dr. Gunya well, and were his associate to help us to …"

"I don't know anything about Dr. Gunya." Sarah snapped in.

Opiyo stopped and stared at the hug sitting in front of them.

"You see Madam as I said earlier on, that is if you cooperate with us in this matter you will be released to go and catch your bus to Mombasa as soon as possible, but if you make the position difficult for us, then we shall have no option, but to try all ways to make sure you do what we want. You said you don't know anything about Dr. Gunya. Well that is correct but we are checking on the fingerprints of all his girl friends. We have here an album which contains all the photographs of his girl friends. It happened you also appeared in the album, well we have proved beyond doubt that you were his girl friend. You were seen in his house many times which of course tell us that you were lovers. Now all we want from you is your fingerprints and when we get it we shall let you go your way. Simple isn't it?" We have already checked on all the other girls. Infact you are the last on the list to be checked." Opiyo lied

Abudu sighed and rubbed his thick nose and stared at his daughter. She returned the stare of her father and said.

"I am not giving you my prints."

"You are doing what?" Opiyo remarked. "I am not giving you my fingerprints."

"Well then you don't go to Mombasa, by order." Opiyo said annoyed.

"Why?" Abudu interjected.

"Because she has refused to cooperate with police investigation of a muder case.

"Why should I give you my fingerprints?" "Routine police check on suspects."

Salim in the room of Abudu pressed his ears on the door and lisent to the argument going on in the living room between Opiyo and Sarah. He knew Shara and Abudu were banking on him for her escape from the mess. He knew they knew he was there with the gun. If he could get rid of these two men, Sarah and everyone

The Director Murdered

else might have to escape to Kampala and then to Mombasa before the news about their death spread all over the town. Salim eased the door inch by inch and leered at the side of the door and saw Lwanga sitting unconcerned with the argument going on between Sarah and Opiyo.

I don't know if they have guns but if I bust on them, there is going to be no chance for them to pull out their guns even if they have some. They are two we are many we could give them quite a tough going. Salim thought and kept on easing the door inch by inch.

When he sat looking unconcerned with what was going on between Sarah and Opiyo, Lwanga has studied the set up of the house and especially the living room where they were, should there be a sudden attack from anywhere. His fear of a surprise attack was hightened by the minx of Sarah. He knew she was up to something with them and escape to Mombasa without giving them here fingerprints. Their car was already out of the garage and was parked ready to be packed and take off. The suitcases which Lwanga saw as possible weapon of defence, stood very near him ready to be taken out. As he sat he saw Salim edging the door slowly. He pretended that he did not see it. He remained calm but ready for action. Salim erronusly thought that he was going to surprised them bust in the living room pointing at them with the 0.38 pistol. He was opening his mouth to give them order when Lwanga with one hand snatch the suitcase standing near him and haurled it at him. Salim tried to doge but with only one leg he was too slow. The suitcase got him on the thigh and sent him tumbling down like a bag of sugar thrown of a lorry. He desperately fired at Lwanga but missed. The bullet hit the picture on the wall and shattered the glass, and the flying glasses got Shara at the corner of her eyes. It ripped it open and blood jetted out. She yelled for help. Her father Abudu lumbered forward and tried to hit Opiyo. Opiyo duck down and jabbed him below the chin and lifted him up and he fell down like an elephant "pump" Abudu was scattered to pieces blood oozed from his mouth and nose.

Lwanga in self defence wipped his gun from his coat pocket and fired at Salim the bullet got him on the head. It opened the top of his head pouring the lump of his brain on the floor. Salim died instantly. The children yelled histerically as their mother lumbered out of the kitchen trumpeting like a female elephant came treading, her footfalls rocking the house. She came and saw the open skull of Salim and fainted and fell like a rotten coconut tree. It was a short turmoil. The chaos was hecatic for a good five minutes and the whole place became still and quiet as if nothing happened there. "You are all under arrest." Lwanga said and cuffed all of them on the hands. He rang the police station and police patrol car was immediately in sight. The siren shirling as the red roof light on the car rotated and glowed and all other cars stop to make way for them. In a matter of minutes the entire family of Abudu Abbas was taken to the police station.

Odongkara and Paul left for the Institute and got there when Opiyo and Lwanga were at Mzee. They picked on Miss Catherine the research Officer whose house was directly behind that of Dr. Gunya and Mcdonald the man whose house was behind that of Hajji. The first to be interviewed in the boardroom that morning was Catherine. Catherine a short, squired face, English blonde walked in with the smile a girl with smuggled packet of Marijuana, give at the custom officer to clear her without much ado. Her clear blue eyes darted nerviously from Paul to Odongkara her thin pointed nose whistled as she breathed through it like wind blowing through a narrow open tube. She sat up pivoted on the chair in front of Odongkara like a trapped rabbit.

"Good morning Madam" Odongkara greeted her. "Good morning sirs"

"I am sorry for bothering you this morning." I want to ask you a few questions which I think should straighten my investigation into the murder of your former boss."

"I – I wish I could be of help I would be very grateful."

"Any information you know, and you will give us, are all we need."

"To begin with we would like to know your particulars." "You are?"

"Catherine Ball."

"Catherine how old are you?" "Twenty nine."

"What is your occupation Catherine?"

The Director Murdered

"I am a Senior Research Officer in the Department of Microbiology."

"When did you come to Uganda?"

"In 1968."

"Have you all along been here since then?" "Yes Sir."

"For how long have you worked together with your former Director Doctor Gunya?"

"For the last four years."

"And his deputy Hajji I guess?" "Yes sir."

"You should, I am sure know each of these two people fairly well."

"What do you mean?"

"I mean their attitude towards people of the Institute. Their way of administration and how people feel about each of them. Say if we start with Doctor Gunya. How was he?"

"Catherine paired her palms and said, he was a kind nice gentleman who had the true sense of administration. He never demanded for respect from anyone. Because of that he was a simple man who any member of staff of the Institute was free to approach. He was however, strict on punctuality and obedience among the member of staff. He emphasized that everyone must respect each other in order to achieve good working relationship I think he was liked by all the staff. But his deputy I – I am sorry to say I don't know much about him. He – I think is an introvert and not very popular."

"Why do you think he is not very popular?"

"I - I think he is very demanding. And he doesn't give the junior Officers their due respect and they don't like him for that especially ordering them to do everything he wants done."

"You think this created some misunderstanding between the two that is Dr. Gunya and Hajji!"

"It looked as if it did."

"Did they get along well together as far as you know?"

That, I don't know much. All I know is that, Hajji is most of the time on his own. He doesn't mix freely with other people. Even during coffee break he doesn't sit with us."

"Why do you think that is so?"

"I don't know I was guessing it was because of his belief."

"Muslims eat and drink tea and coffee of course with any other person."

"Well then I don't know why."

"They never had an open quarrel you know?"

"I only heard that one day they quarrelled this was at home and it is about a year ago. I was told this by my house girl who picked the news from the servant of Dr. Gunya."

"Did she tell you why they quarreled?"

"It was over some flowers. It looks, the children of Hajji picked some flowers from Dr. Gunya's flower gardens without his permission and he talked to Hajji to find out why they did that. Then it seemed Hajji didn't think his children were wrong and that angered Dr. Gunya and they exchanged words."

"Then the quarrel strained their relationship?" "I think it did."

'Now one more question about Dr. Gunya – Hajji Relationship. I have heard rumours that you senior members of staff preferred Hajji to Dr. Gunya in administration and you wanted a change in administration that way. Is this true or it is some individual assumptions?"

"I have no idea about that?"

"As far as you are concerned Catherine which of the two men do you think was preferred by the members of staff of this Institute.

"I think there was nothing wrong with Dr. Gunya." "What of Hajji?"

'I don't know much about him but I don't think ......, well, he is a recluse and not very popular and people tend to avoid him. Beside he seems to be very authoritative."

"Now Catherine a little more about the Institute drama which happened in the night of the 31st December 1971. How do you see the ingenuity of the event as revealed to us by many radio stations especially the BBC? That what happened here was the work of the BDM? I am sure you hear a lot from home by attending to the BBC don't you?"

"Well sir I really don't know much about what happened but all I know is, there have been a lot going on about Town concerning the BDM but nothing was heard around this place. We were in a separate world of our own which was very safe and nice. But with the event of the 31st December, we are now worried as any other person in this country."

"You think the act was the work of the BDM?"

"I am not sure. I think, and most people in the Institute think it should be the work of the arm thugs who are roaming the town every night looting, robbing and terriorising the entire town into panic."

"Before we lave the Institute and go to your residence. Do you believe that these gunmen who attacked you last night came in over the wall?"

"That is one of the odds about the event. It is not possible for these men I hear they were about thirteen in number, to have come over the Institute wall unnoticed. Our night guards are always very vigilant."

"Your house is directly behind that of Dr. Gunya is that right?" "Yes Sir."

"If you are in, are you able to hear well whatever happens in the home of Dr. Gunya, I mean loud noises and sounds of that nature."

"If they are ... Yes I think I do."

"Where you in Catherine, on the night of the attack of Dr. Gunya and Hajji, and the Institute." "Yes I was in."

"Were you awake?" "Yes I was."

"So what first alerted you that you were in problems that night?" "Gun blast."

"Where was this?"

"At Dr. Gunya's home."

"That is where you heard the first gun blast?" "Yes."

"You're sure of that."

"If there were other blasts elsewhere, faraway, before that, which I didn't hear, then I don't know."

"Let me take you back a little. If these guns were to blast at Hajji's home first would you have heard it and located the direction?" "Yes. Hajji's house is only a block from Dr. Gunya in front of Mcadonld's house. I am sure I would have."

"So Catherine the first gun shots went off at Dr. Gunya's home and then second?

"There was an interval of about ten minutes then a number of shots went off at Hajji's house."

"But Hajji last time testified that his home was attacked first and Dr. Gunya's home there after."

"I don't believe it. You will find it out from Mcdonold who sleeps right at the back of his house."

"I will do that Catherine. Last question to you ..."

"How I wish it's the last". Catherine said smiling again. The two men Paul and Odongkara also laughed.

"You don't like to chat with us?"

"I don't like to chat with police all over the world in this manner. When not on duty I can chat with them without fear."

"When you are innocent you needn't worry only when you have the law at your back, then there is course to panic. My question is, "I heard that the terrorist, BDM came in with a list of names of people to be obliterated from the world. This list of names included yours and that of Mcdonald and of course Dr. Gunya, Hajji and others. They only killed Dr. Gunya, visited Hajji and the rest of you were never visited. The question is why did the BDM take special interest in you people and visited two people, only frightened one, and killed Dr. Gunya?"Had you a prioknoweldge about their visit and you bought your way?"

"It gives me a qualm in the stomach when I think of that. I just don't know why Macdonold and I should be assassinated by the BDM. And –no- no I had no prioknowledge of the attack and ...." Catherine paused getting red in the face and swallowed slaiva and continued. We are here as expatriates involved in no political activities except our work. I was really shocked to hear that our names were on the death list. Why? I don't know. I think that increases my suspicion that the event of last night was something planned and camouflaged under the umbrella of the BDM."

"Thank you very much Catherine you have been very helpful. You can go back to your work."

"Thank you very much Sir", Catherine said and got up sweeping her blond hair to the back of her head. She straightened her flowery skirt over her flat buttocks and walked out of the boardroom.

Macdonald a storky lanky Scotish, Microbiologist walked into the boardroom towering up to celling.

He had running nose which kept him blowing through the beaky nose, giving the nose a red rose colour. After they had exchanged greetings Macdonald sat down.

"You aren't well?" Odongkara asked.

"No I have a bad cold." Macdonald replied.

"You realy look it." I am sorry for dragging you out of your bed.

I'll make the interview short for you."

"I'll be grateful because I don't feel like sitting up for any minute now."

"I wish I knew you were sick I would have ignored your culture of ladies first and started with you." Odongkara said and they all laughed. As they laughed a telephone rang and Odongkara picked the receiver.

"Yes Odongkara here."

"A call for you from the Police station." He heard the voice of Betty on the line. A moment later he heard the clicking noise at the reception and the voice of Betty was on the line again. "You are through to Mr. Odongkara Sir." she said and connected them.

"Hello Sir." He heard the voice of Opiyo on the line. "Yes, Opiyo how was it."

"Rough."

"What do you mean rough?"

"We had a mini gun battle with the number one. The most wanted man whose shop got burnt and weapon discovered in his shop."

"Really?" Odongkara asked with excitement. "Yes sir." Opiyo replied.

"Then what happened?"

"He was shot dead by Lwanga." "Oh no."

"It was in self defence. He was turning dangerous." "Where was this?"

"In the house of Abudu Abas the father of Sarah. And for your interest, this Abudu Abas was the man looking for you last night."

"Is he?"

"Yes Sir."

"You got him?"

"The entire family is here in the police station."

"That is fine. Good boys. I thought I would meet him, but not as soon as this."

"Sarah was escaping to Mombasa today, now in fact. She didn't want to give in her fingerprints. We wanted to force her when Salim came to his funeral. His top was opened by the gun and the brain shot out like a ball."

"Well Opiyo thank you for ringing. Anyone of you hurt?"

"No we are as clean as you saw us this morning." Opiyo said boastfully.

"Beautiful we shall be with you in a minute." Odongkara said, and cradled the receiver and shook his head and sighed.

"Let's go on with you quickly we have to be at the station immediately."

Odongkara said and went through the same questions he had been through with Catherine. Macdonald precisely answered the questions which were very similar to Catherine so that in fifteen minutes only, Odongkara and Paul were leaving for the police station to go and see the arrested family.

"She has at last given us the fingerprints Lwanga said as Odongkara and Paul walked in the cells were Abudu Abas and his family was remanded.

"She has?"

"Yes."

"And how does it compare."

"It matches well with those on the knife and the gun." "What does she say now?"

"That her father Abudu forced her to have love affair with Dr. Gunya because he wanted her to kill Dr. Gunya. "Why?"

"Because I think Hajji the uncle of her father wanted Dr. Gunya dead and he told Abudu that if Shara could get her way into

The Director Murdered

Dr. Gunya's house, he Hajji, would provide a gun or a knife or both for Sarah to use to kill Dr. Gunya." And if this was accomplished the reward was going to be the butchery on Church Road."

"This is a big catch." Odongkara said nodding his head and added, "I knew we were not far from our target. Even from the interviews with the staff at the Institute, it was becoming clear that Hajji has knowledge about the assassination of Dr. Gunya and he is only acting. This afternoon, I am going to issue a search warrant for Hajji's house. I want his house to be pulled down into bits and pieces. Then he is going to be arrested and charge with the murder of Dr. Gunya." Odongkara said viciously.

It was a shaky afternoon for the Medical Research Institute when Odongkara with his convoy drove into the Institute compound through the main gate.

The Peugeot 504 carrying Odongkara, Paul, Opiyo, Lwanga and three other armed uniformed policemen drove in through the gate, followed by three Land Rovers for police special force packed with dangerously armed men drove in, and the gate closed behind them. They drove and parked in front of the Administrative Office. Odongkara got out while the rest remained where they were and walked to the office and found Hajji in the chair of Dr. Gunya carrying out administration still as Acting Director.

"Good afternoon, Sir." He greeted him seriously and dropped down on an office chair near him without invitation to sit down.

"Good afternoon". You have come back anything I can do for you this afternoon?" Hajji asked worried at the seriousness of Odongkara.

"Yes, plenty. We want to search your house, here is the search warrant." Odongkara said and produced the warrant and presented it to him. Hajji stared at it disbelievingly and his heart slammed heavily in his chest. He shook, and felt a tight twist in his stomach which chuned his bowl, and sent bile up his throat. He tried to spit, but no saliva came. He tried to swallow and he choked instead but tears glittered in his eyes. He looked a baboon caught in a headlamp of a car.

"Why do you want to search my house?" he laboured to talk.

"Routine police search. We are starting with yours and we might go throughout the Institute."

"Okay let's go."Hajji said and got up from the chair and adjusted the turban on his fat big head and walked out after Odongkara.

Since they launched the operation in the Institute with his men. The uniform they used and the guns were all stocked pilled up in his ceilings and the pistol he was keeping in his pillow worried Hajji. He wasn't sure of himself. He didn't know whether luck would be with him.

If they should fail to find any of those weapons and the uniforms, tonight I must dispose them immediately. Hajji thought as he walked out of his office. He was shocked to get an army of men outside waiting for him. He felt warm water seeping in his trouser and hallow feeling in the stomach, which made his legs numb, unable to carry his bulky weight. Odongkara asked the the heavily armed men to drive infront, as he, Paul and Hajji followed in the Peugeot 504 behind the convoy.

"It's hot."Odongkara flattered when he saw Hajji shed sweat from his skin like water.

"Yes it is." He agreed.

"You'd better lower that glass we are going to be roasted in here."

Odongkara said and he saw Hajji, although he also owned a Peugeot 504 of the same model, did not know where the knob for rolling the glass was. Odongkara sneered at him and help him to roll the glass down. They got to his home and the armed policemen in the Land Rover jumped out and took their stand at the corners of the house while the rest went into the house to pull the house into pieces.

Hajati Rajabu was lying on their sofa set bear chested playing with her son on her obesed stomach when the men entered the house. She was shocked to see the armed men moving everywhere in the house.

"I knew the end would be like this." She blurted hysterically and grasped the child, got up and began to run away into the bedroom with the child slung over her shoulder.

The Director Murdered

"Excuse me Madam come back." Odongkara ordered and she stopped as if she ran into a wall.

"Don't be frightened, we are not after a specific home." Odongkara lied. We are doing a routine police check but because your husband is number one of the institute now, we want to start with him. So don't panic" Hajati Rajabu sat down on a chair breathing heavily eyeing her husband hatefully.

The search was mounted two men to every room. Every place was checked even the crevices on the walls were checked. The mattress cussions and pillows were all ransacked and in one of the pillow in Hajji's bedroom, a hard long object about the length of the pillow was detected by Opiyo. He felt the outline of the object and knew it was a gun. He didn't take it out but carried the pillow into the sitting room where Hajji, Hajati Rajabu, Paul and Odongkara were seated. When they saw him come out with the pillow they knew the game was up. Hajati looked at Hajji resentfully and tears dropped from her eyes.

"What is the matter Madam?"Odongkara said and came and held her on the fat meaty shoulder he felt as if he was holding on a catepillar worm. He withdrew his hand slowly with disgust.

"I told him. I warned him, but he would not listen." She screamed sobbing hysterically.

"Okay hold it you will tell us more later." Odongkara said and patted her shoulder which gave him a spongy mattress feel. Everyone else came back to the living room with nothing except Opiyo with his catch.

"Hajji, will you let us see what is in the pillow."

"Yes." He said and with trembling hands he pulled the 0.38 automatic pistol from the pillow and held it in his trembling hand.

"It's a nice weapon." Odongkara said and glared at it without touching it.

"Whose is it", Opiyo asked?" Hajji did not answer the question.

"He will answer that later, take it away from him." Odongkara said.

"Do you have a ladder?" Odongkara asked Hajji. "Yes."

"Could we have it I want to see the inside of your ceiling."

A long wooden ladder about four metres long was brought and inclined against the entrance to the ceiling. Odongkara mounted the ladder and walked right in the ceiling. Hajji's heart was slamming against his chest like a blacksmith fan working the fire in the furnance. He wished the end of the world came there and then. He felt too weak to stand so he collapsed on the chair. There was nothing he could do about it. He closed his eyes and pretended to sleep. Odongkara went in followed by three other armed police men and Lwanga leaving Opiyo and two other armed police men with Hajji and Hajati Rajabu.

With the torch he brought with him Odongkara flashed the light and the dark hot ceiling was brightly illuminated. They were flabbergasted at what they saw. It looked a mini armoury in a barracks. A heap of national army combat uniforms were piled in the corner of the roof. Next to them, were the high neck black army shoes. The automatic machine guns twenty in number were piled next to the shoes camouflage with a heap of fire wood put on them. Ammunition were packed full in a box near the heap of guns, hand grenades twenty four in number were in a box standing next to the box of ammunition. Odongkara and his men stood akimbo and stared at the discovery tongue tied.

"I will let Captain Ben know about this immediately. Let him come and identify these if they are from the barracks. This is incredible I didn't expect it of this man who was shading crocodile tears yesterday over the death of Dr. Gunya. We have all the proof here. He organized the attack and it is him who killed Dr. Gunya. The baboon." Odongkara said furious and added "yesterday he tried to misguide me by putting me off his back. Criminals are tricksters but he, didn't do it very well. From the interview I had conducted yesterday and today I was left with no doubt that he is the one who organized the Institute drama."

In a few minutes Captain Ben with five armed army men two, constables a sergeant and second lieutenant jumped out from the army Land Rover, the radio antenna at the back swang backward and forward as the Land Rover came to a stop. The five men except Captain Ben carried automatic machine guns similar to

The Director Murdered

those found in the ceiling of Hajji Rajabu's house. They trampled into the house their footfall rocking the house off its foundation.

After Odongkara had given him the story about their discovery Captain Ben gave a vicious lethal stare at Hajji Rajabu who virtually was dead, sitting in the chair without his soul. His breath came once in several minutes. Then he recalled what Salim used to tell him, "If you want to be a criminal you must die before you indulged yourself into criminal activities. If you go at it with your life, you won't make it." Then he knew he made a mistake he went into the job with his life and now he was tormented. He didn't know how to extricate himself from the mess.

In a few minutes Captain Ben and his men tramping in the ceiling their footfalls sounding like bombs descended the ladder and stood right infront of Hajji and pointed his first finger at him. You are lucky you ape, this is not my case. I have just been called to identify what you have stolen from our barracks. If I got you myself you would probably be several minutes dead now or you would be cursing your parents why they ever produced you. In any case you will answer for the murder of Captain Dramadri whose uniform and Identity card you have there, Capatain Ben said outrageously, and unconsciously slapped Hajji hard on the cheek. It made a loud dry cracking sound like a calabash trodded under foot and blood spilled from his nose and mouth.

"I am sorry Odongkara you will excuse me for what I did." Captain Ben said trembling with rage. He walked out and his men trampled after him as they walked to their Land Rover and drove off.

Odongkara returned to the house and found that Hajji had ceased to bleed and had sat back on the chair, with red eyes. His wife sat on the chair beside him, speechless. Her child in the hand frightened silly, cringed in her bosom like a young kangaroo in its mothers' pouch.

"Haji, you and your brother's son Salim, who unfortunately has just been shot dead a few hours ago are responsible for the murder of Captain Dramadri, Odongkara said addressing himself to Hajji. You killed him on the night of 24th Wednesday, July 1970. You got him from Rock Hotel bar, his usual drinking place. You capitalized on his dranknness, and picked him up, went and killed him in Abera forest. You used his uniforms, Land Rover and Identity card to rob 15thbattalion barracks. At the quarter guard the Constables guarding the gate were new and they mistook you for Captain Dramadri and got you the keys for the armoury. You decieved them that you were taking those items to rearm the soldiers at Amuru detach unit who were given a surprised attacked by BDM. They were disarmed and all wepons in detach were taken. They were also stripped of their uniforms and boots. Salim was a clever planner. He acted quickly and advised you strike the nail when it's still hot and you went for it. The soldiers at the quarter guard even helped you to remove and packed guns, uniforms, boots, and ammunition and hand grenades in the Land Rover of Captain Dramadri you had come in, and drove away. You packed some of the weapon in the shop of Salim and the rest you brought here. You did this because you wanted to kill Dr. Gunya, with whom you were already having gradges. You disagreed with each other when Gunya came to approach you when your kids went and cut the flowers from his flower garden without his permission. When he confronted you about that, you, instead of warning your children and apologizing to Dr. Gunya, did the exact opposite. Well, this uncalled for attitude was brought about by the fact that you wanted to be the Director of the Medical Research Institute, but to your disappointment the members of staff in the Institute, do not like you because of your authoritative attitude. You demand too much respect from them and you give them none. Dr. Gunya on the contrary demanded none but gave plenty of respect to everyone as a result he was naturally liked, respected and he was a picturesque candidate for the directorship of the Institute. You did not take this lying down you plotted to kill him as I have already told you. You wanted the murder to appear as though it was the work of the BDM. With the help of Salim you organized a number of gangsters. But you got another fear of how all these people would keep their mouth shut. So you tried to go it alone with the help of your niece the daughter of Abudu the Chief Telephone Engineer with the Post and Telecommunication. You told Abudu that if his daughter succeeds in assassinating Dr. Gunya you would give him your butchery as a reward. Abudu fell for your bait he swallowed it right into his stomach. He then forced his daughter to flirt around with Dr. Gunya. Dr. Gunya being a womanizer picked her up and brought her in. But he was a tricky guy no girls he slept with left him without her photo in his album so with your plan to go it alone you gave a pistol 0.38 automatic revolver to Sarah and a knife you also stole from the barracks for her to use as weapon of assassination. But Sarah being a clown took all the weapons and failing to accomplish your aim left the weapons behind full of her fingerprints. Further more she blundered when you wanted to lead us away from you and put us on the tract of Salim. You instructed Sarah to get for herself an official identity card for food and beverage in the name of Salim Rhajabu. Sarah organized one through her cousin Malyamu Mustafa, the personal Secretary to the manager of Food and Beverages and she took this card and dropped it in Dr. Gunya's boot. The first failure of Sarah to murder Dr. Gunya, disappointed you and desparately, as you were in need of killing Dr. Gunya, you fell back on the murder squad because you knew you were going to blame it on the BDM. So with the uniforms and the weapons already in Salim's shop, Salim got for you thirteen thugs from the Town including Juma Isaac one of the bastards of your brother Ibrahim. Because you wanted to blame the incident on the BDM you waited on the Revolution Day so that it would sound that in spite of the heavy security that day the BDM were able to infiltrate and strike in the most secure place in Town and moreover on some one related to the Head of State. That shows the might of BDM isn't it? I am sure they congratulated you for highlighting their profile. So on the day of the operation these young men came in the Institute one by one through the gate they never went over the wall as you said in your interview yesterday. You kept them at your home until night fall. You dressed them up and they were set for action. You put Mustafa on both day and night duties in order that he led the boys to their target at night and during the day to let them in without being detected. You did this because you wanted it to appear that the boys were from outside and they held Mustafa at gunpoint. But the blunder you made was to send the boys to the Medical Research Institute store.

You foolishly thought the fact that Dr. Gunya had advertised the sale of those ramshackle vehicles and the spares were in the store, the public would be wheeled to think that they were really the BDM who burglared in the store because they wanted those spares but you never stopped to think that these men always got their vehicles on the road at gun point. So your store tricks exposed you Hajji. Well your boys went to the gate and according to plan they asked all the guards to lie down. They did. And of course Mustafa had his turban on his head to identify him from the rest of the guards. Your boys began to ask the guards at the gate to lead them to the homes you had listed just as a cover up to show the world that the target was not only Dr. Gunya. The rest of the guards adhered to the regulation, refused to lead your boys to the homes listed, they got a thorough beating and Mustafa pretended it was because of the beating which his friends had, that made him accept to lead them to Dr. Gunya's home. You knew Dr. Gunya was at home that night and when your boys were led passed your place to Dr. Gunya's home and had taken cover at Dr. Gunya's home, you telephoned him. As he received you call, one of your boys aimed at him and fire two shots, which caught him on the chest, and he fell down dead. When you heard the shots, you smiled and knew your plan had been accomplished.

To show your innocence you told the boys to come and fire few shots at your door because you feared if they fired in, some stray bullets might get at you. Your wife screamed and made alarms just to jamboree over the death of Dr. Gunya not that you were in any danger. You and your boys all came back here change into civilian dress left the guns and every weapon behind and you took the boys out through the gate and they went their way.

What you did next was to ring your nephew Abudu in his home. You told him to go to the post office and ring the police that the BDM have broken into the Institute and killed Dr. Gunya. Further you told him to ring these Western media corresponder and tell them the BDM have done it again. Finally you instructed him to jam your line because you didn't want to be suspected of having anything to do with the murder and the information given to the police and the news men.

The Director Murdered

I was here only yesterday afternoon to investigate on the murder of Dr. Gunya, but more so, to proof that it was not the the work of the BDM who is threatening the security of this country only to find out that it is you, Hajji, amusing yourself. You tried to block my investigation by retaining my client I wanted to interview back on duty pretending you had an important call to make and you wanted her around during the time I was supposed to meet her. You failed to do that and you put your nephew on my tail to try to fix me before I talked to my client. He failed to locate me and he came and reported to you. You knew for sure that she would talk all she knew you know about the case. And she did and I am now on you back because of the information I have collected from her and other staff of the institute. You were shedding crocodile tears yesterday with the hope that you would fox me but you foxed yourself.

To complicate things further for you, the shop of Salim, the mini armoury where you had stock piled the weapons went ablaze on the same night you launched the attack and Salim lost his head after his Baby shop got burnt down. He saw no future for himself. The guns in the shop handicapped him from starting anew anywhere. The police were looking for him in all the suspecious dangerous hidouts in Town and at last they turned him up in Aguru 26 where he walked into accidental ambush laid for him. He had just returned from Abera forest where he slew all his family.

The police headquarter was alerted and for fear that there could be more bandits in the flat with the most lethal sophisticated weapons, they sought for help from the army who have arms that match those of the Operating BDM. They went and there was a shoot out. One army personal accidentally lost his life, and the weapons of Salim a gun, he stole from his British Game Ranger master a about fourteen years ago, and a knife you stole from the barracks were captured, but he escaped. He met his stepbrother Abdalla who brought him to your house here. You were here with Abudu and Sarah deciding what to do to the girl as things were getting out of hand. You wanted her to escape and go away to Mombasa and hide there. It wasn't a bad idea if she escaped. But Salim prevented them from having early good sleep. He disturbed them almost throughout the night and they slept late as a result they woke up too late only to welcome the police in their home. Salim tried to break the barrier but his skull was broken instead. Abudu Abas and Sarah are all arrested they are at the police station talking and you are soon joining them there."

Odongkara said and got up walked to the internal telephone of Hajji and phoned Betty.

He lifted the receiver and dialed her number. After a while he heard her voice.

"Medical Research switchboard, can I help you."

"Honey I am through with the Institute's drama the quarry has been tracked up to the den."

"Congratulation honey I am jovial to hear about that."

"Well we shall celebrate the success tonight same time same place."

"Thank you for inviting me again." "Bye for now."

"Bye dear."Odongkara cradled the receiver and came back to where the rest were sitting,

"Okay you are going unfettered." He said addressing himself to Hajji. You are under arrest. Get up and we go to the police station. The house is going to be guarded until we remove these weapons and the uniforms."

Hajji got up and he was walking to the police Peugeot 504 when Odongkara stopped and said "you now need to be protected, go climbe the Land Rover." Hajji timidly walked and climbed the Land Rover and sat between dangerously armed men.

Odongkara always remembers his own philosophy – *criminals are tricksters and you must be a better trickster to encounter their tricks.*